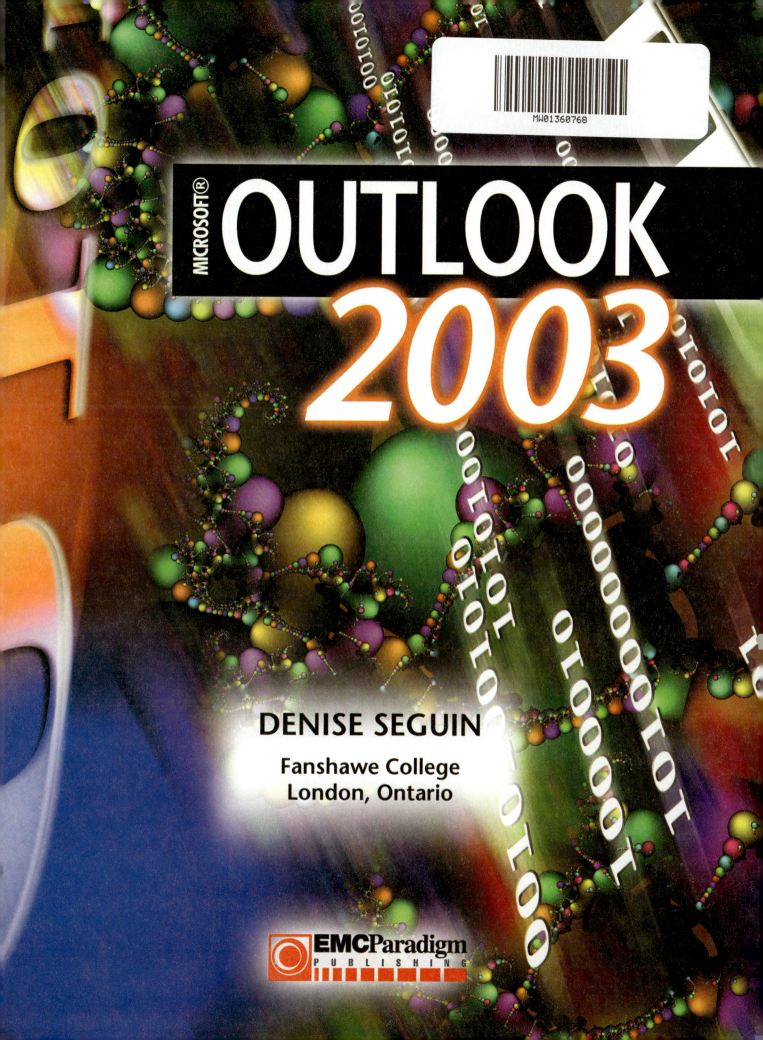

Developmental Editor	James Patterson
Senior Design and Production Specialist	Leslie Anderson
Desktop Production Specialists	Lisa Beller and Erica Tava
Copy Editor and Proofreader	Susan Capecchi
Technical Reviewer	Desiree Faulkner
Indexer	Nancy Fulton

Publishing Team: George Provol, Publisher; Janice Johnson, Director of Product Development; Tony Galvin, Acquisitions Editor; Lori Landwer, Marketing Manager; Shelley Clubb, Electronic Design and Production Manager

Care has been taken to verify the accuracy of information presented in this book. However, the author, editor, and publisher cannot accept any responsibility for Web, e-mail, newsgroup, or chat room subject matter or content, or for consequences from application of the information in this book, and make no warranty, expressed or implied, with respect to its content.

Trademarks: Some of the product names and company names included in this book have been used for identification purposes only and may be trademarks or registered trademarks of their respective manufacturers and sellers. The author, editor, and publisher disclaim any affiliation, association, or connection with, or sponsorship or endorsement by, such owners.

Microsoft and the Microsoft Office Logo are trademarks or registered trademarks of Microsoft Corporation in the United States and/or other countries, and the Microsoft Office Specialist Logo is used under license from owner.

ISBN 0-7638-2154-3
Product Number: 01640

© 2005 by Paradigm Publishing Inc.
Published by **EMC**Paradigm
875 Montreal Way
St. Paul, MN 55102

(800) 535-6865
E-mail: educate@emcp.com
Web site: www.emcp.com

All rights reserved. No part of this book may be reproduced, stored in a retrieval system, or transmitted, in any form or by any means, electronic, mechanical, photocopying, recording, or otherwise, without prior written permission of Paradigm Publishing Inc.

Printed in the United States of America
10 9 8 7 6 5 4 3

CONTENTS

Chapter 1 Using Outlook for E-Mail — 3

- Starting Outlook for the First Time — 4
- Exploring the Outlook Window — 4
- Navigating Outlook Components — 5
- Using Menus and Toolbars — 6
- Creating and Sending E-Mail Messages — 7
    - Using Outlook Connected to Microsoft Exchange Server — 7
    - Using Outlook Connected to an Internet Mail Server — 8
    - Composing a New Mail Message — 8
- Opening, Printing, Replying to, and Forwarding Messages — 11
    - Reading and Printing Messages — 11
    - Replying to a Message — 13
    - Forwarding a Message — 13
- Deleting Messages — 15
- Attaching Files to Messages — 16
- Maintaining Address Books — 18
    - Creating a Personal Address Book — 18
    - Adding Entries to the Address Book — 20
- Assigning Message Options — 23
- Creating a Signature — 26
- Finding a Message — 28
    - Advanced Find — 29
- Flagging Messages — 30
- Arranging Messages in the Contents Pane — 33
    - Filtering Messages — 33
- Applying Color to Message Headers — 34
- Managing Folders — 36
    - Creating a Folder — 36
    - Moving Messages — 37
    - Creating a Rule to Move Messages to a Folder Automatically — 39
    - Understanding the Junk E-Mail Filter — 41
- Using Help — 42
- Chapter Summary — 44
- Features Summary — 45
- Concepts Check — 46
- Skills Check — 47

Chapter 2 Using Calendar for Scheduling — 51

- Scheduling Appointments and Events — 52
    - Recurring Appointments — 55
    - Scheduling Events — 57
    - Natural Language Phrases — 58
    - Editing, Deleting, and Moving Appointments — 58
    - Calendar Coloring — 60
- Changing the Calendar View — 60
    - Displaying the Reading Pane — 61
    - Displaying Views in the Navigation Pane — 63
- Assigning Categories to Appointments — 64
- Automatic Formatting — 66
- Scheduling Meetings — 68
    - Responding to Meeting Requests — 71
    - Updating and Canceling a Meeting — 73
    - Updating Meeting Attendees and Manually Tracking Responses — 76
- Changing Calendar Options — 77
- Working with More Than One Calendar — 79
- Chapter Summary — 81
- Features Summary — 82
- Concepts Check — 83
- Skills Check — 83

Chapter 3 Managing Contacts — 87

- Adding Contacts — 88
- Editing Contacts — 92
- Adding New Contacts from Existing Contacts — 94
- Using the Details and All Fields Tabs — 94
- Adding Pictures to Contacts — 96
- Flagging a Contact for Follow-up — 97
- Sorting Contacts — 99

Filtering Contacts	101
Grouping Contacts into Categories	103
Finding a Contact	106
Find a Contact Text Box	106
Find Bar	107
Advanced Find	108
Changing the Current View	109
Changing Contact Options	111
Sending E-Mail Messages to Contacts	112
Scheduling Appointments from Contacts	113
Creating a Distribution List	114
Maintaining Distribution Lists	117
Expanding the Distribution List in the Message Window	117
Chapter Summary	117
Features Summary	119
Concepts Check	119
Skills Check	120

Chapter 4 Creating Tasks and Notes — 125

Creating and Updating Tasks	126
Updating Tasks	129
Creating a Recurring Task	130
Assigning a Task to Someone Else	132
Responding to a Task Request	134
Tracking and Viewing Assigned Tasks	136
Sending Task Information to Other Users	137
Changing the Task View to Create Task Lists	139
Changing Task Options	141
Creating and Editing Notes	141
Editing and Deleting Notes	143
Placing a Note on the Desktop	143
Assigning a Category to a Note	144
Changing Note Options	145
Changing the Note View	146
Chapter Summary	147
Features Summary	148
Concepts Check	149
Skills Check	149

Chapter 5 Customizing, Integrating, and Archiving Outlook Components — 153

Using and Customizing Outlook Today	154
Specifying the Startup Folder	156
Customizing the Navigation Pane	157
Setting E-Mail Options	160
Changing the Mail Editor and Viewer	165
Customizing Desktop Alerts	167
Understanding Search Folders	168
Creating a Private Appointment	169
Creating a Letter to a Contact	170
Creating a Standard Letter to Multiple Contacts	172
Exporting Data from Contacts to Create a Data Source	172
Completing the Merge in Word	173
Creating a Personal Folders File	176
Archiving Folders	178
Manually Archiving Items	180
Mailbox Cleanup Tool	183
Restoring Archived Items	184
Compacting PST Files	184
Backing Up the PST File	184
Chapter Summary	185
Features Summary	187
Concepts Check	187
Skills Check	188

Index — 192

MICROSOFT® OUTLOOK

Introducing Microsoft Outlook 2003

Organizing your life has never been easier thanks to Microsoft Outlook 2003. Many e-mail messages can be read in the new Reading Pane without even opening the message! Move folders you use often to Favorite Folders and use Outlook's new search folders to easily identify unread mail or messages for follow-up.

Keep track of your appointments in the Calendar and even maintain a separate calendar for personal appointments that you can view side-by-side with your work calendar. Schedule meetings or events and view your schedule by day, week, or month. Reminders make sure you arrive on time.

Locate a person's telephone number or e-mail address in a flash using Contacts. Outlook provides over 100 fields for tracking information about people with whom you communicate. Sort, filter, and group related records as needed. Contact information can be used to print mailing labels and send bulk e-mails or faxes.

Get rid of all those small reminders and notes on your desk and your monitor and track your to-do lists and other reminder notes in Outlook. Even better, assign a task to someone else to do and instruct Outlook to keep you informed of any updates.

Several options are available to customize Outlook to suit your working environment and preferences. Information within the various Outlook components is easily shared between folders and within other products in the Microsoft Office suite.

Get started today. Get organized.

USING OUTLOOK 2003

Microsoft Outlook 2003 is an application that provides tools to send and receive e-mail, organize schedules and events, and maintain contacts lists, to-do lists, and notes. Information in Outlook can be integrated with other applications in the Microsoft Office suite. Using Outlook is different from using other applications such as Word or Excel. In Outlook, you open a folder related to the item you wish to create, edit, or view.

Skills taught in this text:

✔ **Using Outlook for e-mail**
- Create and send an e-mail message
- Reply to, print, and delete e-mail messages
- Attach files to a message
- Create folders and move messages between folders

✔ **Managing schedules**
- Schedule appointments and events
- Schedule recurring appointments
- Change the calendar view
- Print the calendar
- Edit and move appointments
- Use Outlook to schedule meetings

✔ **Managing Outlook folders and contacts**
- Create an appointment from the contacts folder
- Create, print, edit, and delete contacts
- Change the contacts view

✔ **Organizing your work using tasks and notes**
- Create a tasks list
- Mark a task as complete
- Create a recurring task
- Create a note
- Place a note on the desktop

✔ **Customizing Outlook and using advanced features**
- Use and customize Outlook Today
- Perform a mail merge using the contacts list
- Change e-mail options
- Create a private appointment
- Archive folders and archive items

CHAPTER 1

USING OUTLOOK FOR E-MAIL

PERFORMANCE OBJECTIVES

Upon successful completion of Chapter 1, you will be able to:

- Identify Outlook components and display folder contents
- Compose, send, open, and print messages
- Reply to, forward, and delete messages
- Attach a file to a message
- Add and use entries in a personal address book
- Assign importance, sensitivity, and tracking options to a message
- Create a signature
- Find messages
- Apply follow-up flags to messages
- Arrange and filter messages in the Contents Pane
- Apply color to e-mail messages
- Create a folder and move messages from one folder to another
- Create a rule to automatically move messages to a folder
- Modify the junk e-mail settings
- Find information in Microsoft Help resources

(Note: There are two student data files required for this chapter.)

Microsoft Outlook is an application that is often referred to as a ***Desktop Information Management (DIM)*** or a ***Personal Information Manager (PIM)*** program. Information management programs organize items such as e-mail messages, appointments or meetings, contacts, to-do lists, and notes. Data stored within Outlook can be integrated to and from the other applications within the Microsoft Office suite. In this chapter you will explore the basic features of Outlook and the Inbox component that is used for managing e-mail messages.

Starting Outlook for the First Time

The screen that you see when you start Outlook 2003 for the first time depends on whether or not a prior version of Outlook existed on the computer to which Outlook 2003 has been installed. If a prior version of Outlook existed, you will see a message indicating that Outlook is migrating the information from the old Outlook data file to the new Outlook data file. Existing messages are transferred to Outlook 2003 since you already have an e-mail profile.

On a computer for which no prior version exists, you will be presented with the Outlook 2003 Startup Wizard. In this wizard you are guided through the steps required to set up your e-mail profile. An e-mail profile contains the settings required to send and receive e-mail such as your e-mail address and the addresses of the e-mail servers to which your incoming and outgoing messages are routed. Your e-mail provider can provide the server type and server name settings for this process.

Exploring the Outlook Window

Outlook

To start Outlook, click the Start button on the Taskbar, point to All Programs, point to Microsoft Office, and then click Microsoft Office Outlook 2003. The Microsoft Office Outlook application window appears similar to the one shown in Figure 1.1. Depending on your system configuration you may also be able to launch Outlook by clicking an Outlook icon on your desktop, or by clicking E-mail in the first column of program names that appears after you click the Start button if you are using Windows XP.

FIGURE 1.1 *Microsoft Office Outlook 2003 Window*

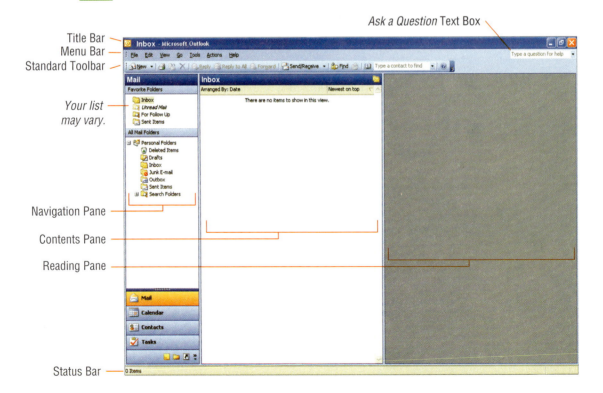

The Outlook window contains elements standard to Windows-based applications such as the Title bar, Menu bar, Standard toolbar, and Status bar that contain features similar to those found in the other programs within the Microsoft Office suite. Please note that the screens shown throughout this book display Outlook 2003 operating within the Windows XP environment.

By default, Mail is the active component with Inbox the active folder within Mail when Outlook is first started. In Outlook, information items within each component are stored within a separate folder for that component. For example, mail messages when received are initially stored within the Inbox folder and appointments are stored within the Calendar folder. Click Mail, Calendar, Contacts, or Tasks in the Navigation Pane to display the items within the folder in the Contents Pane. Table 1.1 describes the type of items that are stored within each Outlook folder.

TABLE 1.1 Outlook Folders

Folder Name	Contents Stored within Folder
Inbox	E-mail messages that have been received. Other folders used for mail messages are Deleted Items, Drafts, Junk E-mail, Outbox, and Sent Items. These folder names display in the *All Mail Folders* section of the Navigation Pane when Mail is active.
Calendar	Scheduled appointments, events, and meetings.
Contacts	Information such as name, address, telephone, e-mail address, and other data about the individuals with whom you regularly communicate. Mail distribution lists will also appear within Contacts.
Tasks	Descriptions of activities that you need to complete of which you want to keep track.
Notes	Reminders or other pieces of unstructured information of which you want to keep track.

Navigating Outlook Components

The Navigation Pane contains icons to the four commonly used folders in Outlook: Mail, Calendar, Contacts, and Tasks. Clicking an icon in the Navigation Pane changes the active folder and displays the folder's contents in the Contents Pane. The top two sections of the Navigation Pane change content depending on the active folder.

exercise 1

VIEWING FOLDER CONTENTS

1. Click the Start button on the Taskbar, point to All Programs, point to Microsoft Office, and then click Microsoft Office Outlook 2003.
2. If necessary, type your user name and password to connect to your mail server. Following this exercise, it will be assumed that you are working with Outlook already connected and your account authenticated by the mail server.
3. Change the active folder using the Navigation Pane by completing the following steps:
   a. Click Calendar in the Navigation Pane. The current day is displayed with time slots for each hour of the day, and the top section of the Navigation Pane changes to the Date Navigator which contains a calendar for the current month.
   b. Click Contacts in the Navigation Pane and then view the layout of the Outlook window.
   c. Click Tasks in the Navigation Pane and then view the layout of the Outlook window.
   d. Click the *Notes* icon in the Navigation Pane and then view the layout of the Outlook window. The *Notes* icon is the first icon from the left below Tasks.
4. Change the active folder back to the Inbox using the Menu bar by completing the following steps:
   a. Click Go on the Menu bar.
   b. Click Mail at the drop-down menu.

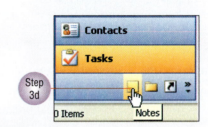

Using Menus and Toolbars

In a default installation of Outlook 2003, the menus and toolbars become personalized as you work with the application. When you click an option on the Menu bar, such as File, the drop-down list of menu items that is shown includes only the options referred to as ***first-rank options***. These are the options that are considered to have the most usage. At the bottom of the menu you will see downward-pointing arrows. This indicates that additional menu items (referred to as ***second-rank options***) are not currently displayed. Use any of the following techniques to expand the menu and see the full list of options.

- Double-click the Menu bar option. For example, double-click File to immediately see the full range of File menu options.
- Click the down-pointing arrows at the bottom of the drop-down menu.
- Rest the mouse pointer over the Menu bar option and within a few seconds, the drop-down menu will expand automatically.

If you click a second-rank option on a menu, the next time you access the same menu, the option will have moved in precedence to a first-rank option and will be visible immediately. This feature is called *adaptive menus*. Complete the following steps if you prefer to work with Outlook with the adaptive menu feature turned off. This means you will see the full list of menu items whenever you click an option on the Menu bar.

1. Click Tools and then Customize.
2. Click the Options tab in the Customize dialog box.
3. Click the *Always show full menus* check box in the *Personalized Menus and Toolbars* section.
4. Click the Close button at the bottom of the Customize dialog box.

Toolbars in Outlook are also adaptive. In some cases you may notice that the Standard and Formatting toolbars are sharing one row within a window, such as a message window. A Toolbar Options button displays which you click to view additional buttons not currently shown. If you prefer you can also customize Outlook to show the toolbars on two rows. With the window active in which the toolbars are sharing a single row, complete Steps 1 and 2 as described above. Click the *Show Standard and Formatting toolbars on two rows* check box in the Customize dialog box and then click Close.

Creating and Sending E-Mail Messages

Electronic mail (e-mail) is communication between individuals by means of sending and receiving messages electronically. E-mail has become the business and personal standard for communication because of its ability to deliver a message within seconds anywhere around the world. The business world embraced e-mail due to the speed of delivery and low cost. Routine business correspondence is now mostly conducted electronically, replacing paper-based letters and memos. Individuals use e-mail regularly to communicate with relatives and friends all around the world.

To send and receive e-mail, you need to have an account on a *mail server*. The mail server acts as the post office—routing messages sent and received to the appropriate recipients. The computer that you use to send messages and read the messages that you have received is called the *mail client*. Connection to a mail server can be through a local area network that is connected to the mail server, or via a modem or other high-speed device such as DSL or cable. If you are using a modem plugged into your telephone line, you may need to manually establish the connection to the server.

Multiple users will be connected to the same mail server just as one post office serves many people within a community. Each individual connected to the mail server is assigned a *user name* and *password* for unique identification and security of mail services.

Using Outlook Connected to Microsoft Exchange Server

Outlook can be used as an e-mail client connected to a server running Microsoft Exchange Server or a server set up as an Internet mail server. Many organizations use Microsoft Exchange Server on a local area network since internal users are provided with additional options such as planning and scheduling meetings, assigning and delegating tasks, and posting notices in public folders. Users

HINT
Use proper business etiquette when using e-mail for business purposes. Many employees mistakenly perceive e-mail as casual correspondence.

QUICK STEPS

Create and Send a Message
1. Click New Mail Message button.
2. Type e-mail address in *To* text box.
3. Type subject in *Subject* text box.
4. Type message in message window.
5. Click Send.

connected to an Exchange Server view all other internal users in a global address list and can send a message to someone else in the organization just by typing the person's name. Messages sent externally require the full e-mail address.

Outlook allows multiple e-mail accounts to be included in the e-mail profile; however, only one Microsoft Exchange Server account can be created. Throughout this book, whenever possible, differences in screens or options that are available for users connected to Microsoft Exchange Server will be identified.

Using Outlook Connected to an Internet Mail Server

If you are not using Outlook as an Exchange Server client, then you are using Outlook as an Internet mail client. When creating your e-mail profile you have the option of setting up your account with the following server types:

- **POP3**. *Post Office Protocol 3* is used by many Internet Service Providers. POP3 accounts download messages to the local computer when the user logs in to the mail server. An option can be set to instruct the server to retain copies of the messages on the mail server; however, many ISPs restrict the size of the mailboxes, and/or have a policy that messages can only be retained for a certain number of days.
- **IMAP**. *Internet Message Access Protocol* accounts store messages on the e-mail server. When the user logs in to the IMAP server, he or she reads the message headers and then chooses the messages to download to the local computer.
- **HTTP**. *Hypertext Transfer Protocol* is the server type for Web mail services such as Hotmail, in which messages are stored as Web pages.

The exercises and assessments in this chapter assume that you are connected to a mail server through a local area network (LAN) at your school. If you are working from home, you need to establish a dial-up connection or have a continuous high speed connection through a cable/digital modem to a service provider that provides the mail server prior to starting an exercise or assessment.

Composing a New Mail Message

New Mail Message

To create a new message, click the New Mail Message button on the Standard toolbar with the Inbox folder active. An Untitled Message window opens as shown in Figure 1.2.

FIGURE

1.2 New Mail Message Window

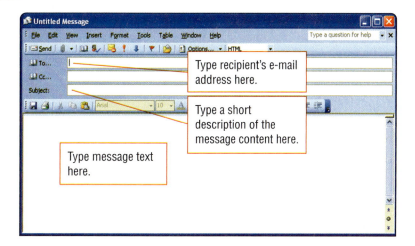

The address that you type in the *To* text box is either the user name of the recipient if you are sending the message to someone on the same mail server as you are, or the full Internet address of the recipient such as *name@mailserver.com* if you are sending the message to someone outside your network. Type multiple addresses separated by a semicolon and one space. For example, *JDoe@school.net; MSmith@mail.net*.

The message window's Title bar initially displays *Untitled Message* until you type text in the *Subject* text box. The subject text then appears in the Title bar of the window. The Formatting toolbar in the message window is used to change the font, font size, font color, font attributes, text alignment, to create a bulleted list, and so on. By default, Outlook is configured to use Microsoft Office Word as the e-mail editor in order to take advantage of the text editing features within Word. Your message window may appear slightly different than the one shown in Figure 1.2 if Word has been disabled as the e-mail editor on the computer that you are using. In Chapter 5, you will learn how to turn this feature on or off.

HINT
Always include a description in the *Subject* box and make it as brief as possible while still accurately describing the purpose of the message.

exercise 2 — CREATING AND SENDING A MESSAGE

(Note: Check with your instructor for specific instructions on whom you should send the e-mail messages to. The instructor may have designated an e-mail partner for each person in the class whom you will send messages to and receive messages from. If necessary, you can send the messages to yourself.)

1. Make sure Inbox is the active folder.
2. Create and send a message by completing the following steps:
   a. Click the New Mail Message button on the Standard toolbar.

Using Outlook for E-Mail

b. Type the e-mail address for the recipient in the *To* text box, for example, *username* or *name@mailserver.net*. Check with your instructor for specific instructions on the person you should send this message to.
c. Press Tab twice to move to the *Subject* text box.
d. Type **Mail Viruses**, and then press Tab to move to the message text window.
e. Type the following as the message text:

As a regular e-mail user, you must always be alert to the risk of infecting your computer with a virus through e-mail. A variation of the virus, called a worm, has become widespread within the last few years. A worm is programmed to replicate a message to addresses within your system, thereby bogging down mail server resources as the message is continually spread. Outlook includes features that will assist with protecting your system from infection.

f. Click the Send button on the message window toolbar to send the message to the recipient. The message window automatically closes once you have clicked Send.

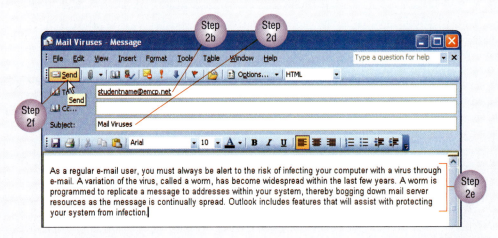

3. Check the mail folders to see where the message has been placed by completing the following steps:
    a. The message will appear in one of two folders. If the mail server is busy, or if your system is not configured to send messages immediately, the message will be queued in the Outbox folder. If the message has already been routed through the mail server, the message will be in the Sent Items folder. Look next to Outbox in the *All Mail Folders* section of the Navigation Pane. If the message is queued in the Outbox, the folder name is displayed in bold and the number of messages waiting to be sent is shown in green text next to the folder name. Click Outbox in the *All Mail Folders* section of the Navigation Pane.
    b. If the message is queued in the Outbox, click the Send/Receive button on the Standard toolbar to send the message immediately to the mail server. If the message has already been sent, Outbox displays the message *There are no items to show in this view*.
    c. Click Sent Items in the *All Mail Folders* section of the Navigation Pane. Messages that have been routed to the mail server are displayed in the Contents Pane.
4. Click Inbox in the *All Mail Folders* section in the Navigation Pane to redisplay the Inbox folder.

Opening, Printing, Replying to, and Forwarding Messages

Messages appear in the Contents Pane of the Inbox grouped by date with the most recent message at the top of the list. The message headers for messages that have not yet been opened are in bold text. The sender's name and subject text appear in the message header. By default, messages are arranged by the date in which they were received with messages received *Today* displayed first. The time the message arrived will also be shown next to the sender's name.

If you are online when a new mail message is received, by default a chime will sound and a ***desktop alert*** appears in the bottom right corner of your screen. The desktop alert displays the sender's name, the subject, and the first two lines of text within the message as shown in Figure 1.3. The alert is set to display for seven seconds, giving you time to read the alert text and decide whether you need to go to the message immediately to read and/or respond to its contents. Click the alert to open the message. The time interval can be increased or decreased, or you may choose to turn off the alert feature. If an alert appears that you want to keep visible longer than the current time interval, rest the mouse pointer over the alert before it disappears from view. In Chapter 5, you will learn how to customize the alert settings.

Print a Message
1. Double-click message header in Contents Pane.
2. Click Print button.
3. Close message window.

Reply to a Message
1. Double-click message header in Contents Pane.
2. Click Reply button.
3. Type reply message.
4. Click Send.

FIGURE 1.3 Desktop Alert for New Message Received

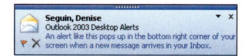

An icon of an envelope will also appear in the system tray at the right edge of the taskbar and the pointer will change briefly to an icon of an envelope as the message is placed in the Inbox.

Reading and Printing Messages

In many cases the contents of a message can be read without having to open the message by viewing the message text within the Reading Pane. The Reading Pane is initially set to approximately one-third the width of the Outlook window. The width of the pane can be widened or narrowed by dragging the blue vertical bar separating the Reading Pane from the Contents Pane as shown in Figure 1.4. Drag the bar left to increase the current width or right to decrease it.

Forward a Message
1. Double-click message header in Contents Pane.
2. Click Forward button.
3. Type recipient's e-mail address.
4. Type explanatory message.
5. Click Send.

FIGURE 1.4 Adjusting the Size of the Reading Pane

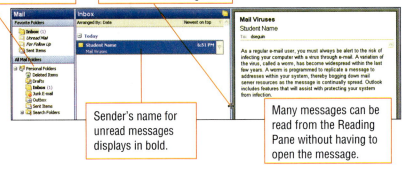

For longer messages, double-click the message header in the Contents Pane to open the message in a message window where you can read the full content. The Standard toolbar in the message window contains buttons to Reply, Reply to All, Print, or Forward the message to someone else as shown in Figure 1.5.

FIGURE 1.5 Opened Message Window

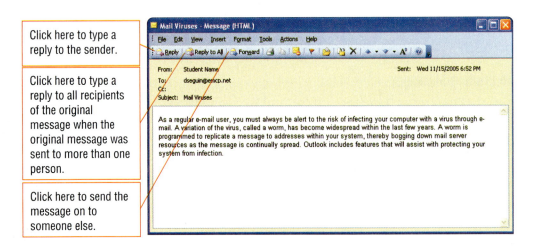

Click the Print button on the message window toolbar to print a hard copy of the message on the default printer. If you want to print from the Contents Pane, click the message header for the message you want to print to select it and then click the Print button on the Standard toolbar.

Replying to a Message

When you click the Reply or Reply to All button on the Standard toolbar, a new message window opens layered over the original message with the sender's e-mail address already entered in the *To* text box, and *RE:* inserted in front of the *Subject* text. The original message text is copied at the bottom of the message window a few blank lines below the insertion point. The original message is included in the reply so that the reader will see the source text. This is referred to as a **thread** and is very beneficial to someone who sends or receives several messages in a day and may not immediately recall what she or he had sent to you. Reply text is displayed in blue above the original message text.

If you are replying to a message that was sent to multiple recipients and you would like all of them to read your reply to the sender, click the Reply to All button to have the sender's e-mail address and the e-mail addresses of the other recipients of the original message automatically inserted in the *To* text box.

Reply

Reply to All

HINT
Exercise good judgment before using Reply to All—make sure *all* of the other recipients really need to see your response!

Forwarding a Message

When you click the Forward button on the Standard toolbar, a new message window opens layered over the original message with the insertion point positioned in the *To* text box, and *FW:* inserted in front of the *Subject* text. The original message text is copied a few blank lines below the beginning of the message window so that the reader can read the threaded text.

Type the e-mail address of the person to whom you want to forward the message and if necessary, include a few explanatory lines of text in the message window above the original message for the benefit of the recipient. Text typed at the top of the editing window of a Forwarded message is displayed in blue.

Forward

HINT
Be careful that you do not forward a message if the sender would object to it being forwarded.

OPENING, PRINTING, REPLYING TO, AND FORWARDING A MESSAGE

(Note: To complete this exercise another student must have sent you the message created in Exercise 2.)

1. Make sure Inbox is the active folder and that a new message appears in the Contents Pane.
2. Open, print, and reply to the message by completing the following steps:
   a. Double-click the message header to open the message and then read the message text.
   b. Click the Print button on the toolbar in the message window to print a hard copy of the message on the printer.
   c. Click the Reply button on the toolbar in the message window.
   d. With the insertion point automatically positioned at the top left of the message text window, type the following reply text:

   Thanks for the information. I have been hearing about computer viruses for some time now. We should investigate this further so that we know how to protect our computers.

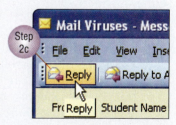
Step 2c

e. Click Send. The reply message window closes and you are returned to the original message window. A gray information box above the sender's name displays the message that you replied to and shows the date and time you sent the reply.

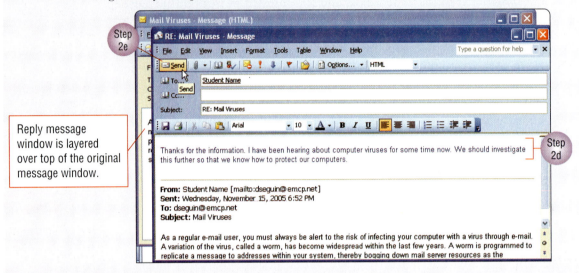

Reply message window is layered over top of the original message window.

   f. Click the Close button on the message window Title bar.
3. Now that you have read and replied to the message, you decide to send both the original message and your reply to someone else by completing the following steps:
   a. Click Sent Items in the *All Mail Folders* section of the Navigation Pane.
   b. Double-click the message header for the message you just sent in Step 2 in the Contents Pane. *(Note: If the message does not appear in the Sent Items folder, it is in the Outbox folder. Click the Send/Receive button on the Standard toolbar to upload the message to the mail server. In a few seconds, the message should appear in the Contents Pane.)*
   c. Click the Forward button on the toolbar in the message window.
   d. With the insertion point positioned in the *To* text box, type the e-mail address of the person to whom you want to forward the message.
   e. Click at the top of the message text window and then type the following text:

   I thought you might be interested in reading this information on e-mail viruses.

   f. Click Send. The forward message window closes and you are returned to the original message window. A gray information box above the sender's name indicates you forwarded the message and displays the date and time you sent the message.
   g. Click the Close button on the message window Title bar.
4. Display the contents of the Inbox folder. The icons in the Contents Pane next to sender's names reflect the message status as follows: opened envelope when a message has been read; a left-pointing purple arrow on an opened envelope when you have replied to the message; and a right-pointing blue arrow on an opened envelope when you have forwarded the message.

Deleting Messages

The mail messages stored in the Inbox and Sent Items folders are stored permanently. After a period of time these folders will become filled with messages that are no longer needed and should be deleted. To delete a message, click the message header to select the message and then press the Delete key on the keyboard or the Delete button on the Standard toolbar. The message will be moved to the Deleted Items folder. The message can be opened, replied to, or forwarded to someone else while it resides in the Deleted Items folder.

Delete

More than one message can be deleted at one time by following standard Windows conventions as follows:

- If the messages to be deleted are a group of adjacent messages, click the message header to select the first message in the list, hold down the Shift key, and then click the message header of the last message in the list.
- If the messages to be deleted are not adjacent, click the message header to select the first message, and then hold down the Ctrl key while clicking the remaining messages.

Delete a Message
1. Click message header in Contents Pane.
2. Click Delete button on toolbar.

Empty *Deleted Items* Folder
1. Right-click *Deleted Items* folder name.
2. Click Empty "Deleted Items" Folder.
3. Click Yes.

From time to time the Deleted Items folder should also be cleared out using the same techniques that you used to delete the messages from the original folder. To delete all of the messages in the Deleted Items folder in one step, complete the following steps:

1. Right-click the Deleted Items folder name.
2. Click Empty "Deleted Items" Folder at the shortcut menu.
3. Click Yes at the message box asking if you are sure you want to permanently delete all of the items in the Deleted Items folder.

DELETING MESSAGES AND EMPTYING THE DELETED ITEMS FOLDER

1. With the Inbox folder active, change to the Sent Items folder.
2. Delete the message that you sent in Exercise 2 by completing the following steps:
   a. Click the message header in the Contents Pane for the message you sent in Exercise 2.
   b. Click the Delete button on the Standard toolbar.
3. Delete the two messages that you sent in Exercise 3 by completing the following steps:
   a. Click the message header in the Contents Pane for the first message that you sent in Exercise 3.
   b. Hold down the Shift key and then click the message header for the second message that you sent in Exercise 3. Both messages are now selected.

c. Press the Delete key.
4. Display the Deleted Items folder and then empty the folder by completing the following steps:
    a. Click Deleted Items in the *All Mail Folders* section of the Navigation Pane.
    b. Notice the messages you deleted in Steps 2 and 3 are displayed in the Contents Pane.
    c. Right-click the Deleted Items folder name.
    d. Click Empty "Deleted Items" Folder at the shortcut menu.
    e. Click Yes at the message asking if you are sure you want to permanently delete all of the items and subfolders in the "Deleted Items" folder.
5. Change the active folder to the Inbox.

QUICK STEPS — Attaching Files to Messages

Attach a File to a Message
1. Click Insert, File in message window.
2. Browse to location of file in Insert File dialog box.
3. Double-click file name.

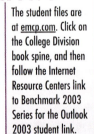

HINT The student files are at emcp.com. Click on the College Division book spine, and then follow the Internet Resource Centers link to Benchmark 2003 Series for the Outlook 2003 student link.

A file that you want to send to another individual can be attached to an e-mail message. Office documents created in Word or Excel, pictures, and other types of documents are routinely distributed by e-mail. To attach a file to a message, click the Insert File button on the message window toolbar, or click Insert on the message window Menu bar and then click File. Browse to the location of the desired document in the Insert File dialog box and then double-click the file name for the file that you want to attach.

The recipient of the e-mail with a file attachment can choose to open the file from the mail server or save it to disk. To open a file attachment from the mail server, double-click the file name next to *Attachments* in the Reading Pane, or open the message and double-click the file name in the message window. Depending on the size of the file and the purpose, saving an attachment to disk is often preferable. A message with a file attachment is displayed with a paper clip icon below the day and time the file was received in the Contents Pane.

Due to the proliferation of viruses and worms, Outlook blocks many file types that are commonly known to carry a virus. A blocked file attachment message displays in the message header.

exercise 5 — ATTACHING A FILE TO A MESSAGE

(Note: Make sure you have copied the student data files from the Benchmark Outlook 2003 Internet Resource Center Student link before completing this exercise.)

1. With Inbox the active folder, click the New Mail Message button on the Standard toolbar.
2. With the insertion point positioned in the *To* text box, type the e-mail address for the person to whom you want to send the message with the file attachment.
3. Click in the *Subject* text box and then type E-Mail Virus Tips.
4. Click in the message editing window and then type the following text:

> I created this Word document with a few tips on how to protect your computer from infection as a result of an e-mail virus. Let me know if you have any additional tips I should add to the list.

5. Attach the Word document named **Virus_Tips.doc** to the message by completing the following steps:
   a. Press Enter twice to move down the message editing window a few lines.
   b. Click the Insert File button on the message window toolbar, or click Insert on the message window Menu bar and then click File.
   c. At the Insert File dialog box, click the down-pointing arrow next to the *Look in* list box, and then click *3½ Floppy (A:)* in the drop-down list. *(Note: Select a different location if your student data files are stored on a drive and/or folder other than the 3½ Floppy.)*

   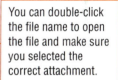

   d. Double-click the file named **Virus_Tips.doc** in the file list box. An *Attach* field is added below the *Subject* text box with the name of the file and the file size.

   You can double-click the file name to open the file and make sure you selected the correct attachment.

6. Click Send.

exercise 6 — SAVING A FILE ATTACHMENT TO DISK

(Note: To complete this exercise another student must have sent you the message created in Exercise 5.)

1. With the Inbox folder active, look at the message header in the Contents Pane for the message received with the subject *E-Mail Virus Tips*. Notice the paper clip icon below the time the message was received.

2. Click to select the message and then look at the message in the Reading Pane. Attachments can be opened directly from the Reading Pane by double-clicking the file name and then clicking Open at the Opening Mail Attachment dialog box. However, depending on the settings for your anti-virus software, saving the file to disk is a better practice. In the next step you will save the file attachment to disk.

   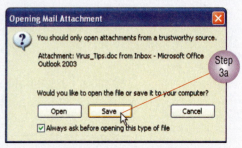

3. Save the Word document to disk by completing the following steps:
   a. Double-click the file name **Virus_Tips.doc** in the Reading Pane and then click Save at the Opening Mail Attachment dialog box.

b. With **Virus_Tips.doc** already selected in the *File name* text box of the Save As dialog box, type **ch1ex6.doc**.
   c. Click the down-pointing arrow next to the *Save in* list box, and then click *3½ Floppy (A:)*.
   d. Click the Save button.

4. Open the file attachment saved to disk by completing the following steps:
   a. Click Start, point to All Programs, point to Microsoft Office, and then click Microsoft Office Word 2003.
   b. Click the Open button on the Standard toolbar.
   c. If necessary, change the *Look in* location to *3½ Floppy (A:)*.
   d. Double-click the file named **ch1ex6.doc**.
   e. Read the text in the document.
   f. Add another tip of your own as a fifth item at the end of the document. If necessary, discuss e-mail virus prevention tips with another student in your class to gain ideas on what you can add.
   g. Type your name at the bottom of the document and then click the Print button on the Standard toolbar.
5. Exit Microsoft Word. Click Yes when prompted to save the changes to the document.

Maintaining Address Books

Address Book

QUICK STEPS

Add Names to Address Book
1. Click To button in message window.
2. Change *Show Names from the* to the address book in which to store the name.
3. Click Advanced, click New.
4. Click Other Address, OK.
5. Type **Display name and e-mail address**.
6. Type **smtp** in *E-mail type*, then click OK.

The ***Address Book*** is used to store the names and e-mail addresses of people to whom you send mail often. Addresses can be stored in Outlook in different locations. In a default installation of Outlook, the address book is dynamically linked to the Contacts folder. Adding an entry in the Address Book while in the Inbox folder is essentially creating a record in the Contacts folder.

If you wish to keep track of some e-mail addresses independently from the Contacts folder, one personal address book can be created that is stored separately from Contacts. A personal address book is created using the E-mail Accounts Wizard.

If the computer you are using for Outlook is connected to a Microsoft Exchange Server, a third address list called the ***Global Address List*** is shown in the Address Book. This list is stored on the server and contains the names of all of the mail accounts created on the server. Modifying addresses in the Global Address List is usually performed by the system administrator for the Exchange mail server.

Creating a Personal Address Book

A personal address book is a file stored outside Outlook with the file name extension of *.PAB*. You might want to create a PAB file to store personal addresses that are separate from business contacts. Complete the following steps to create a personal address book that stores addresses outside the Contacts folder.

1. Click Tools and then click E-mail Accounts.
2. Click *Add a new directory or address book* and then click Next.
3. Click *Additional Address Books* and then click Next.
4. Click *Personal Address Book* in the *Additional Address Book Types* list box and then click Next.
5. If necessary, change the properties for the new address book.
6. Click OK to close the Personal Address Book dialog box.
7. Exit Outlook. You have to exit and restart Outlook for the new address book to take effect.

When you are creating a message to someone with an entry in the Address Book, click the To or Cc buttons in the message window and the Select Names dialog box will open as shown in Figure 1.6.

FIGURE 1.6 Select Names Dialog Box

Click the name in the *Name* list box for the person to whom you want to send the message, and then click the To, Cc, or Bcc button in the *Message Recipients* section to add the selected name to the message. Click OK to close the Select Names dialog box when you are finished choosing names. The names displayed in the message window will appear underlined indicating they were selected from an address book. When you send the message, the e-mail address stored in the address book for the displayed name is used to deliver the message.

If you are working on a computer that is connected to a Microsoft Exchange Server, the names of the other accounts connected to the same mail server will appear when you open the Address Book under the Global Address List. To display names that are stored in your own personal address book or the Contacts folder, click the down-pointing arrow next to the *Show Names from the* list box, and then click Contacts or Personal Address Book.

Adding Entries to the Address Book

New names and e-mail addresses can be added to the address book by clicking Tools, Address Book, or clicking the Address Book icon on the Standard toolbar. If a message window is open, click the To button, click the Advanced button at the bottom left of the Select Names dialog box, and then click New at the drop-down menu.

By default, Outlook will store new entries to the Address Book in the Contacts folder. Open the Address Book, click Tools and then Options to change the storage location if you want a new entry to be stored in the Personal Address Book.

exercise 7

CREATING A PERSONAL ADDRESS BOOK

(Note: In this exercise you will be creating a personal address book (PAB) file saved to the disk in the floppy disk drive. Following completion of this exercise, whenever you start or exit Outlook, you must ensure the same floppy disk is in the drive or an error message will display that data has been lost. Check with your instructor for instructions on saving the PAB to an alternate storage location if you do not want to use the floppy disk.)

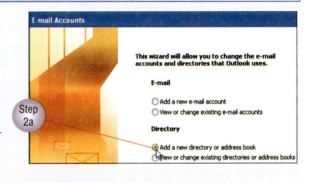

1. With the Inbox folder active, click Tools and then click E-mail Accounts.
2. Create a new personal address book using the E-mail Accounts wizard by completing the following steps:

    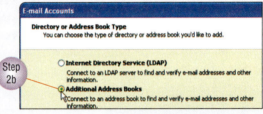

    a. At the first E-mail Accounts dialog box, click *Add a new directory or address book* and then click Next.
    b. At the second E-mail Accounts dialog box, click *Additional Address Books* and then click Next.
    c. At the third E-mail Accounts dialog box, click *Personal Address Book* in the *Additional Address Book Types* list box and then click Next.

    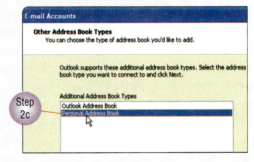

d. At the Personal Address Book dialog box, click the Browse button next to the *Path* text box.
e. Change the *Look in* location to *3½ Floppy (A:)*, leave the default file name **mailbox.PAB** as is, and then click the Open button.
f. Click OK to close the Personal Address Book dialog box.
g. Click OK at the Add E-mail Account message box that indicates you have to exit and restart Outlook for the new account to start.
h. Click File and then click Exit.
3. Start Outlook. If necessary, enter your user name and password to log back in to the mail server.

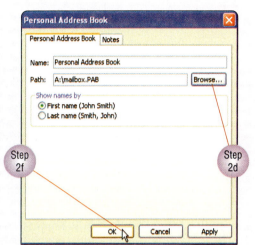

Step 2f

Step 2d

exercise 8

ADDING AN ENTRY TO THE PERSONAL ADDRESS BOOK WHILE CREATING A MESSAGE

1. With the Inbox folder active, click Tools, Address Book, or click the *Address Book* icon on the Standard toolbar.
2. Specify the Personal Address Book as the default location to store new entries to the Address Book by completing the following steps:
   a. Click Tools and then Options.
   b. At the Addressing dialog box, click the down-pointing arrow next to the *Keep personal addresses in* list box and then click *Personal Address Book*.
   c. Click OK to close the Addressing dialog box.
   d. Click the Close button on the Address Book window Title bar.

   This entry may show *Global Address List* if you are connected to a Microsoft Exchange Server.

3. Add a new entry to the Personal Address Book while creating a new message by completing the following steps:
   a. Click the New Mail Message button on the Standard toolbar.
   b. Click the To button in the Untitled Message window.
   c. At the Select Names dialog box, click the down-pointing arrow next to the *Show Names from the* list box and then click *Personal Address Book*.

Step 2a

Step 2b

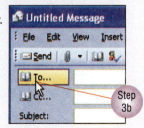

Step 3b

Step 3c

OUTLOOK

Using Outlook for E-Mail 21

d. Click the Advanced button at the bottom left of the Select Names dialog box and then click New.
e. With *Other Address* already selected in the *Select the entry type* list box at the New Entry dialog box, click OK.
f. With the insertion point positioned in the *Display name* text box, type the name of the student for whom you are creating an entry.
g. Press Tab or click in the *E-mail address* text box and then type the full e-mail address of the student for whom you are creating an entry.
h. Press Tab or click in the *E-mail type* text box and then type **smtp**. **SMTP** is the acronym for **Simple Mail Transfer Protocol**. Protocols are standards that were developed to facilitate communication between computers over the Internet. Most mail servers use SMTP to send messages from one server to another. In addition, SMTP is generally used as the protocol to send messages from a mail client to a mail server.
i. Click OK to close the New Other Address Properties dialog box.

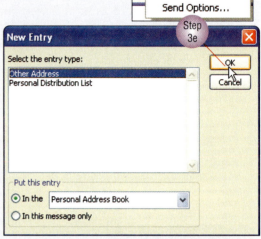

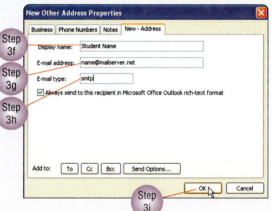

4. With the name of the recipient already entered in the *To* text box, click in the *Subject* text box and then type **Outlook Address Books**.
5. Click in the message editing window and then type the following text:

   Use a personal address book to store names and e-mail addresses for individuals that you do not want to keep track of through the Contacts folder. One suggestion is to use Contacts for business associates and a personal address book for friends and relatives.

6. Click Send.

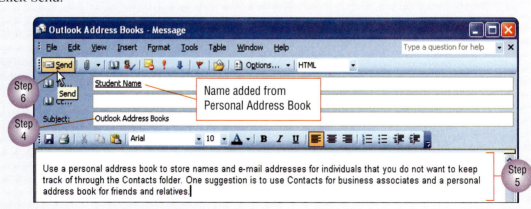

Assigning Message Options

With a message window open, click the Options button on the message window toolbar to display the Message Options dialog box shown in Figure 1.7. The Message Options dialog box is used to change settings, security, voting and tracking, and delivery options for the message you are creating.

Options

The *Message settings* section contains options for you to indicate to the recipient the message priority if it is to be treated unlike a normal message by attaching an Importance level of *High* or *Low*; and/or the Sensitivity is *Personal*, *Private*, or *Confidential*. Outlook also provides on the message window toolbar an Importance: High button and an Importance: Low button. Click the Security Settings button in the Security section to specify encryption or add a digital signature to the outgoing message.

Importance High

Importance Low

FIGURE 1.7 Message Options Dialog Box

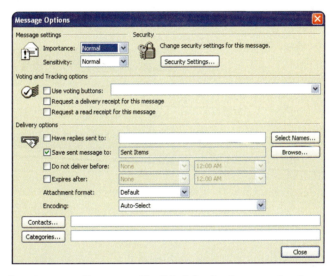

Voting buttons display Approve/Reject or Yes/No/Maybe buttons in the message window at the Recipient's end. These can be used to obtain feedback from recipients of your message on an issue described within the message. Delivery and read receipts can be attached to the message so that the sender will be notified when the message is delivered to the recipient's mailbox, and also when the recipient opens the message so that you will know they have read it.

In the *Delivery options* section you can direct replies to your message to someone else. For example, if you are going to be away and want a message that is replied to looked at in your absence, type an assistant's e-mail address in the *Have replies sent to* text box. Click the Select Names button to choose the alternate recipient from the Global Address List, Contacts, or Personal Address Book. Sent messages can be directed to a different folder in the *Save sent messages to* box. Use the Browse button to navigate to a different folder other than Sent Items. Use the *Do not deliver before* option to specify a date and time that you want the message sent if you do not want immediate delivery to take place. The message will be retained in the Outbox folder until the delivery date and time specified occurs.

Assign Message Options
1. Click Options button in message window.
2. Add required options as necessary.
3. Click Close.

The *Expires after* text box can be used to enter a date and time on which the message will expire. After the specified date and time, the message will no longer be available.

The Attachment format can be changed from *Default* to *MIME, UUEncode,* or *BINHEX*. The Encoding method is set to *Auto-Select* which means Outlook will automatically choose the appropriate character set for messages. To change the Encoding method, you have to close the message window, disable Microsoft Word as the mail editor, and then clear the Auto-Select option in the International Options dialog box of the Mail Format tab in the Options dialog box.

The Contacts button is used to display a list of contacts for which you can link the message. Later, you will be able to view the message by the Contacts name. The *Categories* text box is used to type in words that you want to associate the message with in order to find or group related messages at a later time.

exercise 9

ASSIGNING MESSAGE OPTIONS

1. With the Inbox folder active, click the New Mail Message button on the Standard toolbar.
2. Click the To button in the Untitled Message window to display the Select Names dialog box. Change *Show Names from the* to *Personal Address Book*, and then double-click the name of the student you added to the Personal Address Book in Exercise 8. Double-clicking inserts the student's name in the *To* text box in the *Message Recipients* section.

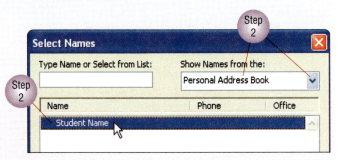

3. Click OK to close the Select Names dialog box.
4. Click in the *Subject* text box and then type **E-Mail Viruses**.
5. Click in the message editing window and then type the following text:

   E-mail viruses are a common occurrence. We need to be sure we are completely informed on the latest news regarding viruses and share a common strategy for protecting our systems.

6. Assign message options to the message by changing the Importance and Sensitivity settings and request a read receipt by completing the following steps:
   a. Click the Importance: High button ❗ on the message window toolbar. This button is a toggle. When it is turned on, the button is shaded with a light orange background.

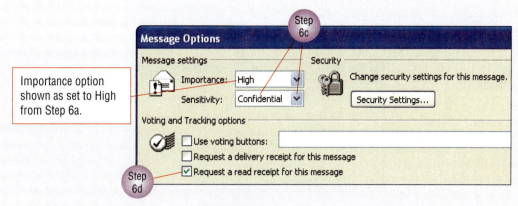

b. Click the Options button [Options...] on the message window toolbar.
c. At the Message Options dialog box, click the down-pointing arrow next to *Sensitivity* in the *Message settings* section and then click *Confidential*.
d. Click the *Request a read receipt for this message* check box in the *Voting and Tracking options* section.
e. Click the Close button at the bottom right of the Message Options dialog box.
7. Click Send.

The recipient of a message that has the Importance High option attached to it will see a red exclamation mark below the time the message was received in the Contents Pane. In the Reading Pane for the message, a gray information box displays below the sender's name informing the recipient of the options that have been assigned to the message as shown in Figure 1.8.

FIGURE 1.8 *Message Options Information Box in Reading Pane*

When a message has been sent to you with a read receipt attached to it, you will be notified that a read receipt has been requested by the sender. You will have the option of whether or not to send a read report as shown in Figure 1.9. If you click Yes at the Microsoft Outlook message box to send the receipt, a read report message similar to the one shown in Figure 1.10 is returned to the sender.

HINT
Click Tools, Options, E-mail Options, and then Tracking Options to control how your system handles read requests.

FIGURE 1.9 Message Box to Recipient for Read Receipt Message

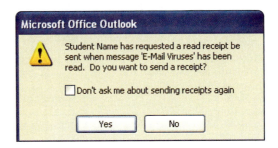

FIGURE 1.10 Read Report Message Sent to Sender Who Requested Read Receipt as Shown in Reading Pane

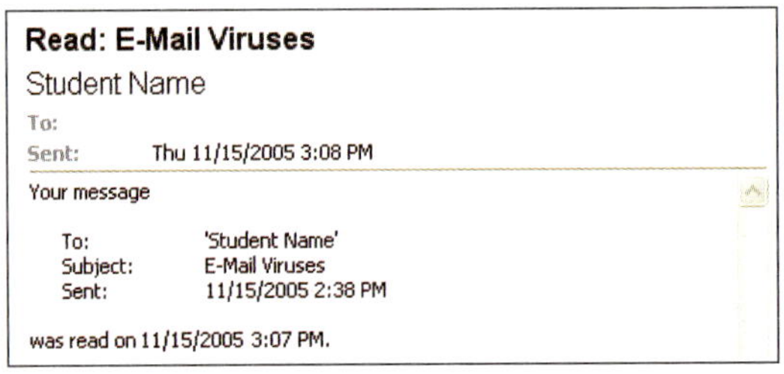

QUICK STEPS

Create a Signature
1. Click Tools, Options, Mail Format.
2. Click Signatures button.
3. Click New.
4. Type name for signature text.
5. Click Next.
6. Type text and change options as desired.
7. Click Finish.
8. Click OK twice.

Some mail servers do not support read reports to the sender. If you do not receive a read report message after sending a message with a read receipt attached, it does not always mean that the message was not opened by the recipient. One possibility is that the recipient's mail server does not support this feature. If you are sending and receiving mail using Microsoft Outlook connected to a Microsoft Exchange Server, then the read receipt feature should be operational. Contact your system administrator if you are not sure.

Creating a Signature

A signature is a closing that you would like automatically inserted at the bottom of each message that you create. Signature text usually includes information about the sender such as name, title, department, company name, and contact numbers. Some people include additional information such as office hours, assistant's name, or alternative contact names. An advantage to creating a signature is that each message you send contains a consistent closing. Multiple signatures can be created in case you want one signature for external contacts and another one for internal business mail. Once a signature has been created, Outlook inserts the text automatically at the end of each message you create.

exercise 10

CREATING A SIGNATURE

1. With the Inbox folder active, click Tools and then Options.
2. Click the Mail Format tab in the Options dialog box.
3. Click the Signatures button in the *Signatures* section near the bottom of the dialog box.
4. Create a new signature by completing the following steps:
   a. Click New in the Create Signature dialog box.
   b. Type **External Signature** in the *Enter a name for your new signature* text box in the Create New Signature dialog box.
   c. Click Next.
   d. Click the Font button in the Edit Signature - [External Signature] dialog box and then change the font, font size, and font color of the signature text by completing the following steps:
      1) Scroll down the *Font* list box and then click *Comic Sans MS*.
      2) Click *12* in the *Size* list box.
      3) Click the down-pointing arrow next to the *Color* list box and then click *Navy*.
      4) Click OK to close the Font dialog box.
   e. Click in the white text box above the Font button and then type the following signature text substituting your name, school name, and address for those shown:

      Student Name
      School Name
      City, StateorProvince,
      ZIPorPostalCode

   f. Click Finish.
   g. Click OK in the Create Signature dialog box. *External Signature* is automatically inserted in the *Signature for new messages* list box in the Options dialog box.
   h. Click OK to close the Options dialog box.
5. Create and send a new message with the external signature automatically inserted by completing the following steps:
   a. Click the New Mail Message button. Notice the external signature text is automatically inserted at the bottom of the message window.
   b. Click the To button and then insert the student name from your personal address book.

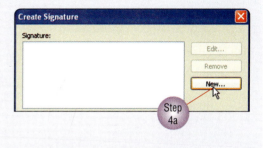
Step 4a

Step 4b
Step 4c

Step 4e
Step 4d
Step 4f

OUTLOOK
Using Outlook for E-Mail

c. Type **Outlook Signatures** in the *Subject* text box.
d. Click in the message window above the signature text and then type the following text:

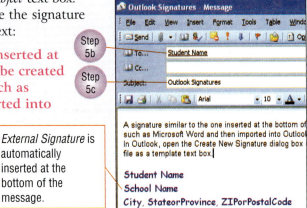

A signature similar to the one inserted at the bottom of this message can be created in another software program such as Microsoft Word and then imported into Outlook. To do this, create the signature text in a Word document. In Outlook, open the Create New Signature dialog box and then browse to the Word document name in the Use this file as a template text box.

External Signature is automatically inserted at the bottom of the message.

6. Click Send.

Find a Message
1. Click Find button.
2. Type search criteria in *Look for* text box.
3. Click folder to search in *Search In* drop-down list.
4. Click Find Now.

Once a signature has been created it can be edited or deleted. To do this, display the Create Signature dialog box by completing Steps 1 to 3 from Exercise 10. In the Create Signature dialog box, click the signature name that you want to edit if more than one signature exists, and then click the Edit button to open the Edit Signature dialog box where you can change the content or format. To delete the signature, click the signature name in the Create Signature dialog box and then click the Remove button.

Finding a Message

Once you have been sending and receiving messages for a while, the Contents Pane can be filled with a large number of messages in each of your mail folders. To locate and review a message that you sent or received in the past may be difficult. When the Contents Pane becomes filled with messages, scrolling through the list can also be a time-consuming process.

With the Find feature, Outlook will return a filtered list of all the messages that contain a keyword or phrase that you specify. The messages that do not meet the search criteria are temporarily hidden from view. To begin a Find, click Tools, point to Find, and then click Find, or click the Find button on the Standard toolbar to open the Find bar shown in Figure 1.11.

Find

FIGURE 1.11 *Find Bar*

The Find button toggles the Find bar on or off.

Find Bar

Type the word or phrase in the *Look for* text box that you want Outlook to search for within the messages. By default, the *Search In* list box contains the name of the current folder. Click Search In to display the drop-down list with the options *Inbox, All Mail Folders, Mail I Received, Mail I Sent,* or *Choose Folders.* The *Choose Folders* option will open the Select Folders dialog box where you can select which folders to search from the folder list. Click Find Now to begin the search. Outlook will list only those messages that meet the search criteria in the Contents Pane. Click Clear to remove the filter and restore the folder to the original list.

exercise 11 — FINDING A MESSAGE

1. With the Inbox folder active, click the Find button on the Standard toolbar to open the Find bar.
2. Search for messages that you sent that contain the keyword *protect* by completing the following steps:
    a. With the insertion point positioned in the *Look for* text box, type **protect**.
    b. Click Search In on the Find bar and then click *Mail I Sent* in the drop-down list.
    c. Click Find Now on the Find bar. Outlook searches through the messages in the Sent Items folder and displays in the Contents Pane only those messages that have the text string *protect* somewhere within the message.

Step 2a   Step 2b

3. Click each message in the Contents Pane and read through the message in the Reading Pane to make sure the text *protect* exists within the message. Notice in one message, the word found is *protecting*, a form of the word in the *Look for* text box.
4. Click Clear on the Find bar. The Contents Pane is restored to the previous list.
5. Click the Find button on the toolbar to close the Find bar.

Advanced Find

To use the Advanced Find feature, click Options at the right end of the Find bar and then click Advanced Find to open the Microsoft Office Outlook dialog box shown in Figure 1.12. The Messages tab of the dialog box contains options to locate messages by restricting the search to individual names, to search by specific fields in a message, or restrict the search to messages within a specific time frame. To search in additional folders for the search criteria, click the Browse button to select folder names from a list. In the *Folders* list box, click the check boxes next to the folders that you want to search, and then click OK. The folder names will appear separated by semicolons in the *In* text box.

The More Choices tab can be used to locate messages by the category they have been assigned, the read status, the attachments, the importance setting, or the color of the flag that has been applied. The case of the text within the search string can be matched, or the messages can be filtered by the message size.

The Advanced tab can be used to enter conditional statements which Outlook must satisfy to filter the message list.

FIGURE 1.12 Microsoft Office Outlook Dialog Box with Advanced Find Options

Use these buttons to search for messages sent or received from a specific individual.

Flagging Messages

Flag a Message
1. Right-click flag in Flag status column.
2. Click flag color to apply to message.

A message that you have received can be flagged as a reminder to follow up on an item or a message can be flagged as you are creating it to request someone else to perform an action. Outlook provides six colored flags that you can apply to messages for organizing your follow-up activities: red, blue, yellow, green, orange, and purple. For example, you can apply a red flag to messages that need immediate follow-up and green flags to messages that can be followed up next week. Reminder dates can be added to flags to indicate the date by which the follow-up activity should be completed. When the follow-up is complete, you can change the flag status to Flag Complete which causes a gray check mark to display in the flag status column, or you can clear the flag from the message.

When a recipient receives a flagged message, a gray information box appears at the top of the message with the purpose of the flag. If a reminder date has been set, the date will also appear in the information box.

Mark Flag Complete
1. Right-click flag in Flag status column.
2. Click Flag Complete.

To flag a message that you have already received with the default red flag, click in the Flag status column next to the message header in the Contents Pane. The flag automatically changes to red and the message is linked to the For Follow Up folder in the *Favorite Folders* section of the Navigation Pane. To choose a flag color other than red, right-click in the Flag status column in the Contents Pane and then click the desired flag color at the drop-down list. Assign a reminder date for a flagged message by right-clicking the flag and then clicking Add Reminder at the drop-down list. At the Flag for Follow Up dialog box, enter the reminder date in the *Due by* text box.

Message Flag

To add a flag to a message that you are sending to someone else, click the Message Flag button on the message window toolbar. The Flag for Follow Up dialog box opens where you can set the flag type and due date.

exercise 12

ATTACHING A FOLLOW UP FLAG TO A MESSAGE AND FLAGGING MESSAGES IN THE CONTENTS PANE

1. With the Inbox folder active, click the New Mail Message button.
2. Click the To button and then insert the student name from your personal address book.
3. Type **Virus Protection Strategy** in the *Subject* text box.
4. Click in the message window above the signature text and then type the following text:

   Let's meet soon to discuss the E-Mail Virus Tips document and formalize a strategy that we can all use to protect our systems.

5. Attach a Follow up Flag with a due date to the message by completing the following steps:
   a. Click the Message Flag button [icon] on the message window toolbar.
   b. With *Follow up* the default flag type in the *Flag to* text box, drag across the text *None* in the *Due by* text box and then type **one week from today**. *(Note: This text is referred to as a natural language phrase. You can also use the down-pointing arrow to click a specific date from a drop-down calendar.)*
   c. Click OK. A gray information box appears above the recipient's name with the Follow up message and due date.
6. Click Send.
7. Apply colored flags to messages in the Inbox folder to indicate follow-up action is required by completing the following steps:
   a. Click the flag icon next to the message header in the Contents Pane for the message with the subject text *E-Mail Virus Tips*. The flag color changes to red, a gray Follow up message is added to the top of the message in the Reading Pane, and the For Follow Up folder in the *Favorite Folders* section of the Navigation Pane displays in bold with [1] in green text. *(Hint: If Favorite Folders does not contain the For Follow Up folder name, expand the Search Folders folder name in the All Mail Folders section, and then drag For Follow Up just above Sent Items in the Favorite Folders section.)*
   b. Right-click the flag icon in the Flag status column next to the message header in the Contents Pane for the message with the subject text *Outlook Signatures* and then click Blue Flag at the drop-down list. The flag color changes to blue, and the For Follow Up folder now indicates that two messages require follow-up action.

OUTLOOK

Using Outlook for E-Mail — 31

c. Click the For Follow Up folder name in the *Favorite Folders* section of the Navigation Pane. The Contents Pane displays the two messages that have been assigned Follow up flags. By default, Outlook arranges the flagged messages with red flagged messages first.

Step 7c

8. Change the active folder to Inbox.

Clear Flag
1. Right-click flag in Flag status column.
2. Click Clear Flag.

To clear a flag from a message, right-click the Flag icon in the Flag status column of the Contents Pane and then click Clear Flag at the drop-down list. To mark a flag activity as completed, right-click the *Flag* icon and then click Completed at the drop-down list. Completed flags display with a check mark in the Flag status column.

exercise 13

MARKING A FLAGGED MESSAGE COMPLETE AND CLEARING A FLAG

(Note: To complete this exercise another student must have sent you the message created in Exercise 12.)

1. With Inbox the active folder, click the message header for the message with the Subject text *Virus Protection Strategy* with the Follow up Flag that was sent to you in Exercise 12. A gray information box appears at the top of the message in the Reading Pane indicating the due date for the follow-up activity.
2. Assume you have held the meeting and want to mark the follow-up activity finished by completing the following step:
   a. Right-click the red flag in the Flag status column and then click Flag Complete at the drop-down list. The flag icon changes to a gray check mark and the date the activity was completed is added to the gray information box at the top of the message in the Reading Pane.

Step 2a

3. Assume you have decided you do not need to do any follow-up action on the message that you flagged for follow-up with a red flag in Exercise 12. Clear the flag on the message by completing the following step:
   a. Right-click the red flag in the Flag status column next to the message header in the Contents Pane for the message with the subject text *E-Mail Virus Tips*, and then click Clear Flag at the drop-down list. The flag is removed from the message and the number next to the For Follow Up folder updates to reflect that only one message remains flagged.

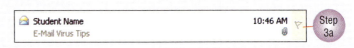

Step 3a

Step 4

4. Click For Follow Up in the *Favorite Folders* section of the Navigation Pane. Only one message displays, which is the Outlook Signatures message with the blue flag applied.
5. Change the active folder to the Inbox.

Arranging Messages in the Contents Pane

By default, Outlook displays messages in the Contents Pane grouped by the date they were received with the most recent message displayed at the top of the list. A collapse button appears next to each grouped day's blue heading (i.e., Today). Click the collapse button (button with minus symbol) to remove from display the messages for that day. The collapse button changes to an expand button (button with plus symbol) when a day's messages have been collapsed. Click the expand button to redisplay the messages below the group heading.

Click *Newest on top* in the gray header bar at the top of the Contents Pane to reorder the messages to *Oldest on top*. Click *Oldest on top* to change the order back to *Newest on top*. Click *Arranged By: Date* in the gray header bar at the top of the Contents Pane to display a drop-down list of options for grouping messages in the Contents Pane. For example, you can group the messages in the Contents Pane by the *From* field, meaning the messages will be arranged in alphabetical order by the sender's name. Each sender's name will become a group heading with a collapse button.

Arrange Messages
1. Click View, Arrange By.
2. Click option to group messages.

Filtering Messages

Click View on the Menu bar, point to Arrange By, point to Current View and then click a filter option such as Unread Messages or Last Seven Days. The current setting displays with a check mark in a light orange box next to the active menu option. *Unread Messages* filters the Contents Pane to display only those messages with an unread status on them—messages in the current folder that have been read are not listed when this view is active. To redisplay all the messages afterwards, select Messages from the Current View menu.

exercise 14 — ARRANGING THE CONTENTS PANE AND FILTERING MESSAGES

1. With the Inbox folder active, group the messages by the importance option by completing the following steps:
   a. Click Arranged By: Date in the gray header bar at the top of the Contents Pane.
   b. Click Importance at the drop-down list.
   c. With the messages grouped in the Contents Pane by the Importance option, click the collapse button next to the category *(none)*. The Contents Pane now displays only those messages that have the High Importance option and the collapse button next to *(none)* changes to an expand button (plus symbol).
   d. Restore the full list of messages by clicking Arranged By: Importance in the gray header bar at the top of the Contents Pane and then clicking Date at the drop-down list.
2. Filter the Contents Pane to display only those messages that are unread by completing the following step:
   a. Click View, point to Arrange By, point to Current View, and then click *Unread Messages in This Folder*. Outlook will display only those messages that have not yet been opened. If you have read all of your messages, the Contents Pane will be empty as shown below. Notice the message *(Filter Applied)* at the right edge of the folder banner.

3. Click View, point to Arrange By, point to Current View, and then click Messages. All of the messages reappear in the Contents Pane.
4. Click View and then click AutoPreview. AutoPreview displays the first three lines of the message text below the message headers as shown.
5. Click View and then click AutoPreview. The Contents Pane is restored to its original setting.

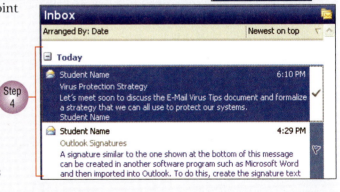

Applying Color to Message Headers

Having messages from selected individuals display in a different color will allow you to manage your Inbox folder by distinguishing those that might need immediate attention. For example, you might choose to have all messages where your boss is the sender display in Green. To do this, click Tools and then click Organize to display the Ways to Organize Inbox pane. Click Using Colors and then change the settings as required in the *Color messages* section.

Figure 1.13 shows the Ways to Organize Inbox pane with Using Colors selected. Messages can be colored based on the individual that the message is *from* or the individual the message is *sent to*. By default, the name of the sender in the message that is currently selected in the Contents Pane is automatically inserted in the name text box. Click the down-pointing arrow next to the color list box (displays *Red* by default) and then choose a color from the drop-down list. Click the Apply Color button and then close the Ways to Organize Inbox pane by clicking Tools and then Organize.

The option to change the color for *Show messages sent **only to me** in [Blue]* will help you to distinguish between messages where you are the only recipient and messages where you are part of a distribution list of recipients.

F I G U R E

1.13 Way to Organize Inbox Pane with Using Colors Selected

exercise 15

APPLYING COLOR TO MESSAGES

1. With Outlook open and the Inbox folder active, apply color to the message headers in the Contents Pane for the messages received from the student from whom you have been receiving e-mail in this chapter by completing the following steps:
   a. Click any message header in the Contents Pane for a message received from the student that you have been receiving e-mail from for this chapter's exercises.
   b. Click Tools and then click Organize.
   c. Click Using Colors in the Ways to Organize Inbox pane. The student's name is automatically inserted in the *from* text box next to *Color messages*.

   d. Click the down-pointing arrow next to the color list box (currently displays Red), and then click *Green* in the drop-down list.
   e. Click the Apply Color button. The message *Done!* appears next to the Apply Color button and the messages are now colored green in the Contents Pane for all messages received from the student whose name was entered in the *from* text box.
   f. Click Tools and then click Organize to close the Ways to Organize Inbox pane.
2. Create and then send a message to yourself to test the color application by completing the following steps:
   a. With Inbox the active folder, click the New Mail Message button on the Standard toolbar.

b. With the insertion point positioned in the *To* text box, type your own e-mail address.
c. Click in the *Subject* text box and then type Apply Color to Messages.
d. Click in the message editing window and then type the following text:

This message is to test the color applied to messages as they arrive in the Inbox.

e. Click Send.
f. If necessary, click the Send/Receive button on the Standard toolbar to have the message delivered immediately. In a few seconds, the message you sent yourself appears at the top of the Contents Pane. Notice the message header is black since the color green applies only to messages received from the student whose name you added to the Ways to Organize Inbox pane.

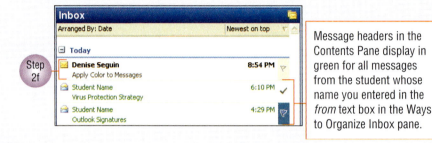

Message headers in the Contents Pane display in green for all messages from the student whose name you entered in the *from* text box in the Ways to Organize Inbox pane.

Apply Color to Message Headers
1. Click message header for sender to which you want color applied.
2. Click Tools, Organize.
3. Click Using Colors.
4. Change color option.
5. Click Apply Color.
6. Click Tools, Organize.

When apply coloring to messages is turned on for a selected individual in the Ways to Organize Inbox pane, Outlook creates a message ***rule***. A message rule is an action that you want Outlook to perform based upon a condition. In this case, the action is the application of the color green to a message header based upon the condition that the sender is the student name that you specified in the *Color messages from* text box.

To turn off the message rule for the color application, click Automatic Formatting in the Ways to Organize Inbox pane, click *Mail received from Student Name* in the *Rules for this view* list box, click Delete, and then click OK.

Managing Folders

Throughout this chapter you have been working with four folders set up in Outlook to organize mail messages: Inbox for mail that has been received; Outbox for mail that has been created but not yet uploaded to the mail server; Sent Items for messages that have been uploaded to the server and delivered to the recipient; and Deleted Items for messages that you have deleted. Frequently, you will want to manage the messages in your folders by organizing related items together in a separate folder with a descriptive name. For example, if you are working on an assignment and have been sending and receiving several messages about the assignment, you might want to create a folder specifically for the assignment work and then move all of the messages about the assignment to the folder.

Creating a Folder

The folder list in the *All Mail Folders* section of the Navigation Pane displays the names of the Outlook mail folders similar to a Windows Explorer folder list. A plus symbol next to a folder name in the list indicates the folder contains subfolders.

Click the plus symbol to expand the list and view the names of the subfolders within it. Complete the following steps to create a new folder or subfolder:

1. Right-click the folder name in the *All Mail Folders* section for which you want the new folder created as a subfolder. For example, right-click Inbox if you want to create a new subfolder from the Inbox folder.
2. Click New Folder at the shortcut menu.
3. Type the name for the new folder in the *Name* text box in the Create New Folder dialog box as shown in Figure 1.14.
4. Click OK.

Create a Folder
1. Right-click folder name in which to create new folder.
2. Click New Folder.
3. Type name for new folder.
4. Click OK.

FIGURE 1.14 *Create New Folder Dialog Box*

If you elect to place the new folder within an existing folder, such as Inbox, the new folder will appear in a hierarchial arrangement below the existing folder name.

Moving Messages

Once you have created new folders to organize messages, Outlook provides several methods for moving messages from one folder to another:

- With the message headers displayed in the Contents Pane, drag the message headers from their current location to the desired folder name.
- Click to select the message in the Contents Pane; click Edit and then click Move to Folder. At the Move Items dialog box, click the destination folder name and then click OK.
- Right-click the message header in the Contents Pane and then click Move to Folder at the shortcut menu. At the Move Items dialog box, click the destination folder name and then click OK.

Multiple messages can be moved in one operation using the multiple select keys of Ctrl + click for nonadjacent messages and Shift + click for adjacent messages.

exercise 16 — CREATING A NEW FOLDER AND MOVING MESSAGES

1. With Inbox the active folder, create a subfolder within Inbox by completing the following steps:
   a. Right-click Inbox in the *All Mail Folders* section of the Navigation Pane and then click New Folder at the shortcut menu.
   b. With the insertion point positioned in the *Name* text box, type **E-Mail Viruses**.
   c. With *Folder contains* already set to *Mail and Post Items* and *Inbox* already selected in the *Select where to place the folder* list box, click OK.

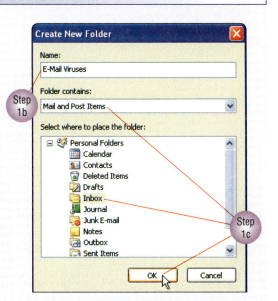

2. Move messages using the drag and drop method from the Inbox folder to the E-Mail Viruses folder by completing the following steps:
   a. Click the message header in the Contents Pane for the first message received with the subject *Mail Viruses*.
   b. Hold down the Ctrl key and then click each additional message header with *Virus* or *Viruses* within the subject text. If you click a message by mistake, simply click the message header a second time with the Ctrl key held down and the message will be deselected.
   c. Move the mouse pointer within the highlighted area for any of the selected messages, hold down the left mouse button, drag the mouse to the folder name E-Mail Viruses in the *All Mail Folders* section of the Navigation Pane and then release the left mouse button.

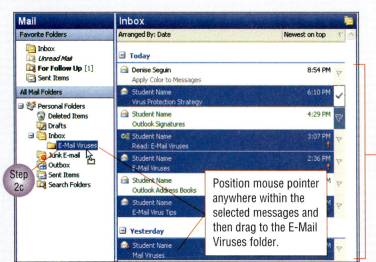

Your list may vary.

Position mouse pointer anywhere within the selected messages and then drag to the E-Mail Viruses folder.

38 Chapter One OUTLOOK

3. Click E-Mail Viruses in the *All Mail Folders* section to view the folder contents to make sure the messages have been placed in the correct location.
4. Click Inbox to make Inbox the active folder.

Mail messages should be organized in folders in a manner similar to how you manage documents on your hard disk. Create folders and/or subfolders and routinely move related messages from the Inbox to the appropriate folder name. In addition, make it part of your routine to delete messages when they are no longer needed and empty the deleted items folder. Imagine if you receive just 10 messages a day. Assuming a five-day work week and four weeks in a month, your Inbox will have 200 messages in the Contents Pane!

Creating a Rule to Move Messages to a Folder Automatically

When you applied the color green to all messages received from the student whose name you added to the *Color messages from* text box, you created a message rule, which is an action that is performed on messages based on a condition that you specify. In the color rule, the condition was the message was from a specific individual and the action to be performed was to color the message header green. Similar rules can be created that cause Outlook to move messages to specific folders automatically. The condition that causes the message to be moved can be based on a name, a subject, a message setting such as the Importance option, and so on.

The easiest method with which to create a rule that is based on a sender's name or subject is to select a message in the Contents Pane that meets the condition and then click the Create Rule button on the Standard toolbar. Outlook opens the Create Rule dialog box where you can choose the condition and the action you want performed. Information from the currently selected message is displayed next to the condition options as shown in Figure 1.15.

HINT
Set aside a time on the same day each week to clean up your Inbox so that the folder stays a manageable size.

Create Rule

QUICK STEPS

Create a Rule
1. Click message header that meets condition.
2. Click Create Rule button.
3. Change condition options as required.
4. Click *Move e-mail to folder* check box.
5. Click folder name to move messages.
6. Click OK to close Rules and Alerts dialog box.
7. Click OK at Create Rule dialog box.
8. Click OK at Success message.

FIGURE 1.15 Create Rule Dialog Box

exercise 17
CREATING A NEW FOLDER AND MESSAGE RULE

1. With Inbox the active folder, create a new subfolder within Inbox by completing the following steps:
   a. Right-click Inbox in the *All Mail Folders* section of the Navigation Pane and then click New Folder at the shortcut menu.
   b. With the insertion point positioned in the *Name* text box, type **Outlook Tips**.
   c. With *Folder contains* already set to *Mail and Post Items* and *Inbox* already selected in the *Select where to place the folder* list box, click OK.

2. Create a rule to move messages received in the Inbox that are related to Outlook information to the Outlook Tips folder by completing the following steps:
   a. Select the message header in the Contents Pane with the subject *Outlook Signatures*.
   b. Click the Create Rule button on the Standard toolbar.
   c. Click the *Subject contains* check box in the *When I get e-mail with all of the selected conditions* section of the Create Rule dialog box.
   d. Click the insertion point in the white text box next to *Subject contains* and then delete the word *Signatures* so that the entry in the text box consists of only the word *Outlook*.
   e. Click the *Move e-mail to folder* check box in the *Do the following* section of the Create Rule dialog box. The Rules and Alerts dialog box automatically opens.
   f. At the Rules and Alerts dialog box, click the expand button next to Inbox (plus symbol) in the *Choose a folder* list box, click *Outlook Tips*, and then click OK.
   g. Click OK at the Create Rule dialog box to complete the rule.
   h. Click OK at the Success message box indicating that the rule has been created.

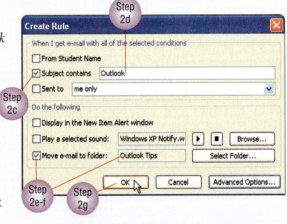

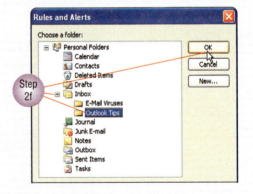

3. New rules that are created are applied automatically to messages as they are received. Manually apply the message rule created in Step 2 to the existing messages in the Inbox by completing the following steps:

40 Chapter One

OUTLOOK

a. Click Tools and then click Rules and Alerts.
b. At the Rules and Alerts dialog box, click the Run Rules Now button.
c. At the Run Rules Now dialog box, click the *Outlook* check box in the *Select rules to run* list box and then click the Run Now button. Outlook applies the rule to the existing messages and moves messages that meet the specified condition.
d. Click the Close button to close the Run Rules Now dialog box.
e. Click OK to close the Rules and Alerts dialog box.

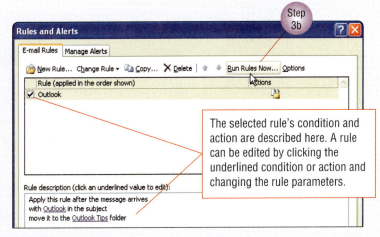

Rules are a powerful message management tool for controlling the size of your Inbox. If you receive many messages in a day and several that are related in some way, consider creating folders and rules to have the messages directed to a location in which you can easily view and manage the content.

Understanding the Junk E-Mail Filter

You have probably noticed the Junk E-mail folder in the *All Mail Folders* section of the Navigation Pane. You will be prompted when messages that are received have been automatically moved to the Junk E-mail folder. It is a good idea to check the folder periodically to review its contents and see if legitimate messages have been moved to Junk E-mail by mistake. In an attempt to better manage spam, a new feature of Outlook 2003 is the Junk E-mail Filter rule. By default, junk message filtering is turned on at the low protection level setting. This setting catches obvious spam messages. The filter works on two levels: Junk E-mail lists and artifical intelligence technology that evaluates a message based on factors such as the time sent and the content within the message in an effort to determine the probability that the message is spam.

To view and/or change the filter settings, click Tools and then click Options. At the Options dialog box with the Preferences tab selected, click the Junk E-mail button to open the Junk E-mail Options dialog box shown in Figure 1.16.

Change Junk E-mail Options
1. Click Tools, Options.
2. Click Junk E-mail button.
3. Change options as required.
4. Click OK.

FIGURE 1.16 Junk E-mail Options Dialog Box with Options Tab Selected

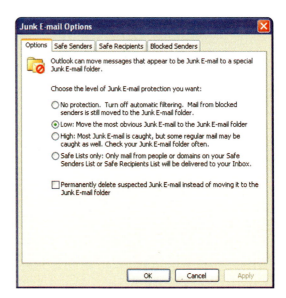

At the Junk E-mail Options dialog box with the Options tab selected you can choose to change the protection level from *Low* to *No protection, High,* or *Safe Lists only*. You can also choose to have messages identified as junk e-mail permanently deleted instead of moved to the Junk E-mail folder.

Add e-mail addresses or domain names to the lists on the Safe Senders or Safe Recipients tabs to make sure messages received or sent to or from members of the list are never treated as junk e-mail. E-mail address or domain names added to the list on the Blocked Senders tab will always be treated as junk e-mail. Click OK after making changes in the Junk E-mail Options dialog box.

Using Help

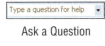

Ask a Question

Use Help
1. Click in *Ask a Question* text box.
2. Type word or phrase for which you need help.
3. Press Enter.
4. Click topic links in Search Results task pane.

An extensive help resource is available whenever you are working in Outlook by clicking in the *Ask a Question* text box, typing a word or phrase related to the topic you require assistance with, and then pressing Enter. A list of Help topics that have been associated with the keyword(s) appears in the Search Results task pane. By default Outlook searches the resources available from Microsoft Office Online as long as you are connected to the Internet. If you are not operating Help while online, you will still have access to help topics but the search results list will not be as extensive. Click a hyperlinked topic in the Search Results task pane and a Microsoft Office Outlook Help window opens with information about the topic. Once the Help window is open, you can continue to click topic links in the Search Results task pane until you find the information that you need. Help topics can be printed for future reference.

In addition to the Help facility within Outlook, the Microsoft Office Online option on the Help drop-down menu starts Microsoft Internet Explorer and automatically connects you to the Microsoft Office Online Web page. From this site you can obtain training and templates for Outlook, download updates, and search for information about a problem you may be encountering with a feature.

exercise 18 — USING HELP

1. With Inbox the active folder, search the help resources for information on how to send a message to someone without the recipient's name showing to other recipients (referred to as a *blind carbon copy*) by completing the following steps:
   a. Click in the *Ask a Question* text box at the right end of the Menu bar, type **recipient name not shown**, and then press Enter.
   b. Click Send a message without the recipient's name showing in the list of topics that appears in the Search Results task pane. A Microsoft Office Outlook Help window will open with information about the selected topic.
   c. Read the steps presented in the Help window. Notice that the text *Bcc* appears in blue in Step 3 indicating that the word is hyperlinked and more information can be displayed.
   d. Click Bcc to expand the topic and display information about blind carbon copy. Read the definition that appears in green below the hyperlink.
   e. Click Tip at the bottom of the topic text and then read the information presented below the hyperlink.
2. Click the Print button on the Microsoft Outlook Help window toolbar and then click Print at the Print dialog box.
3. Click the Close button on the Microsoft Office Outlook Help window Title bar.
4. Close the Search Results task pane.

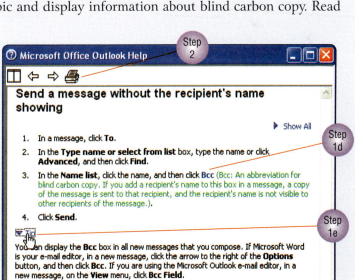

Using Outlook for E-Mail

CHAPTER summary

- Microsoft Outlook is an application that includes all of the tools needed to organize your work or personal environment including e-mail, calendar, contacts, tasks, and notes.
- Information in Outlook is organized in folders. Click Mail, Calendar, Contacts, Tasks, or Notes in the Navigation Pane to view the contents of the folder in the Contents Pane.
- Outlook can be used as an e-mail client connected to a Microsoft Exchange Server or an Internet Mail Server that supports POP3, IMAP, or HTTP protocols.
- Click the New Mail Message button on the Standard toolbar to create and send an e-mail message.
- Messages received are placed in the Inbox. Display the contents of the Inbox, and then click a message header in the Contents Pane to read the message text in the Reading Pane. In most cases, messages can be read without opening the message in a window.
- Double-click a message header in the Contents Pane to open the message in a message window.
- Print, Reply to, or Forward a message using buttons on the toolbar in the message window.
- Deleted messages are moved from the current folder to the Deleted Items folder where they remain until you empty the Deleted Items folder.
- Files such as Office documents can be e-mailed by attaching the file to a message.
- A file attachment can be opened directly from the mail server or saved to disk.
- Create a Personal Address Book (PAB) to store names and e-mail addresses of individuals that you do not want to store in the Contacts folder.
- Enter a name in the message window from your Address Book by opening the Select Names dialog box.
- The Message Options dialog box is used to assign importance levels, sensitivity, security, and delivery options.
- A read receipt can be sent to you indicating the date and time the recipient opens your e-mail message by tracking the message.
- Create a signature that is automatically added to the end of each message in the Mail Format tab of the Options dialog box.
- Display the Find bar to locate a message by entering a search criterion.
- Messages can be flagged for follow-up action by applying colored flags to the message headers in the Contents Pane. Outlook provides six colored flags that can be used to organize follow-up action.
- A flag can have a due date assigned for the follow-up action to be completed.
- Once a follow-up flag activity is complete, the flag can be marked as completed, or you can clear the flag.
- Mail items in the the Contents Pane can be grouped and individual groups expanded and collapsed. By default, items in the Contents Pane for mail folders are grouped by date with the most recent date at the top of the list.
- Options on the Current View menu can be used to filter messages.
- Apply color to messages in the Ways to Organize Inbox pane with the *Using Colors* section active. Click Tools and then click Organize to open the Ways to Organize Inbox pane.

- Mail messages are stored in one of five folders: Inbox, Outbox, Sent Items, Junk E-mail, and Deleted Items.
- Create new folders to organize related messages by opening the Create New Folder dialog box. Folders can be created in a hierarchial arrangement below existing folders. A folder created within another folder is called a subfolder.
- Move messages from one folder to another by dragging and dropping the message header from the current folder to the desired folder name in the *All Mail Folders* section of the Navigation Pane.
- Create a rule to instruct Outlook to automatically move messages to a specific folder as they are received. A rule analyzes the message as it is received to determine if it meets the specified condition for which the message should be placed in a folder other than the Inbox.
- Junk e-mail filters are included with Outlook 2003 that work on two levels: junk e-mail lists and artificial intelligence to determine the likelihood that the message is spam. Check the Junk E-mail folder periodically to make sure legitimate messages have not been placed in the folder.
- Display the Junk E-mail Options dialog box to change the protection level, or add e-mail addresses or domain names to the Safe Senders, Safe Recipients, or Blocked Senders lists.
- Outlook contains an extensive help resource that can be accessed by typing a word or phrase in the *Ask a Question* text box.

FEATURES summary

FEATURE	BUTTON	MENU	KEYBOARD
Address book	📖	Tools, Address Book	Ctrl + Shift + B
Apply color to messages		Tools, Organize	
Arrange messages		View, Arrange By	
Attach a file to a message	📎	Insert, File	
Create a message rule		Tools, Rules and Alerts	
Create a new folder		File, New, Folder; or right-click folder name, New Folder	Ctrl + Shift + E
Create a new mail message	New	File, New, Mail Message	Ctrl + N
Create a new signature		Tools, Options, Mail Format, Signatures	
Delete a message	✕	Edit, Delete	Ctrl + D
Filter messages		View, Arrange By, Current View	
Find a message	Find	Tools, Find, Find	Ctrl + E
Flag a message	⚑	Actions, Follow Up	

OUTLOOK
Using Outlook for E-Mail

FEATURE	BUTTON	MENU	KEYBOARD
Forward a message	Forward	Actions, Forward	Ctrl + F
Help	Type a question for help	Help, Microsoft Office Outlook Help	F1
Junk E-mail Options		Tools, Options, Preferences, Junk E-mail; or Actions, Junk E-mail	
Message handling options	Options...		
Print message	🖨	File, Print	Ctrl + P
Reply to a message	Reply	Actions, Reply	Ctrl + R
Reply to all recipients	Reply to All	Actions, Reply to All	Ctrl + Shift + R

CONCEPTS check

Completion: On a blank sheet of paper, indicate the correct term, command, symbol, or explanation for each description.

1. Information in Outlook is stored in these. *Folders*
2. Click an icon in this pane to display the to-do list in the Tasks folder. *Outlook bar*
3. Most messages can be read in this pane without opening them. *Reading Pane*
4. When replying to or forwarding a message, this information is included and is called a thread. *Original message txt.*
5. Deleted messages are moved to this area. *Deleted Items Folder.*
6. These two actions can be done to a file attached to a message. *File can be opened directly from the mail server or it can be saved to a disk.*
7. Names and e-mail addresses of individuals with whom you frequently send messages can be stored here if you do not want to use the Contacts folder. *Address book.*
8. Set the sensitivity level of a message at this dialog box. *Message options.*
9. Attach this request to a message to receive a report when the recipient opens the message. *Read receipt*
10. This feature automatically inserts stored text at the end of each message. *Signature.*
11. Messages can be located by typing a word or phrase that exists within the message in the *Look for* text box of this feature. *For Followup. Find bar*
12. Message headers that have a flag applied to them are automatically linked to this folder name in the *Favorite Folders* section. *For Follow up.*
13. Messages within a group can be removed from view by clicking this button next to the group heading. *Collapse. ⊖ sign*
14. Apply color to messages from a specific individual by opening this panel. *Ways to organize Inbox.*
15. Move messages to a new location using the mouse by this method. *Drag Message Header to destination folder name in Folder List.*
16. This is the term used to describe the feature in Outlook that automatically moves messages to a specified folder based on a condition. *Junk E-mail lists & artificial Intelligence technology that evaluate each message.* / *Message Rule.*

17. Junk e-mail moves messages to the Junk E-mail folder based on these two levels of analysis. _Messages are evaluated based on factors such as time sent & content._
18. Type a word or phrase in this text box to access the Microsoft Office Outlook Help resources. _Ask a question._

Assessment 1

1. Create and send a new message to a student in your class as follows:
    a. Select the student's name from your personal address book.
    b. Type **More Info on E-Mail Viruses** as the subject text.
    c. Type the following text in the message window:

    I just read an article about e-mail viruses on the Web. Here is a summary of what I read.

    Viruses are not replicated by means of an e-mail message since a message is based on text and text does not transmit a virus. Your computer becomes infected with a virus from a file attached to a message. You have to open the attached file for it to infect your computer. This is why it is always preferable to choose the option to save the attachment to disk and then scan the file with antivirus software prior to opening it.

    d. Print and then send the message.

Assessment 2

1. Copy the message received in your Inbox from Assessment 1 to the E-Mail Viruses folder and then open the message. *(Hint: To copy a message using the drag and drop method, hold down the Ctrl key while dragging.)*
2. Send a reply to the originator of the message with the following text:

    Thanks for the information. If I find any new tips while browsing the Web, I will send them to you.

3. Display the Sent Items folder, open the message sent in Step 2 and then forward it to another student as follows:
    a. Type the following text at the top of the message:

    Are you interested in sharing information you find on e-mail viruses with us?

    b. Print and then send the message.
4. Display the Inbox folder and then delete the message you received from Assessment 1.
5. Empty the Deleted Items folder.
6. Make sure Inbox is the active folder.

Assessment 3

1. Create and send a new message with a file attachment to a student in your class as follows:
    a. Send the message to the student you added to your personal address book.
    b. Type **Picture for Political Science Project** as the subject text.
    c. Type the following text in the message window:

    I have attached a picture of the White House for our project's title page. Let me know if you need help with inserting the picture in Word.

    d. Attach the file named **WhiteHouse.jpg** from the Internet Resource Center to the message.
    e. Print and then send the message.

Assessment 4

1. Create a new message to a student in your class as follows:
    a. Send the message to the student you added to your personal address book.
    b. Type **Security Options** as the subject text.
    c. Type the following text in the message window:

    Digital IDs or Certificates are documents that allow you to prove your identity for electronic transactions. The Security tab in the Options dialog box is where you can import or export digital IDs and set other security options.

    Have a look at this tab in the Options dialog box and let me know if you want further information on any of the other security features.

2. Assign the following message handling and tracking options to the message:
    a. Set the importance level of the message to High.
    b. Set a tracking option on the message so that you receive a read receipt when the recipient opens the mail message. *(Note: Remember that not all mail servers process read receipts.)*
3. Apply a Follow up flag to the message with a due date of two weeks from today.
4. Print and then send the message.

Assessment 5

(Note: Skip this assessment if you did not complete Exercise 10.)

1. Edit the content and format of the signature named *External Signature* as follows:
    a. Select the text in the Edit Signature dialog box, change the font to 10-pt Tahoma Regular, and select Maroon as the font color.
    b. Add the title *Outlook Professional* between your name and the school name.
    c. Delete the City, StateorProvince, and ZIPorPostalCode information.
2. Create a new message to a student in your class as follows:
    a. Send the message to the student you added to your personal address book.
    b. Type **Send/Receive Options** as the subject text.
    c. Type the following text in the message window:

> You can set the time interval for Outlook to automatically check for new mail. Open the Options dialog box and click the Mail Setup tab. Click the Send/Receive button. In the Send/Receive Groups dialog box the default is set to 5 minutes. Have you found anything interesting?

　　d. Print and then send the message.

Assessment 6

1. Select the new messages received in the Inbox that contain information about Outlook options, and then use the drag-and-drop method to move the messages to the Outlook Tips folder.
2. Make Outlook Tips the active folder.
3. Apply a purple flag to the message headers for the messages with the word *Options* in the subject text.
4. Apply a green flag to the message header for the message with *Outlook Signatures* in the subject text.
5. Apply a yellow flag to the message header for the message with *Outlook Address Books* in the subject text.
6. Arrange the messages in the Outlook Tips folder by flag.
7. Click File and then click Print. Click *Table Style* in the *Print style* section of the Print dialog box and then click OK.
8. Arrange the messages in Outlook Tips by date with newest on top.
9. Make E-Mail Viruses the active folder and then arrange the messages by subject.
10. Print the message list in *Table Style*.
11. Make Inbox the active folder.

Assessment 7

1. Add the domain name for your home ISP to the Safe Senders list in the Junk E-mail Options by completing the following steps:
    a. Click Tools and then Options.
    b. If necessary, click the Preferences tab in the Options dialog box.
    c. Click the Junk E-mail button in the *E-mail* section.
    d. Click the Safe Senders tab in the Junk E-mail Options dialog box.
    e. Click the Add button.
    f. Type the domain name for the ISP you use for home Internet access to the *Enter an e-mail address or Internet domain to be added to the list* text box. For example, type aol.com or msn.com. If you do not have Internet access at home, add the domain name for your school.
    g. Click OK to close the Add address or domain dialog box.
    h. Click OK to close the Junk E-mail Options dialog box.
2. Click OK to close the Options dialog box.

Assessment 8

(Note: Skip this assessment if you did not complete Exercise 10.)
1. Delete the signature created in this chapter by completing the following steps:
    a. Click Tools and then Options.
    b. Click the Mail Format tab in the Options dialog box.
    c. Click the Signatures button.
    d. With *External Signature* already selected in the Create Signature dialog box, click Remove.
    e. Click Yes at the message asking if you are sure you want to permanently remove this signature.
    f. Click OK to close the Create Signature dialog box.
2. Click OK to close the Options dialog box.

Assessment 9

(Note: Skip this assessment if you did not complete Exercise 17.)
1. Delete the message rule created in this chapter by completing the following steps:
    a. Click Tools and then Rules and Alerts.
    b. Click *Outlook* in the *Rule* list box.
    c. Click the Delete button.
    d. Click Yes at the message box asking if you want to delete the rule.
2. Click OK to close the Rules and Alerts dialog box.

Assessment 10

(Note: Skip this assessment if you did not complete Exercise 15.)
1. Delete the message rule that applies the color green to all messages received from the student whose name you specified in the *Using Colors* section of the Ways to Organize Inbox pane by completing the following steps:
    a. Make sure Inbox is the active folder, click Tools and then Organize.
    b. Click Using Colors in the Ways to Organize Inbox pane.
    c. Click Automatic Formatting near the top right of the Ways to Organize Inbox pane.
    d. Click *Mail received from Student Name* in the *Rules for this view* list box.
    e. Click the Delete button.
    f. Click OK.
2. Click the Close button near the top right of the Ways to Organize Inbox pane.

CHAPTER 2

USING CALENDAR FOR SCHEDULING

PERFORMANCE OBJECTIVES

Upon successful completion of Chapter 2, you will be able to:
- Schedule appointments and events
- Schedule recurring appointments
- Edit, move, and delete appointments
- View and print daily, weekly, and monthly calendars
- Change the current view to filter appointments and events
- Turn on the Reading Pane and view appointment details
- Assign a category to an appointment and view appointments by category
- Apply formatting to appointments based on a category
- Schedule meetings by sending meeting requests
- Accept and decline a meeting request
- Update a meeting
- Change calendar options
- Create a new calendar folder to store items separately from the main calendar
- View two calendars side-by-side

(Note: There are no student data files required for this chapter.)

The Calendar component of Outlook is used to schedule appointments and events such as conferences and meetings. Appointments or meetings that occur on a regular basis can be created as recurring items that need to be entered only once. Reminders can be established to display messages and sound a chime at a set interval before the time of the appointment, event, or meeting.

Meetings are integrated with e-mail so that an individual can send a meeting request to others by e-mail message. When the invitee responds to the message by accepting a meeting request, the details are automatically added in his or her calendar.

Schedule an Appointment Using Click and Type
1. Click date for appointment in Date Navigator.
2. Click next to time for appointment in Appointment area.
3. Type description of appointment.
4. Press Enter or click outside appointment box.

Multiple calendars can be displayed side-by-side in Outlook to keep track of appointments, events, and meetings separately.

Scheduling Appointments and Events

Click Calendar in the Navigation Pane to display the contents of the Calendar folder as shown in Figure 2.1. The default view for the Calendar is Day, which displays the current day's appointments beginning at 8 a.m. The top section of the Navigation Pane is the Date Navigator which shows the current month with directional arrows to browse backward and forward to previous and succeeding months. The current date is shaded in the Date Navigator and other days within the current month that have appointments, events, or meetings scheduled display in bold. Depending on your monitor size and/or screen resolution setting, the Navigation Pane may display one month or two within the Navigation Pane.

FIGURE 2.1 **The Calendar Window**

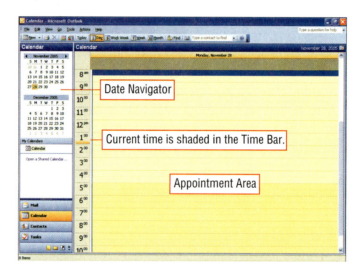

New Appointment

To schedule a new appointment, click the date of the appointment in the Date Navigator, click next to the time of the appointment in the Appointment area, and then type a short description of the appointment details. The appointment length will default to one half-hour. To lengthen the appointment time, point to the bottom border of the appointment box until the pointer changes to an up- and down-pointing arrow. Drag the box up or down to lengthen or shorten the appointment duration.

Display the Appointment window shown in Figure 2.2 to enter more detailed information about an appointment. To enter a new appointment using the Appointment window, click next to the desired time in the Appointment area and then do one of the following actions:

- Click the New Appointment button on the Standard toolbar.
- Double-click next to the appointment starting time in the Appointment area.
- Click File, point to New, and then click Appointment.
- Click Actions, New Appointment.

52 Chapter Two

OUTLOOK

FIGURE 2.2 Appointment Window

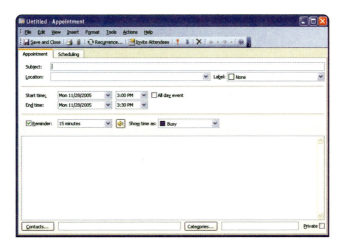

Type a description of the appointment in the *Subject* text box, and the location where the appointment will take place in the *Location* text box. The *Label* list box allows you to color code the appointment box for quick identification when you view your calendar as to the appointment's significance. Click the down-pointing arrow next to the *Label* list box and then choose from the following options: *Important, Business, Personal, Vacation, Must Attend, Travel Required, Needs Preparation, Birthday, Anniversary,* or *Phone Call.* The appointment box will be shaded with the color for the associated label in the Appointment area.

The Start time will display the day and time that you selected in the Calendar before opening the Appointment window. You can change the start day and time by clicking the down-pointing arrow next to the day or time text box, and then clicking the correct entry. The times are displayed in half-hour blocks. If necessary, you can drag across the current time entry to select it and then type a specific time of your own such as *10:50 AM.*

Enter the end time for the appointment by clicking the down-pointing arrow next to the *End time* text box, and then clicking the correct time in the drop-down list. The *Reminder* check box in Figure 2.2 is set to display a reminder message and play a chime 15 minutes before the scheduled appointment.

The *Show time as* list box is used to assign a color code for *Busy, Free, Tentative,* or *Out of Office* in the scheduled time slot. This option displays as a colored border at the left edge of the appointment box in your calendar. When others view your calendar to plan a meeting the time slot will appear as a colored bar dependent on the *Show time as* setting.

If you want to store additional information about the appointment, type the text in the white editing window below the *Reminder* check box. An appointment can be linked to a contact name in the *Contacts* text box or associated with a category by typing the category name in the *Categories* text box. Click the *Private* check box to prevent others who may have access to your calendar from viewing the appointment details. When all the required entires have been made, click the Save and Close button.

QUICK STEPS

Schedule an Appointment Using Appointment Window
1. Click date for appointment in Date Navigator.
2. Click next to time for appointment in Appointment area.
3. Click New Appointment button on Standard toolbar.
4. Type description in *Subject* text box.
5. Type location in *Location* text box.
6. Change other options as required.
7. Click Save and Close.

exercise 1

SCHEDULING APPOINTMENTS

1. With Outlook open and Inbox active, click Calendar in the Navigation Pane.
2. Add a new appointment to the Calendar using the click and type method by completing the following steps:

    a. Click the right- or left-pointing arrow in the Date Navigator to scroll to the month of October 2005.
    b. Click Friday, October 14, 2005 in the Date Navigator.
    c. Click next to 10:00 am in the Appointment area. The time 10:00 to 10:30 am is selected as shown by the blue box.
    d. Type **Human Resources dept - review benefits plan.**
    e. Point at the bottom blue border of the appointment box until the pointer changes to an up- and down-pointing arrow, drag the appointment time down to the 11:00 am time boundary, and then release the left mouse button.

    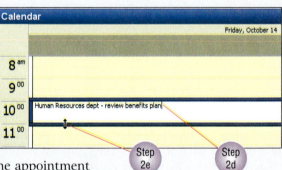

    f. Click in the appointment area outside the appointment box. The appointment is displayed in a white box with a blue border at the left. Blue is the color displayed for times in the calendar that are specified as *Busy*. By default, a reminder is set for 15 minutes prior to the appointment as shown by the bell icon next to the description.

3. Add a new appointment using the Appointment window by completing the following steps:

    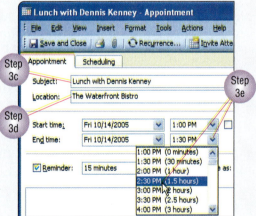

    a. With Friday, October 14, 2005 the active date, click next to 1:00 pm in the Appointment area.
    b. Click the New Appointment button on the Standard toolbar. An Untitled - Appointment window opens.
    c. With the insertion point positioned in the *Subject* text box, type **Lunch with Dennis Kenney**.
    d. Press Tab or click in the *Location* text box and then type **The Waterfront Bistro**.
    e. Click the down-pointing arrow next to the *End time* time text box and then click *2:30 PM (1.5 hours)* in the drop-down list.
    f. Click the down-pointing arrow next to the *Show time as* list box and then click *Out of Office* in the drop-down list.

    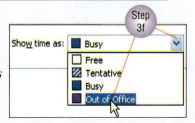

54 Chapter Two

g. Click the Save and Close button. The appointment appears in the Appointment area with a purple border at the left edge of the appointment box. Purple is the color displayed for times in the calendar that are specified as *Out of Office*.
4. Click the Print button on the Standard toolbar. With *Daily Style* selected in the *Print style* section of the Print dialog box, click OK.

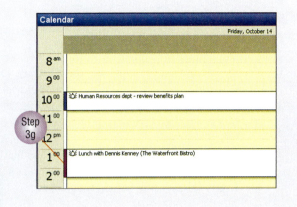

Recurring Appointments

Recurrence

An appointment that occurs on a regular basis at fixed intervals need only be entered once and then Outlook will automatically schedule the remainder of the appointments within the recurrence pattern. To schedule a recurring appointment, open the Appointment window, enter the details for the first appointment, and then click the Recurrence button on the Appointment window toolbar, or click Actions on the Menu bar and then click New Recurring Appointment to open the Appointment Recurrence dialog box shown in Figure 2.3.

FIGURE 2.3 *Appointment Recurrence Dialog Box*

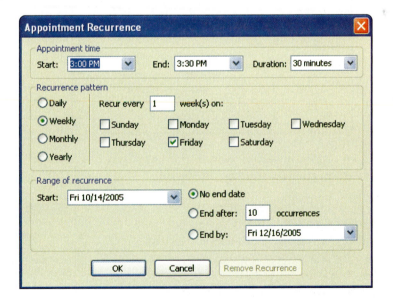

The *Start*, *End*, and *Duration* details in the *Appointment time* section will display the settings entered in the Appointment window. If necessary, change these options for the recurring appointment. Click the frequency options in the *Recurrence pattern* and the *Range of recurrence* sections and then click OK.

OUTLOOK Using Calendar for Scheduling 55

exercise 2

SCHEDULING A RECURRING APPOINTMENT

1. With Calendar active and the date Friday, October 14, 2005 displayed in the Appointment area, schedule a recurring appointment by completing the following steps:
   a. Click Thursday, October 13, 2005 in the Date Navigator.
   b. Click next to 3:00 pm in the Appointment area.
   c. Click the New Appointment button on the Standard toolbar.
   d. With the insertion point positioned in the *Subject* text box, type **Project status meeting**.
   e. Press Tab or click in the *Location* text box and then type **Conference room**.
   f. Click the Recurrence button on the Appointment window toolbar.
   g. Drag to select the value *1* in the *Recur every [] week(s) on* text box in the *Recurrence pattern* section and then type **2**.
   h. Click OK to close the Appointment Recurrence dialog box and accept all other default settings. The current recurrence settings appear in the Appointment window below the *Location* text box.

   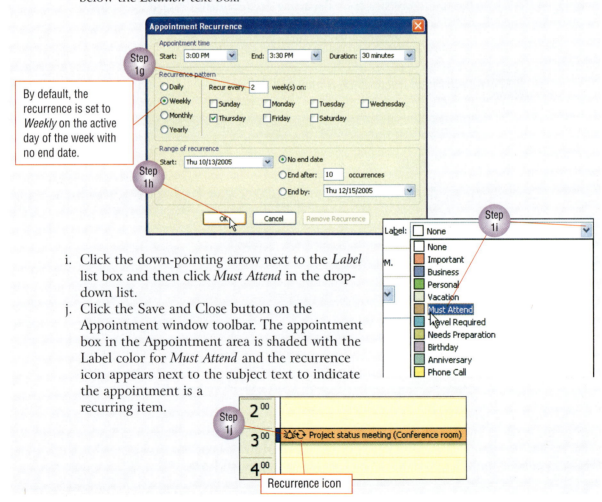

   i. Click the down-pointing arrow next to the *Label* list box and then click *Must Attend* in the drop-down list.
   j. Click the Save and Close button on the Appointment window toolbar. The appointment box in the Appointment area is shaded with the Label color for *Must Attend* and the recurrence icon appears next to the subject text to indicate the appointment is a recurring item.

56 Chapter Two

Scheduling Events

An event differs from an appointment in that it is an activity that lasts the entire day or longer. Examples of an event might include a seminar, training session, conference, trade show, or vacation. Other occasions that you might like to enter in the Calendar as an event are birthdays and anniversaries. An event does not occupy a time slot on the day it is scheduled. It appears in the banner for the scheduled day at the top of the Appointment area below the date.

To schedule an event, double-click the date at the top of the Appointment area, or click Actions on the Menu bar, and then New All Day Event. The Event window is similar to the Appointment window with the exception there are no text boxes for entering times.

HINT
Create an event for any date for which you want to be reminded—a birthday, an anniversary, car maintenance, bill payment, and so on.

QUICK STEPS
Schedule an Event
1. Click date for event in Date Navigator.
2. Double-click date in banner at top of Appointment area.
3. Type event description in *Subject* text box.
4. Change other options as required.
5. Click Save and Close.

exercise 3 — ADDING AN EVENT

1. With Calendar active and the date Thursday, October 13, 2005 displayed in the Appointment area, schedule a one-day conference as an event by completing the following steps:
   a. Double-click the date *Thursday, October 13* at the top of the Appointment area. An Untitled - Event window opens.
   b. With the insertion point positioned in the *Subject* text box, type **Project Management Conference**.
   c. Press Tab or click in the *Location* text box and then type **Downtown Metro Center**.
   d. Click the *Reminder* check box to remove the check mark. *(Note: Skip this step if the Reminder check box is already deselected.)*
   e. Click the down-pointing arrow next to the *Show time as* list box and then click *Out of Office*.
   f. Click the down-pointing arrow next to the *Label* list box and then click *Important*. *(Note: A message box may appear above the subject text indicating that this event conflicts with another appointment in your Calendar. Since this event has been established as an out of office event, the meeting at 3:00 PM is in conflict.)*

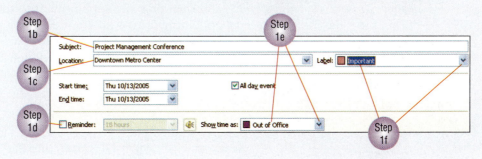

OUTLOOK
Using Calendar for Scheduling

g. Click Save and Close. The event subject and location details appear below the date at the top of the Appointment area. In addition, a purple colored bar has been added to the entire day since the event is defined as occurring out of the office.

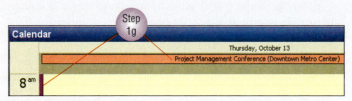

Step 1g

Natural Language Phrases

In day or time text boxes within Outlook's appointment or event windows you can type natural language phrases and Outlook will convert the phrase to the appropriate entry for the field. For example, in the *Start time* day text box you can type *next Monday* and Outlook will automatically enter the date for the Monday following the current day. In the time text box you can type *ten o'clock am* and Outlook will convert the entry to *10:00 AM*.

Delete

Editing, Deleting, and Moving Appointments

Double-click an existing appointment in the Appointment area to open the Appointment window, or right-click the appointment box and then click Open at the shortcut menu to change the details for an appointment or event. Edit the text and/or day and time settings as required and then click Save and Close. To delete an appointment, position the arrow pointer on the colored bar at the left edge of the appointment box until the pointer changes to the four-headed arrow move icon, and then click the left mouse button. The appointment box displays the colored bar as a border around the entire box indicating the appointment has been selected. Press Delete or click the Delete button on the Standard toolbar. Alternatively, right-click the appointment box and then click Delete at the shortcut menu.

To move an appointment to a new time on the same day, position the arrow pointer on the colored bar at the left edge of the appointment box until the four-headed arrow move icon appears, and then drag the appointment to the new time slot on the same day. To move an appointment to a different day, drag the appointment while the Calendar is displayed in Week or Month view. An appointment can also be moved by opening the Appointment window and then changing the *Start time* and *End time* settings.

EDITING, DELETING, AND MOVING APPOINTMENTS

1. With the Calendar folder active and the date Thursday, October 13, 2005 displayed in the Appointment area, change the starting time for the Project status meeting by completing the following steps:
   a. Double-click over the shaded appointment box for *Project status meeting* at 3:00 pm.

b. Since the appointment is one of a recurring series of appointments, Outlook displays the Open Recurring Item dialog box asking if you want to open this occurrence only or the entire series. Click *Open the series* and then click OK.

c. Click the Recurrence button on the Project status meeting - Recurring Appointment window toolbar.

d. Click the down-pointing arrow next to the *Start* text box in the *Appointment time* section of the Appointment Recurrence dialog box and then click *4:30 PM* in the drop-down list. The *End* time automatically changes to *5:00 PM* since *Duration* is set to *30 minutes*.

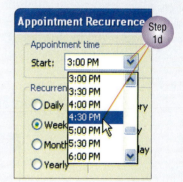

e. Click OK to close the Appointment Recurrence dialog box.

f. Click Save and Close.

2. Delete the lunch appointment on Friday, October 14 by completing the following steps:
   a. Click Friday, October 14 in the Date Navigator.
   b. Position the mouse pointer on the purple colored bar at the left of the appointment box for *Lunch with Dennis Kenney* until the pointer changes to the four-headed arrow move icon and then click the left mouse button. The appointment is selected as indicated by the purple border surrounding the appointment box.

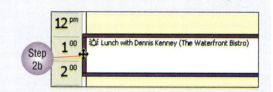

   c. Press the Delete key, or click the Delete button on the Standard toolbar.

3. Move the appointment with the Human Resources department to 1:00 pm on the same day using the drag and drop method by completing the following steps:
   a. Position the mouse pointer on the blue colored bar at the left of the appointment box for *Human Resources dept – review benefits plan* until the pointer changes to the four-headed arrow move icon.
   b. Hold down the left mouse button, drag the appointment box to the 1:00 pm boundary and then release the mouse. The pointer displays with a gray shaded box attached as you drag the mouse.

4. Click the Print button on the Standard toolbar. Click *Weekly Style* in the *Print style* section of the Print dialog box and then click OK.

Calendar Coloring

Calendar Coloring

Click to select an appointment and then click the Calendar Coloring button on the Standard toolbar to assign a label to an appointment after the appointment has been created. The appointment box will be shaded with the color of the label chosen from the drop-down menu.

Click Edit Labels from the Calendar Coloring drop-down menu to change the label text associated with a color in the menu. For example, if you prefer to use purple to shade sales appointments, click Edit Labels at the Calendar Coloring menu. At the Edit Labels dialog box shown in Figure 2.4, drag to select the text *Birthday* in the text box next to the purple color box, and then type *Sales*. Click OK to close the Edit Calendar Labels dialog box.

> **HINT**
> Use label colors sparingly. Applying several colors to appointments may make it difficult to remember which color corresponds with which label.

FIGURE 2.4 Edit Calendar Labels Dialog Box

Changing the Calendar View

> **QUICK STEPS**
> **Change Current View**
> 1. Click View, point to Arrange By, point to Current View.
> 2. Click desired view.

The Standard toolbar includes buttons to change the view for the calendar to Work Week, Week, or Month. Click View, point to Arrange By, and then point to Current View to display the menu shown in Figure 2.5.

FIGURE 2.5 Calendar Current View Menu

Active Appointments, Events, Annual Events, and Recurring Appointments will filter the calendar to display only the items that match the option in a table format so that all related items can be viewed and printed on one page.

Displaying the Reading Pane

Click View, point to Reading Pane, and then click Right or Bottom to turn on the Reading Pane at the right edge or bottom of the Calendar window. Click an appointment to view the details within the Reading Pane. Figure 2.6 shows the Reading Pane at the bottom of the window with the details shown for the recurring project status meeting on Thursday, October 13, 2005.

FIGURE 2.6 Calendar with Reading Pane at Bottom of Window

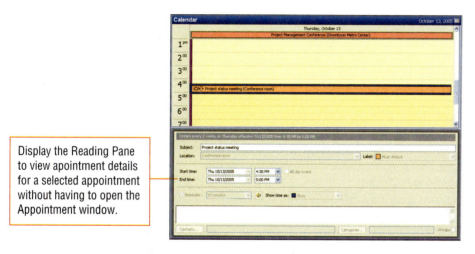

Display the Reading Pane to view apointment details for a selected appointment without having to open the Appointment window.

Click View, point to Reading Pane, and then click Off to turn off the display of the Reading Pane if you no longer need to view appointment details while scrolling through the calendar.

exercise 5

CHANGING THE CURRENT VIEW; USING GO TO DATE; DISPLAYING THE READING PANE

1. With Calendar active and the date Friday, October 14, 2005 displayed in the Appointment area, change the current view to display Active Appointments only, increase the column width, and print the view by completing the following steps:
   a. Click View, point to Arrange By, point to Current View, and then click Active Appointments. The calendar displays in a table format with the appointments grouped by the recurrence pattern. Notice that the information in some columns is not entirely visible.

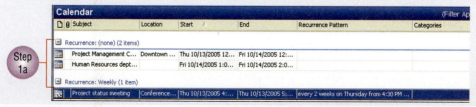

Step 1a

OUTLOOK Using Calendar for Scheduling 61

b. Position the pointer on the column boundary to the right of the column heading *Subject* until the pointer changes to a vertical line with a left- and right-pointing arrow, hold down the left mouse button, drag right approximately 1 inch, and then release the mouse button. Dragging a column boundary right or left increases or decreases the column width. A black vertical line indicates the new right column boundary position as you drag the mouse.
c. Position the pointer on the column boundary to the right of the column heading *Start* until the pointer changes to a vertical line with a left- and right-pointing arrow and then double-click the left mouse button. Double-clicking the column boundary increases the column width to accommodate the longest entry in the column.
d. Position the pointer on the column boundary to the right of the column heading *End* until the pointer changes to a vertical line with a left- and right-pointing arrow and then double-click the left mouse button.
e. Click the Print button on the Standard toolbar. With *Table Style* selected in the *Print style* section of the Print dialog box, click OK.
2. Change the current view to examine two other formats for displaying the calendar by completing the following steps:
   a. Click View, point to Arrange By, point to Current View, and then click Events. Only items that are events are shown in a table format and the message *Filter Applied* displays in the Folder banner near the top right of the window to indicate that the current view is not displaying all items.

   b. Click View, point to Arrange By, point to Current View, and then click Recurring Appointments. Only recurring items are displayed in a table format.

3. Click View, point to Arrange By, point to Current View, and then click Day/Week/Month to restore the calendar to the default display.
4. Scroll to display a specific date in the Appointment area using the Go To Date dialog box by completing the following steps:
   a. Click Go and then click Go to Date.

b. With the current date selected in the *Date* text box in the Go To Date dialog box, type 10/13/2005, and then press Enter or click OK.
5. Click the Month button on the Standard toolbar to view the month of October 2005.
6. Turn on the display of the Reading Pane and view appointment details by completing the following steps:
   a. Click View, point to Reading Pane, and then click Bottom.
   b. Point at the entry on October 14 near 1:00 pm until the pointer displays as a four-headed arrow and then click the left mouse button. This selects the entry and displays the appointment details in the Reading Pane.
   c. Point at the entry on October 27 near 4:30 pm until the pointer displays as a four-headed arrow and then click the left mouse button. Read the appointment details in the Reading Pane.
   d. Click the Week button on the Standard toolbar.
7. Click View, point to Reading Pane, and then click Off.
8. Click the Day button on the Standard toolbar to return to the default view and then click Thursday, October 13, 2005 in the Date Navigator.

Displaying Views in the Navigation Pane

If you need to switch views often while working in the Calendar, you may prefer to display the Current View options in a separate section in the Navigation Pane so that you can switch views with just one mouse click. To do this, click View, point to Arrange By, and then click Show Views in Navigation Pane. A *Current View* section is added to the Navigation Pane as shown in Figure 2.7.

QUICK STEPS

Display *Current View* Section in Navigation Pane
1. Click View, point to Arrange By.
2. Click Show Views in Navigation Pane.

FIGURE 2.7 *Current View Section in Navigation Pane*

With the *Current View* section added to the Navigation Pane, you can switch views with just one mouse click.

QUICK STEPS

Assign a Category to an Appointment
1. Open appointment window.
2. Click Categories button.
3. Click desired category names.
4. Click OK.

Assigning Categories to Appointments

Appointments can be associated with a keyword in the category list and can then be grouped, sorted, or filtered by category. The *By Category* option on the Current View menu will group appointments by the catgeory they have been assigned. The list of appointments can then be expanded and collapsed by category. The Categories dialog box is shown in Figure 2.8. Click the Categories button in the Appointment window and then click the category check box for the category that you want to assign to the appointment. An appointment can be associated with more than one category.

FIGURE 2.8 *Categories Dialog Box*

If a suitable category name for the appointment does not appear in the *Available categories* list box, you can add your own category to the Master Category List. To do this, type the category name in the *Item(s) belong to these categories* text box and then click the Add to List button.

To assign a category to an existing appointment, right-click the appointment in the Appointment area and then click Categories at the shortcut menu to open the Categories dialog box.

exercise 6

ASSIGNING CATEGORIES TO APPOINTMENTS; VIEWING APPOINTMENTS BY CATEGORY

1. With Calendar active and the date Thursday, October 13, 2005 displayed in the Appointment area, assign a category to existing appointments by completing the following steps:
    a. Right-click over the *Project status meeting* appointment box, and then click Categories at the shortcut menu.

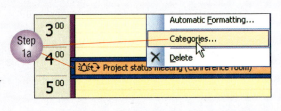

64   Chapter Two

b. Click *Business* in the *Available categories* list box and then click OK.
c. Click Friday, October 14, 2005 in the Date Navigator.
d. Double-click over the *Human Resources dept - review benefits plan* appointment box.
e. Click the Categories button at the bottom of the Appointment window.
f. Click *Personal* in the *Available categories* list box and then click OK. The category name *Personal* appears in the *Categories* text box in the Appointment window.
g. Click Save and Close.

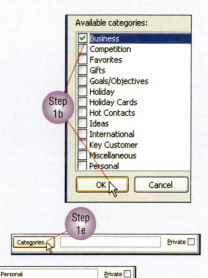

2. Schedule a new appointment by dragging in the Appointment area for the time duration and assign a category by completing the following steps:
   a. Click Tuesday, October 11, 2005 in the Date Navigator.
   b. Position the mouse pointer next to 11:00 am in the Appointment area, hold down the left mouse button, drag to the 1:00 pm time boundary and then release the mouse. This selects a two-hour time duration for the new appointment.
   c. Type **Employee interviews** and then click outside the appointment box.
   d. Right-click over the *Employee interviews* appointment box, and then click Categories at the shortcut menu.
   e. Click *Business* in the *Available categories* list box and then click OK.

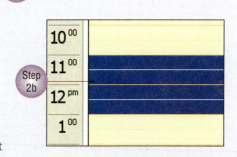

3. Display the *Current View* section in the Navigation Pane, group the appointments in the calendar by category, and collapse a category by completing the following steps:
   a. Click View, point to Arrange By, and then click Show Views In Navigation Pane.
   b. Click *By Category* in the *Current View* section of the Navigation Pane. Outlook displays the appointments in table format arranged in group headings with each group automatically expanded to display all items below the group heading.
   c. Widen column widths as necessary for the *Subject, Start,* and *End* column headings.

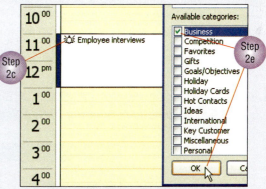

d. Click the collapse button (minus symbol) next to the group heading *Categories: Personal*. The collapse button changes to the expand button when the group is collapsed.
e. Click the Print button on the Standard toolbar. With *Table Style* selected in the *Print style* section of the Print dialog box, click OK.
4. Click *Day/Week/Month* in the *Current View* section of the Navigation Pane.
5. Display the date Friday, October 14, 2005 in the Appointment area using the Go To Date dialog box by completing the following steps:
   a. Click Go and then click Go to Date.
   b. Type **10/14/2005** in the *Date* text box and then press Enter or click OK.

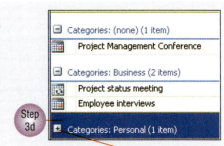

Step 3d

Collapse button (minus symbol) changes to Expand button (plus symbol) when a group has been collapsed.

Automatic Formatting

When your Calendar becomes filled with appointments, meetings, and events, it might be desirable to format certain items based on a category or keyword to make them easily identifiable to you. Formatting can include changing the color and/or font of the text, or shading the appointment box a different color. In Outlook, automatic formatting can be applied to items in folders by creating a rule for the current view. The rules are stored with the view so that you can have different rules for different views. As you learned in Chapter 1, a rule performs an action on an item based on a condition you specify. Recall that you used rules in Chapter 1 to apply color to message headers and to automatically move an item to a folder.

Calendar Coloring

In the Calendar, consider using a rule to instruct Outlook to automatically shade all appointment boxes a label color that have been assigned a specific category such as *Personal*. To do this, display the folder in the desired view, click Edit and Automatic Formatting, or click the Calendar Coloring button on the Standard toolbar and then click Automatic Formatting at the drop-down menu to open the dialog box shown in Figure 2.9.

FIGURE 2.9 Automatic Formatting Dialog Box

Click Add to create a new rule for the current view. Outlook displays the name *Untitled* in the *Name* text box in the *Properties of selected rule* section. Type a name to identify the rule and then choose the color to shade the appointment in the *Label* list box. Click the Condition button to open the Filter dialog box and set the criteria upon which the appointment is to be formatted. The *Label* list box changes to *Font* dependent on the active view when the Automatic Formatting dialog box is opened.

QUICK STEPS

Apply Formatting Automatically to Appointments
1. Display Calendar in desired view.
2. Click Edit, Automatic Formatting.
3. Click Add.
4. Type name for new rule.
5. Choose color in *Label* list box.
6. Click Condition.
7. Choose filter criteria.
8. Click OK twice.

exercise 7 — AUTOMATICALLY FORMATTING APPOINTMENTS

1. With Calendar active in Day view and the date Friday, October 14, 2005 displayed in the Appointment area, create a rule to automatically format personal appointments with a color label by completing the following steps:
   a. Click the Calendar Coloring button on the Standard toolbar and then click Automatic Formatting at the drop-down menu.
   b. Click the Add button in the Automatic Formatting dialog box. A new rule named *Untitled* appears checked in the *Rules for this view* list box and in the *Name* text box in the *Properties of selected rule* section.
   c. With the text *Untitled* already selected in the *Name* text box, type **Personal Appointments**.
   d. Click the down-pointing arrow next to the *Label* list box and then click *Personal*.
   e. Click the Condition button.
   f. At the Filter dialog box, click the More Choices tab.
   g. Click in the *Categories* text box and then type **Personal**.
   h. Click OK to close the Filter dialog box.
   i. Click OK to close the Automatic Formatting dialog box.

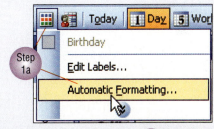

Step 1a

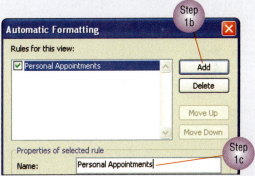

Step 1b

Step 1c

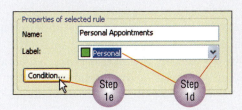

Step 1e   Step 1d

Step 1f

Step 1g

OUTLOOK
Using Calendar for Scheduling 67

2. Schedule a new personal appointment on Wednesday, October 12, 2005 by completing the following steps:
   a. Click Wednesday, October 12, 2005 in the Date Navigator.
   b. Position the mouse pointer next to 9:00 am, hold down the left mouse button and then drag to the 10:00 boundary.
   c. Type **Doctor's appointment** and then press Enter.
   d. Right-click the *Doctor's appointment* appointment box and then click Categories at the shortcut menu.
   e. Click *Personal* in the *Available categories* list box and then click OK in the Categories dialog box. The appointment box is automatically shaded green as the automatic formatting rule is applied to the new appointment.
3. Click the Week button on the Standard toolbar.
4. Click the Print button on the Standard toolbar. With *Weekly Style* selected in the *Print style* section of the Print dialog box, click OK.
5. Click the Day button on the Standard toolbar and then click Friday, October 14, 2005 in the Date Navigator.

Scheduling Meetings

Schedule a Meeting
1. Click date for meeting in Date Navigator.
2. Click next to time for meeting in Appointment area.
3. Click down-pointing arrow on New Appointment button.
4. Click Meeting Request.
5. Add invitees' names in *To* text box.
6. Type description of meeting in *Subject* text box.
7. Type location in *Location* text box.
8. Change other options as required.
9. Click Send.

Scheduling a meeting in Outlook is essentially setting up an appointment to which you invite people by e-mail. When you create a meeting request, you identify the individuals that you want to attend, the subject, the location, and the meeting day and time. Individuals are notified of the meeting via an e-mail message. Responses to the organizer's meeting request are automatically tracked and can be viewed in the meeting window. To create a new meeting request, do one of the following actions:

- Click File, point to New, and then click Meeting Request.
- Click Actions, New Meeting Request.
- Click the down-pointing arrow on the New Appointment button on the Standard toolbar and then click Meeting Request at the drop-down menu.
- Open a new Appointment window and then click the Invite Attendees button on the Appointment window toolbar.

An Untitled - Meeting window opens which is similar to an Appointment window. The gray information box near the top of the window displays the message *Invitations have not been sent for this meeting*, the *To* text box is added above the *Subject* text box to include the e-mail addresses of the attendees, and the Save and Close button is replaced with the Send button to send e-mail messages for the meeting as shown in Figure 2.10.

FIGURE 2.10 Meeting Window

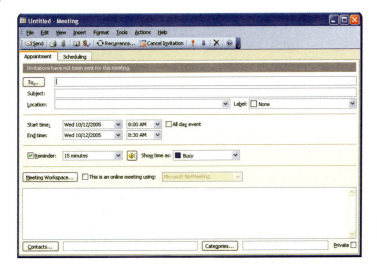

HINT
Consider typing the meeting's agenda in the white text box in the meeting window to inform attendees as to what is expected to be covered at the meeting.

exercise 8

SCHEDULING A MEETING

(Note: In this exercise, and in several remaining exercises and assessments, you will be sending a meeting request by e-mail to the student you added to the Personal Address Book [PAB] in Chapter 1. Check with your instructor if necessary for alternate instructions on to whom you should send the meeting requests.)

1. With Calendar active and the date Friday, October 14, 2005 displayed in the Appointment area, schedule a meeting by completing the following steps:

    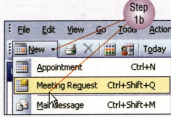

    a. Click next to 3:00 pm in the Appointment area.
    b. Click the down-pointing arrow on the New button on the Standard toolbar and then click Meeting Request.

    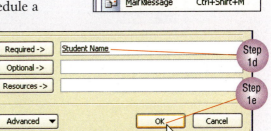

    c. Click the To button. At the Select Attendees and Resources dialog box, click the down-pointing arrow next to *Show Names from the* and then click *Personal Address Book*.
    d. Double-click the name of the student you added to the PAB in Chapter 1 to add his or her name to the *Required* text box.
    e. Click OK to close the Select Attendees and Resources dialog box.

OUTLOOK Using Calendar for Scheduling 69

f. Press Tab twice or click in the *Subject* text box and then type **Project change request meeting**.
g. Press Tab or click in the *Location* text box and then type **Room 101E**.
h. Click the down-pointing arrow next to the *End time* time text box and then click *4:00 PM (1 hour)*.
i. Click the Send button. The meeting is scheduled in your calendar and an e-mail message is sent to the student who was selected as a required attendee.

2. View the Scheduling and Tracking information that Outlook maintains in the Meeting Request window by completing the following steps:
    a. Double-click the appointment box for *Project change request meeting* at 3:00 pm. The message *No responses have been received for this meeting* appears above the *To* text box.

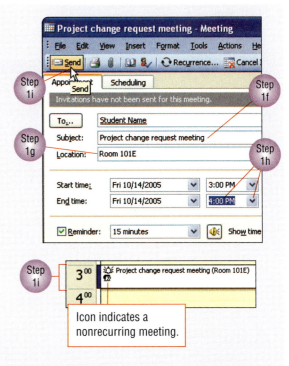

    b. Click the Scheduling tab in the Meeting window. The window next to the attendees list contains the calendar information for each attendee. At the bottom of the window are editing options to Add Others to the list of attendees, change the calendar Options, AutoPick different meeting times, and alter the meeting start and end times. *(Note: Click Cancel if a Microsoft Office Internet Free/Busy dialog box displays prompting you to Join the Internet Free/Busy service.)*

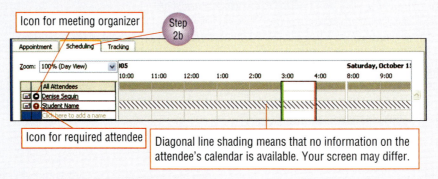

    c. Click the Tracking tab in the Meeting window. The responses from attendees are logged on this tab.

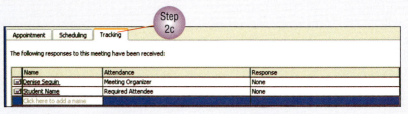

    d. Click the Close button on the Meeting window Title bar.
3. View the meeting request e-mail message sent by completing the following steps:
    a. Click Mail in the Navigation Pane.

b. Click *Sent Items* in the *All Mail Folders* section of the Navigation Pane.
c. Click the message header for the meeting request message sent in Step 1.
d. View the message in the Reading Pane.
4. Click Inbox in the *All Mail Folders* section of the Navigation Pane.

Responding to Meeting Requests

Individuals who have been invited to a meeting via a meeting request receive notification by e-mail. The message window contains buttons for responding to the request as shown in Figure 2.11. The invitee can choose to click Accept, Tentative, Decline, or Propose New Time. Within the Reading Pane, buttons to respond to the meeting request message also appear above the subject text.

> **QUICK STEPS**
>
> **Accept a Meeting Request**
> 1. Display the Inbox mail folder.
> 2. Double-click message header for meeting request.
> 3. Click Accept.
> 4. Click *Edit the response before sending* and then type a short message or choose not to type a message and just send the acceptance notification.

FIGURE 2.11 Meeting Request Message

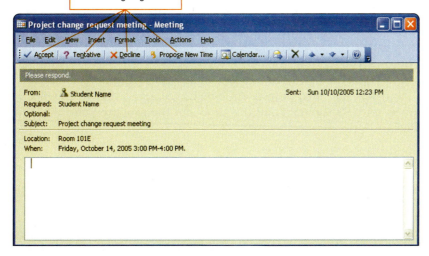

When the respondent clicks Accept, Tentative, or Decline, a Microsoft Outlook message window appears with the information that the meeting has been scheduled in the calendar for Accept or Tentative; or moved to the Deleted Items folder for Decline. The respondent has the option to *Edit the response before sending* so that a few words of explanation can be appended; *Send the response now* so that the meeting organizer receives the default response message of *User name has accepted*; or *Don't send a response*. Figure 2.12 shows the dialog box that appears after clicking the Accept button.

If you send a meeting request to a recipient using an Internet mail address, Outlook exports the meeting information as an iCal (Internet Calendar) item. The recipient will not see the buttons shown in Figure 2.11; however, he or she can respond using the Reply feature.

> **HINT**
>
> Always respond promptly to meeting requests so that the meeting organizer is not left wondering if you are attending or not.

FIGURE 2.12 Accept Meeting Response Dialog Box

HINT
The Microsoft Office Internet Free/Busy Service allows you to publish the blocks of time when you are available. This service allows users to schedule meetings with others who are not on the same server or who do not have access to each other's calendar.

The meeting organizer receives the responses from the invitees by means of e-mail messages. In addition, Outlook updates the Tracking tab of the Meeting window so that the organizer can view all invitee responses in one place.

If an invitee is unavailable at the requested meeting day and time, he or she may choose to propose a new time for the meeting rather than send a decline message. To do this, click the Propose New Time button on the message window toolbar. At the Propose New Time dialog box, change the meeting start time and end time parameters and then click the Propose Time button. A message window opens in which the invitee can type a short explanation to the meeting organizer and then click the Send button. An e-mail message is sent to the meeting organizer with the original day and time and the proposed new day and time particulars.

exercise 9

ACCEPTING A MEETING REQUEST

(Note: To complete this exercise another student must have sent you a meeting request from Exercise 8.)

1. With Inbox active, respond to a meeting request by accepting the meeting day and time by completing the following steps:
   a. Double-click the message header in the Contents Pane for the message with the subject *Project change request meeting*.
   b. Click the Accept button on the message window toolbar.
   c. At the Microsoft Office Outlook dialog box, click *Edit the response before sending* and then click OK.

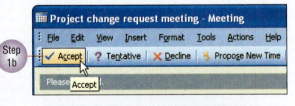

Chapter Two

d. With the insertion point positioned in the message editing window, type the following text:

   Please send the new material estimates so that I can update the budget before the meeting.

e. Click the Print button on the message window toolbar.

f. Click Send. A message is sent to the meeting organizer with the subject text *Accepted: Project change request meeting* below the invitee's name.

2. Display the Calendar with the active date Friday, October 14, 2005. Notice Outlook added the meeting to your Calendar. *(Note: You will have two meetings scheduled for 3:00 p.m. on Friday, October 14 if you have completed both Exercises 8 and 9—one as a meeting organizer and the other as a meeting invitee.)*

Updating and Canceling a Meeting

From time to time meetings might need to be rescheduled, canceled, or the list of individuals attending a meeting may need to be revised. Complete the following steps to make changes to a meeting:

1. Open the meeting window in the Calendar.
2. Change the details as required in the meeting window.
3. Click the Send Update button.

Outlook will send an e-mail message to each attendee with the word *Updated* in the subject line to highlight the message contents. Each attendee can then choose to accept or decline the revision. If the meeting organizer closes the meeting window without clicking the Send Update button, Outlook will prompt the user with a message that the attendees have not been notified.

To cancel a meeting, open the meeting window and then click Actions, Cancel Meeting, or click to select the appointment box in the Appointment area and then press the Delete key. If you are the meeting organizer and you delete a meeting from your calendar, Outlook displays the message box shown in Figure 2.13. Outlook sends each attendee an e-mail message with the word *Canceled* in the subject line. Each attendee can then choose to open the message and remove the meeting from his or her calendar by clicking the Remove from Calendar button on the message window toolbar.

Update a Meeting
1. Open meeting window.
2. Change attendees or otherwise edit the meeting details.
3. Click Send Update.

Canceled meeting messages are sent as High Priority items.

FIGURE 2.13 *Delete Meeting Message Box to Meeting Organizer*

If you delete a meeting from your Calendar for which you were invited by meeting request and you accepted, Outlook displays the message box shown in Figure 2.14. You can choose to delete the meeting from your Calendar with or without sending a message to the meeting organizer.

FIGURE 2.14 *Confirm Delete Meeting Message Box to Attendee*

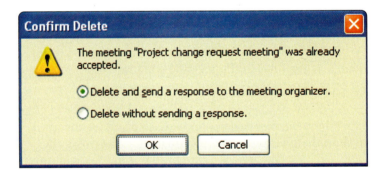

exercise 10 — SCHEDULING AND UPDATING A MEETING

1. With Calendar active and the date Friday, October 14, 2005 displayed in the Appointment area, click Monday, October 10, 2005 in the Date Navigator.
2. Schedule a new meeting by completing the following steps:
   a. Drag to select from 1:00 to 3:00 pm in the Appointment area.
   b. Click Actions on the Menu bar and then click New Meeting Request.

c. Click the To button. At the Select Attendees and Resources dialog box, change *Show Names from the* to the *Personal Address Book*, double-click the student name added to your PAB in Chapter 1 to add his or her name to the *Required* text box, and then click OK.
d. Click in the *Subject* text box and then type Project resource planning meeting.
e. Click in the *Location* text box and then type Room 101E.
f. Change the *Label* to *Important*.
g. Click Send.

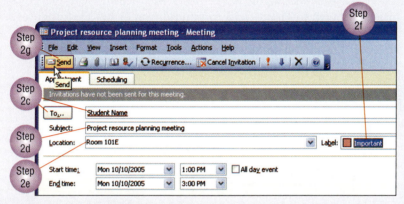

3. Update the meeting request sent in Step 2 to change the duration of the meeting by completing the following steps:
   a. Double-click the *Project resource planning meeting* appointment box.
   b. Click the down-pointing arrow next to the *End time* time text box and then click *4:00 PM (3 hours)*.
   c. Click the Send Update button on the message window toolbar. Outlook sends an e-mail message to each attendee with the updated information and automatically adjusts the appointment within your calendar.

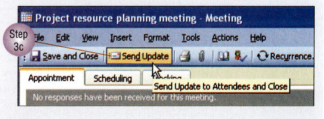

4. Read the meeting request and update meeting e-mail messages by completing the following steps:
   a. Click Mail in the Navigation Pane.
   b. Click *Sent Items* in the *All Mail Folders* section of the Navigation Pane.

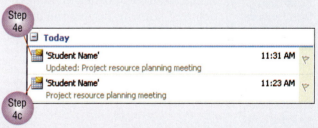

   c. Click the message header for the meeting request message sent in Step 2.
   d. Read the message in the Reading Pane.
   e. Click the message header for the updated message sent in Step 3.
   f. Read the message in the Reading Pane.
5. Click Calendar in the Navigation Pane and then display *Monday, October 10, 2005* in the Appointment area.
6. Click the Print button on the Standard toolbar, click *Weekly Style* in the *Print style* section of the Print dialog box, and then click OK.

Updating Meeting Attendees and Manually Tracking Responses

If after sending a meeting request, a new attendee is to be invited to the meeting, open the meeting window, type the e-mail address of the new attendee in the *To* text box, or click the Scheduling or Tracking tab. Click in the *Name* column over *Click here to add a name* and then type the name or e-mail address of the person that is being added to the meeting attendee list. To remove an attendee from the meeting, right-click the mouse over the name of the individual and then click Cut at the shortcut menu.

When the meeting organizer closes the meeting window, Outlook displays the message shown in Figure 2.15 to remind him or her that updates should be sent. You can choose to send an update message only to the individuals who have been added or deleted, or to all of the meeting participants.

FIGURE 2.15 *Send Update to Attendees Message Box*

HINT
Outlook tracks meeting responses automatically when all attendees are connected to a Microsoft Exchange Server. For attendees not connected to an Exchange Server, you may need to update the responses yourself depending on whether or not all attendees use Outlook as their mail client and send responses in rich text format.

Outlook tracks the responses received from attendees when they open the message and click one of the response buttons. The replies can be viewed by the meeting organizer in the Response column of the Tracking tab in the meeting window. If, however, an attendee contacts the meeting organizer by telephone or a subsequent e-mail with a change in their status, the meeting organizer can manually change the response status. To do this, click in the *Response* column next to the attendee's name and a down-pointing arrow appears. Click the down-pointing arrow to display the drop-down list shown in Figure 2.16, and then click the new status for the attendee.

F I G U R E 2.16 Manually Tracking Response Options

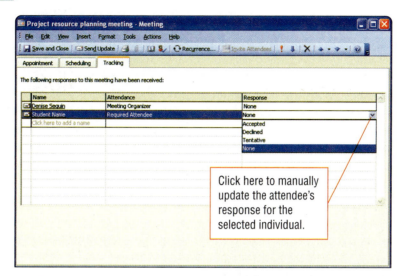

Changing Calendar Options

You can customize the Calendar in Outlook by changing options in the Calendar Options dialog box. For example, if you work a nonstandard work week, select the days that apply to you in the *Calendar work week* section of the Calendar Options dialog box. Click Tools, Options, and then click the Calendar Options button in the Options dialog box with the Preferences tab selected to display the Calendar Options dialog box shown in Figure 2.17.

QUICK STEPS

Change Calendar Options
1. Click Tools, Options, Preferences tab.
2. Click Calendar Options.
3. Change options as desired.
4. Click OK twice.

F I G U R E 2.17 Calendar Options Dialog Box

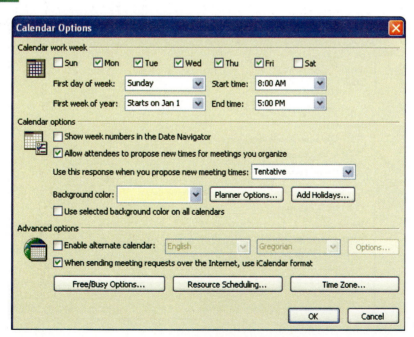

To change the way the calendar displays in the Date Navigator, change the options in the *Calendar work week* section. For example, if you change the *First day of week* entry from *Sunday* to *Saturday*, the Date Navigator will display calendars with the first day in each week as Saturday. The weeks would display in columns labeled S S M T W T F. Changing the *Start time* and *End time* entries will cause the Appointment area background color for workday hours to shorten or lengthen to reflect the length of the new workday.

The *Calendar options* section of the Calendar Options dialog box includes the capability to display week numbers in the Date Navigator, to provide the ability for attendees to propose alternate meeting times to your meeting requests, set the default response when proposing new meeting times, set the Appointment area background color, change Planner Options, and Add Holidays for a specific country.

Use the *Advanced options* section to set Free/Busy Options, Resource Scheduling options, and change the Time Zone.

exercise 11

CUSTOMIZING THE CALENDAR APPEARANCE

1. With Calendar active and the date Monday, October 10, 2005 displayed in the Appointment area, change the start and end times for the workday, show week numbers in the Date Navigator, and change the Calendar's background color by completing the following steps:
    a. Click Tools, Options, and then click the Calendar Options button in the Options dialog box with the Preferences tab selected.
    b. Click the down-pointing arrow next to the *Start time* text box in the *Calendar work week* section, and then click *9:00 AM*.
    c. Click the down-pointing arrow next to the *End time* text box in the *Calendar work week* section, and then click *6:00 PM*.
    d. Click the *Show week numbers in the Date Navigator* check box in the *Calendar options* section.
    e. Click the down-pointing arrow next to the *Background color* list box in the *Calendar options* section and then click the white color bar.

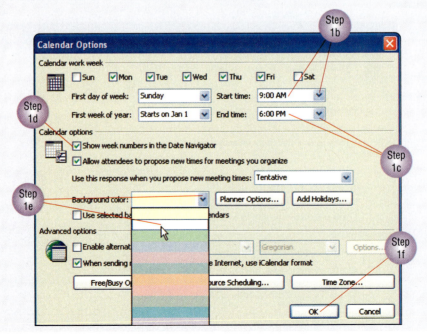

f. Click OK to close the Calendar Options dialog box.
g. Click OK to close the Options dialog box.
2. View the new options in the Calendar window. The background color of the Appointment area should be white for the new workday times between 9:00 am and 6:00 pm. Week numbers should be added to the months displayed in the Date Navigator section.

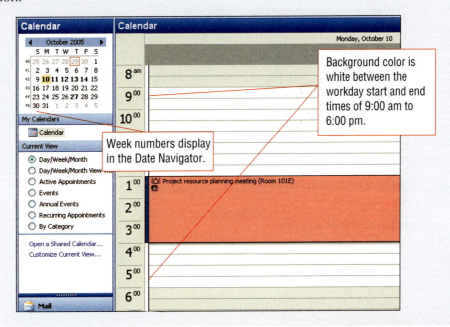

Working with More Than One Calendar

Create New Calendar Folder
1. With Calendar active, click File, New, Folder.
2. Type new folder name.
3. Click OK.

In Outlook 2003, you can view more than one calendar at the same time. Outlook displays multiple calendars side-by-side in the Appointment area with all calendars synchronized so that you can view the same day or time period simultaneously. For example, you may want to maintain a separate calendar for a special project that you are working on to keep the project activities separate from your main job. Another example might be that you want to maintain personal appointments separate from your business appointments.

To create a new Calendar you create a new folder in which to store the new calendar items. Outlook adds the name of the new calendar in the *My Calendars* section of the Navigation Pane. Click the check box next to the calendar name in the *My Calendars* section to display the new calendar beside the existing calendar.

exercise 12   DISPLAYING TWO CALENDARS SIDE-BY-SIDE

1. With Calendar active and the date Monday, October 10, 2005 displayed in the Appointment area, create a new folder in which to store calendar items by completing the following steps:
   a. Click View, point to Arrange By, and then click Show Views In Navigation Pane to remove the *Current View* section from the Navigation Pane.

b. Click the down-pointing arrow next to the New button on the Standard toolbar and then click Folder.
c. At the Create New Folder dialog box, with the insertion point positioned in the *Name* text box, type **Project Calendar**.
d. With *Calendar Items* already selected in *Folder contains,* and *Calendar* selected in *Select where to place the folder,* click OK.
e. Click the *Project Calendar* check box in the *My Calendars* section of the Navigation Pane. Outlook opens the Project Calendar and displays it to the right of the main calendar with the same day and time displayed in the Appointment area as shown below. Outlook differentiates the two calendars by displaying different background colors for each calendar.

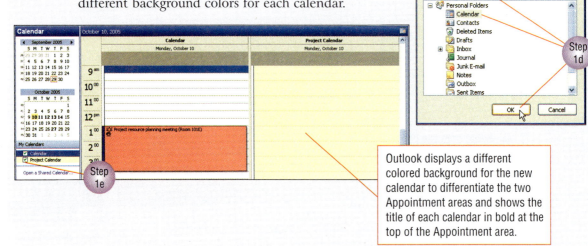

Outlook displays a different colored background for the new calendar to differentiate the two Appointment areas and shows the title of each calendar in bold at the top of the Appointment area.

2. Click Tuesday, October 11, 2005 in the Date Navigator. Notice both calendars display the same day simultaneously.
3. Schedule an appointment in the Project Calendar by completing the following steps:
   a. With Tuesday, October 11, 2005 the displayed date, click next to 9:30 am in the Appointment area for the Project Calendar.
   b. Type **Project vendor meeting** and then press Enter.

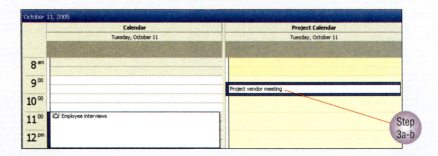

4. Click the *Project Calendar* check box in the *My Calendars* section of the Navigation Pane to close the Project Calendar and display only the main calendar.

CHAPTER summary

- The Calendar folder is used to schedule appointments, events, and meetings.
- An event differs from an appointment in that it is an activity that lasts the entire day or longer.
- An appointment that occurs on an ongoing basis can be set up as a recurring appointment.
- Edit appointment details by double-clicking the Appointment box to open the appointment window.
- An appointment can be moved to another day and/or time by dragging the Appointment box or by changing the start and end times.
- The Standard toolbar contains buttons to change the view from Day to Work Week, Week, or Month.
- The Current View menu contains options such as *Active Appointments* and *Events* that will filter the calendar and display the items in a table format.
- Appointments can be grouped by a keyword in the category list and can then be expanded or collapsed in groups in table format using the *By Category* option in the *Current View* section of the Navigation Pane.
- Outlook can apply automatic formatting to appointments, meetings, or events which can include changing the color and/or font of the text, or shading the appointment box. Formatting is applied based on a rule that is stored with the current view.
- Scheduling a meeting in Outlook is similar to setting up an appointment, with the exception that you identify the meeting attendees that you want to attend. Attendees are notified of the meeting via an e-mail message.
- The attendee can choose to click Accept, Tentative, Decline, or Propose New Time in the meeting request e-mail message.
- Responses to the organizer's meeting request are automatically tracked by Outlook.
- Open the meeting window and edit the details to reschedule or change the attendees. Click the Send Update button to notify the meeting attendees of the changes that have been made.
- To cancel a meeting, open the meeting window and then click Actions, Cancel Meeting.
- Responses to meeting requests can be manually changed on the Tracking tab in the Meeting window.
- You can customize the Calendar in Outlook by changing options in the Calendar Options dialog box.
- Create a new Calendar folder if you want to store appointments, meetings, or events separately from the main calendar.
- When multiple calendars exist, click the check boxes for the calendars you want to display in the *My Calendars* section of the Navigation Pane. Outlook displays a different colored background in each calendar and synchronizes scrolling in the Date Navigator so that each calendar displays the same day and time period.

FEATURES summary

FEATURE	BUTTON	MENU	KEYBOARD
Appointment	New	File, New, Appointment; or Actions, New Appointment	Ctrl + N
Automatic Formatting	▦	Edit, Automatic Formatting	
Calendar Options		Tools, Options, Preferences tab, Calendar Options	
Cancel meeting		Actions, Cancel Meeting in meeting window	
Categories		Edit, Categories	
Change current view		View, Arrange By, Current View	
Create a new folder		File, New, Folder	Ctrl + Shift + E
Delete appointment, event, or meeting	✕	Edit, Delete	Ctrl + D
Event		Actions, New All Day Event	
Go To Date		Go, Go To Date	Ctrl + G
Meeting Request		File, New, Meeting Request; or Actions, New Meeting Request	Ctrl + Shift + Q
Reading Pane		View, Reading Pane	
Recurring appointment	Recurrence...	Actions, New Recurring Appointment	

CONCEPTS check

Completion: On a blank sheet of paper, indicate the correct term, command, symbol, or explanation for each description.

1. This the default view for the Calendar. *Day*
2. Double-click here to create an event. *Date in the banner at the top of the Appointment Area.*
3. Click this button in the appointment window to create an appointment that occurs on an ongoing basis at fixed intervals. *Recurrence*
4. Do this action with the mouse over an appointment box to open the appointment window. *Double click*
5. The Standard toolbar contains four buttons to change the current view: Day, Week, Month, and this button. *Work week*
6. Click this menu sequence to display the *Current View* section in the Navigation Pane. *View, Arrange by, Current View*
7. Associate an appointment with a keyword in this dialog box that will allow you to view appointments grouped by the keyword. *Categories*
8. Open this dialog box to create a rule for the current view in which appointments are formatted based on a condition that you specify. *Automatic Formatting*
9. To view the free/busy times of meeting attendees, click this tab in the meeting window. *Scheduling*
10. An attendee can click this button in the meeting request message window to indicate his or her agreement to attend the meeting at the specified day and time. *Accept*
11. The meeting organizer clicks this button in the meeting window after making changes to the meeting details to inform attendees of the changes made. *Send update*
12. This section of the Calendar options dialog box is where you set the normal start and end times of your workday. *Calendar work week*
13. Click another calendar name in this section of the Navigation Pane to display two calendars side-by-side. *My Calendars*

SKILLS check

Assessment 1

1. With Calendar active in Day view, schedule an appointment at 10:00 a.m. on Monday, October 24, 2005 as follows:
   - Subject — **Budget planning**
   - Location — **Accounting conference room**
   - 1 hour duration
   - No reminder
   - Show time as *Out of Office*
2. Schedule a recurring appointment at 2:30 p.m. on Monday, October 24, 2005 as follows:
   - Subject — **Review sales**
   - Location — **My office**
   - ½ hour duration
   - Reminder at 5 minutes
   - Recurs monthly on the fourth Monday of every month
3. Print the Calendar in *Daily Style*.

Assessment 2

1. With Calendar active and the date Monday, October 24, 2005 displayed, schedule the following events:
   a. A two-day E-learning conference in San Diego starting Tuesday, October 25, 2005. Deselect the *Reminder* option if it is active, show the time as *Out of Office*, and assign the label *Travel Required*.
   b. A vacation day on Friday, October 28, 2005. Deselect the *Reminder* option if it is active, assign the event to the *Personal* category, and show the time as *Out of Office*.
2. Display the Calendar in Week view.
3. Move the Budget planning appointment at 10:00 a.m. on Monday, October 24, 2005 to Thursday, October 27, 2005 by dragging and dropping the appointment from Monday to Thursday while the pointer displays as the four-headed arrow icon.
4. Print the Calendar in *Weekly Style*.
5. Change the current view to display only events.
6. Adjust column widths as necessary to view the event details.
7. Print the events in *Table Style*.
8. Restore the current view to Day view for Monday, October 24, 2005.

Assessment 3

1. With Calendar active and the date Monday, October 24, 2005 displayed, create and send a meeting request at 9:00 a.m. as follows:

Attendee	Student from Personal Address Book
Subject	**Project training**
Location	**My office**
1 hour duration	
10 minute reminder	

2. Print the Calendar in *Daily Style*.

Assessment 4

(Note: To complete this assessment, another student must have sent you the Project training meeting request from Assessment 3.)

1. Click Mail and make sure the Inbox folder is selected.
2. Open the Project training meeting request message.
3. Decline the meeting with the following text typed in the response message:

   I have a personal appointment outside the office on this day. Please reschedule this training at your convenience.

4. Print and then send the response.
5. Display the Calendar for the date Monday, October 24, 2005.

Assessment 5

1. With Calendar active and the date Monday, October 24, 2005 displayed in Day view, add a new rule for automatic formatting of items as follows:
   a. Name the rule *Sales appointments and meetings*.
   b. Assign the label *Important*.
   c. Click the Condition button. Type the word **Sales** in the *Search for the word(s)* text box of the Appointments and Meetings tab in the Filter dialog box and then click OK twice.
2. Change the current view to Active Appointments.
3. Change the current view back to Day view for Monday, October 24, 2005.
4. Display the Calendar in the Week view.
5. Print the Calendar in *Weekly Style*.
6. Display the Calendar in Day view.

Assessment 6

1. With Calendar active, display the date Thursday, October 27, 2005, and then create and send a meeting request at noon as follows:

Attendee	Student from Personal Address Book
Subject	**Meeting with client**
Location	**Client's office**
1.5 hours duration	
No reminder	
Show time as *Out of Office*	

2. Open the meeting window for the meeting scheduled in Step 1 and then edit the meeting details as follows:
   a. Change the location to The Waterfront Bistro.
   b. Change the duration of the meeting to 2 hours.
3. Send the update message.
4. Print the Calendar in *Daily Style*.

Assessment 7

1. With Calendar active and the date Thursday, October 27, 2005 displayed, change the calendar options back to the default settings as follows:
   a. Change the start time for the workday to *8:00 AM*.
   b. Change the end time for the workday to *5:00 PM*.
   c. Deselect the *Show week numbers in the Date Navigator* check box.
   d. Change the background color for the Appointment area to pale yellow.
2. Display the calendar in the Month view.
3. Print the Calendar in *Monthly Style*.
4. Display the calendar in Day view for the current date.

CHAPTER 3

MANAGING CONTACTS

PERFORMANCE OBJECTIVES

Upon successful completion of Chapter 3, you will be able to:
- ➤ Add, edit, and delete contacts
- ➤ Add a new contact from an existing contact
- ➤ Add a picture of a contact to the contact window
- ➤ Flag a contact for follow-up
- ➤ Sort and filter contacts
- ➤ Group contacts into categories
- ➤ Find a contact
- ➤ Change the current view
- ➤ Print contacts in card, booklet, and phone directory style
- ➤ Change contact options
- ➤ Send an e-mail message from the Contacts folder
- ➤ Schedule an appointment from the Contacts folder
- ➤ Create and use a distribution list for e-mail messages

(Note: There are no student data files to copy for this chapter.)

The Contacts folder can be used to maintain all of the information you need about the individuals or companies with whom you regularly communicate by e-mail, fax, letter, or telephone. The information you store can go beyond addresses and telephone numbers to include additional details such as manager's name, assistant's name, spouse's name, children's names, birthday, or anniversary. In Outlook 2003, you can now store a picture of the contact in the form so that you can see the person's picture while looking at his or her name, address, and phone number. Outlook provides several methods for viewing contacts by sorting, filtering, and grouping related records. Any Outlook item such as an e-mail message, appointment, or meeting can be linked to a contact and all activities related to the contact viewed in one window.

Adding Contacts

Add a New Contact
1. Click New Contact button.
2. Type data in required fields.
3. Click Save and Close.

Visualize the Contacts folder as an electronic Rolodex or address book—names, addresses, telephone numbers, and e-mail addresses for individuals with whom you communicate. The Contacts folder is a database, with each contact occupying a *record* in the folder and each unit of information about an individual within the record, such as a telephone number, referred to as a ***field***. Approximately 140 fields are available for storing information about a contact including three different addresses, three different e-mail addresses, and up to nineteen contact telephone numbers. The information can be viewed and printed in a variety of formats and orders.

When you click Contacts in the Navigation Pane, the Contacts window appears as shown in Figure 3.1.

FIGURE

3.1 *Contacts Window*

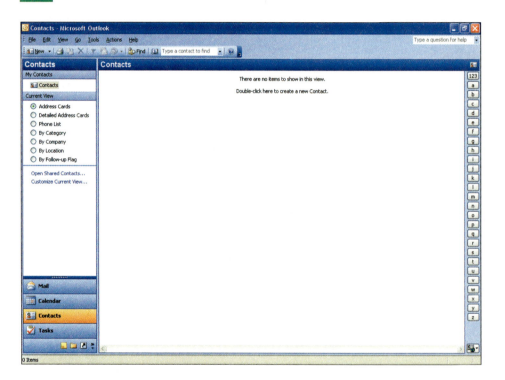

New Contact

To open the Contact window with the General tab selected shown in Figure 3.2, click the New Contact button on the Standard toolbar; click File, point to New, and then click Contact; or click Actions, New Contact. The General tab is used to group the most frequently used fields such as job title, company name, address, telephone numbers, and e-mail, Web, and instant messaging addresses.

FIGURE 3.2 New Contact Window with General Tab Selected

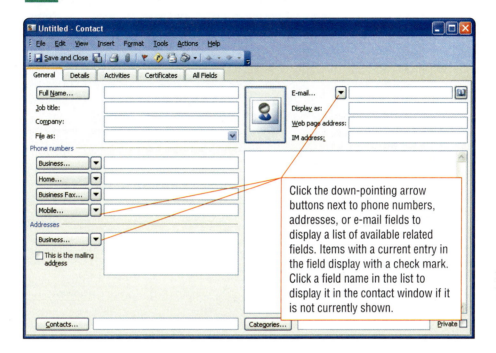

The Details tab contains fields to enter the *Department, Office, Profession, Manager's name,* and *Assistant's name* for the contact's business. If you have personal information about the contact that you would like to keep track of, type entries in the *Nickname, Spouse's name, Birthday,* or *Anniversary* fields. If the contact will be participating in online meetings or sharing calendar information, the server and directory address settings are entered in the Details tab.

Use the Activities tab to view details for the various Outlook actions that are related to the selected contact. For example, you can use the Activities tab to view e-mail messages sent or received by the active contact. The Certificates tab is used to import or export digital IDs that can be used to encrypt mail sent to the contact. Use the All Fields tab to view a group of related fields. For example, you can choose to view only the telephone numbers entered for the contact in the All Fields window.

Additional fields not shown in the previous tabs can be viewed from the All Fields tab by selecting a category of fields from the *Select from* drop-down list. The *All Contact fields* option from the *Select from* drop-down list will show all of the fields in one window for the active contact.

> **HINT**
> Use the white text box below *IM address* to type any free-form notes to yourself about this contact that you want to remember. For example, type the name of a favorite restaurant or vacation destination.

exercise 1 — ADDING NEW CONTACTS

1. With Outlook open, click Contacts in the Navigation Pane.
2. Add a new record to the Contacts folder by completing the following steps:
    a. Click the New Contact button [New] on the Standard toolbar.

b. With the insertion point positioned in the *Full Name* text box, type **Ms. Kayla McAllister** and then press Tab. When you move to the next field, the *File as* text box automatically displays the name with the last name first for sorting purposes.
c. With the insertion point positioned in the *Job title* text box, type **Sales Manager** and then press Tab.
d. With the insertion point positioned in the *Company* text box, type **Worldwide Enterprises**.
e. Click in the *Business* text box in the *Phone numbers* section and then type **6085554555**. After you click in the next field, Outlook converts the telephone number to (608) 555-4555. You can type telephone numbers with or without spaces or hyphens between sections of the number.
f. Click in the *Business Fax* text box in the *Phone numbers* section and then type **6085554556**. If necessary, check with your instructor if a Location Information dialog box appears the first time that you click in the *Business Fax* text box.
g. Click in the *Mobile* text box in the *Phone numbers* section and then type **6085550123**.
h. Click in the *Business* text box in the *Addresses* section and then type the following street address, city, state, and ZIP Code as you would normally type them on a letter or envelope:
   P. O. Box 99A
   1453 Airport Road
   Middleton, WI 53562
i. Click in the *E-mail* text box, type **kmcallister@emcp.net**, and then click in a blank text box to complete the entry. The *Display as* text box automatically converts the e-mail entry to *Kayla McAllister (kmcallister@emcp.net)*.
j. Click the Save and Close button on the Contact window toolbar.

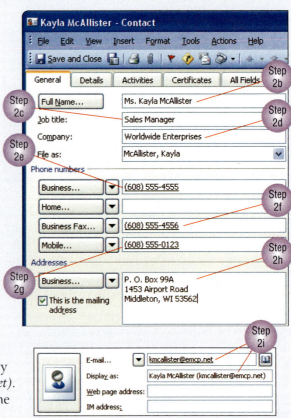

3. By default, the contact displays in the Contents Pane as an Address Card with the name, address, telephone numbers, and e-mail address visible. Review the text entered for Kayla McAllister in Step 2.
4. Add a new record to Contacts using the Check Full Name and Check Address dialog boxes in the contacts window by completing the following steps:
   a. Click the New Contact button on the Standard toolbar.
   b. With the insertion point positioned in the *Full Name* text box, click the Full Name button to open the Check Full Name dialog box.
   c. With the insertion point positioned in the *Title* text box in the *Name details* section, type **Mr.** and then press Tab or click in the *First* text box.
   d. Type **Leslie** in the *First* text box and then press Tab twice or click in the *Last* text box.

e. Type **Taylor** in the *Last* text box and then press Enter or click OK.
f. Click in the *Job title* text box and then type **Sales Representative**.
g. Press Tab or click in the *Company* text box and then type **Globalware Distributors**.
h. Type the following telephone numbers in the fields noted:
   - Business   6085552199
   - Business Fax   6085552200
   - Mobile   6085554975
i. Click the Business button in the *Addresses* section to open the Check Address dialog box.
j. With the insertion point positioned in the *Street* text box in the *Address details* section, type **4532 Dundas Street West** and then press Tab or click in the *City* text box.
k. Type **Madison** and then press Tab or click in the *State/Province* text box.
l. Type **WI** and then press Tab or click in the *ZIP/Postal code* text box.
m. Type **53710** and then press Enter or click OK.
n. Type the following text in the *E-mail* text box:
   ltaylor@emcp.net
o. Click the Save and Close button on the Contact window toolbar.

5. Change the current view to add the job title and company fields by completing the following step:
   a. Click *Detailed Address Cards* in the *Current View* section of the Navigation Pane.

6. Increase the width of the first column of contacts in the Contents Pane by completing the following step:
   a. Position the mouse pointer on the gray line at the right of the first column of contact names until the pointer displays as a left- and right-pointing arrow and then drag the column right approximately 1 inch.

7. Click the Print button on the Standard toolbar. With *Card Style* already selected in the *Print style* section, click OK.

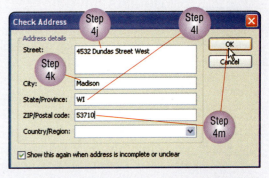

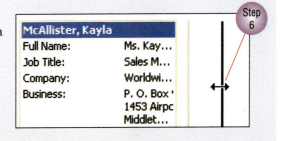

HINT

The Check Address dialog box often appears for international addresses due to differences in ZIP/Postal Codes. To save time, type these addresses directly into the Check Address dialog box.

In Exercise 1, Step 2, you typed text directly into the *Full Name* and *Business* text boxes, while in Step 4, you typed text into the individual fields that comprise the name and address using the Check Full Name and Check Address dialog boxes. Outlook inserts text into the fields based on the input unless it cannot recognize the entry, in which case the Check Full Name or Check Address dialog box opens automatically. Insert and delete text as required to correct the text in the fields or click OK to accept the entries as they were typed. Outlook recognizes the titles *Dr., Miss, Mr., Mrs., Ms.,* and *Prof.* The Check Address dialog box automatically opens when an address has been typed that Outlook does not recognize as containing a valid street, city, state or province, and ZIP or Postal Code.

Editing Contacts

Maintaining contact records involves activities such as changing an address, telephone number, or e-mail address as individuals move or change companies, adding information to fields not previously completed, or deleting contacts for which you no longer require a record in the Contacts folder.

QUICK STEPS

Delete a Contact
1. Click name banner in Contents Pane.
2. Click Delete button.

Double-click a contact name in the Contents Pane to open the contact window. Edit the fields as required and then click the Save and Close button. If the data you need to change is visible in the current view, click the insertion point within the field and make the necessary changes directly within the Contents Pane. Editing in the Contents Pane cannot be done for the name in the contact record banner.

To delete a contact record, click to select the contact name in the banner for the record and then press Delete or click the Delete button on the Standard toolbar.

QUICK STEPS

Edit a Contact
1. Double-click name banner.
2. Edit fields as required in contact window.
3. Click Save and Close.

exercise 2

ADDING AND EDITING CONTACTS

1. With Outlook open and Contacts active in Detailed Address Cards view, add a new contact by completing the following steps:
   a. Click Actions on the Menu bar and then click New Contact.
   b. With the insertion point positioned in the *Full Name* text box, type **Miss Guiseppina D'Allario**.
   c. Press Tab or click in the *Job title* field, and then type **Regional Sales Manager**.
   d. Press Tab or click in the *Company* text box and then type **Eastern Industries**.
   e. Type the following telephone numbers in the fields noted:
      Business   **6085554968**
      Business Fax   **6085554702**
      Mobile   **6085553795**
   f. Click in the *Business* text box in the *Addresses* section and then type the following text:
      44 Queen Street
      Madison, WI 53562
   g. Click in the *E-mail* text box and then type **dallario@emcp.net**.
   h. Click Save and Close.

2. Edit the telephone numbers for Leslie Taylor in the Contents Pane by completing the following steps:

   a. Position the I-beam pointer ⌶, in the *Business* field between *2* and *1* in the record for Taylor, Leslie, and then click the left mouse button. A dotted box appears around the field and an insertion point is placed between *2* and *1*.

   b. Press the Delete key three times to remove *199*, type **267**, and then press Enter.

   c. Click the mouse at the end of the *Business Fax* field (after the last zero), press Backspace four times to delete *2200*, type **2311** and then press Enter.

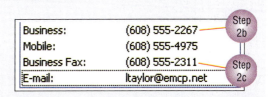

3. Change the street address for Kayla McAllister in the Contact window by completing the following steps:

   a. Double-click the name banner for *McAllister, Kayla*.

   b. Position the I-beam pointer in the *Business* text box in the *Addresses* section at the beginning of the second line and then drag to select the street address *1453 Airport Road*.

   c. Type **18 Forsythia Avenue**.

   d. Click Save and Close.

4. Click the Print button on the Standard toolbar. With *Card Style* already selected in the *Print style* section, click OK.

QUICK STEPS

Add New Contact from Existing Contact
1. Select contact upon which to base new record.
2. Click Actions, New Contact from Same Company.
3. Type data in fields as required.
4. Click Save and Close.

Adding New Contacts from Existing Contacts

When there is more than one person from the same company that you communicate with, you can quickly add the second or third record by basing a new record on an existing one. Outlook inserts the company name and address in the Contact window so that you don't have to retype it. This not only avoids duplication of effort but ensures that records are consistent and reduces the chance of typing errors.

Once one of the contacts has been created for the company, the remaining contacts for the same company can be added by selecting the record, clicking Actions, and then New Contact from Same Company.

exercise 3

ADDING A NEW CONTACT FROM AN EXISTING CONTACT

1. With Outlook open and Contacts active in Detailed Address Cards view, add a new contact by basing the record on an existing contact by completing the following steps:
    a. If necessary, click the name banner for *McAllister, Kayla* to select the contact record.
    b. Click Actions, then New Contact from Same Company.
    c. With the insertion point positioned in the *Full Name* text box, type **Mr. Henry Miele**.
    d. Press Tab or click in the *Job title* text box and then type **Sales Manager, European Division**.
    e. Click in the *E-mail* text box and then type **hmiele@emcp.net**.
    f. Click Save and Close.
2. Click the Print button on the Standard toolbar. With *Card Style* already selected in the *Print style* section, click OK.

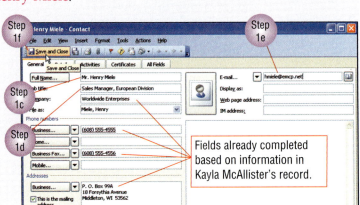

Using the Details and All Fields Tabs

Approximately 140 fields are available for storing information about a contact, including four user-defined fields. The Details tab in the Contact window shown in Figure 3.3 groups fields related to the contact's business and personal relationships. The bottom of the Details tab contains the settings required to participate in online meetings using Microsoft NetMeeting and for sharing calendar information over the Internet.

The All Fields tab provides the ability to view subsets of related fields or all of the contact fields in a table format.

FIGURE

3.3 Contact Window with Details Tab Selected

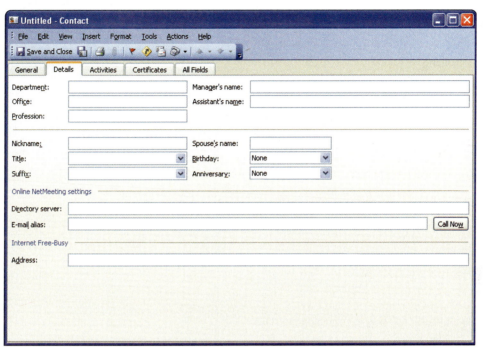

exercise 4

ADDING INFORMATION IN DETAILS AND ALL FIELDS TABS

1. With Outlook open and Contacts active in Detailed Address Cards view, add a new contact with information in the Details tab by completing the following steps:
   a. Click the New Contact button on the Standard toolbar.
   b. Type the following information in the General tab of the Contact window:

Full Name	Dr. Tory Nunez
Job title	Director, Marketing and Sales
Company	Globe Products
Business	6085552689
Business Fax	6085552458
Mobile	6085551598
Address	393 Brentwood Road Madison, WI 53562
E-mail	nunez@emcp.net

   c. Click the Details tab in the Contact window.
   d. With the insertion point positioned in the *Department* text box, type **Marketing**.
   e. Click in the *Manager's name* text box and then type **Kyle Winston**.
   f. Click in the *Assistant's name* text box and then type **Dana Gauthier**.
   g. Click in the *Spouse's name* text box and then type **Chris Greenbaum**.
2. View all of the contact fields and add the names of the children for the contact by completing the following steps:

a. Click the All Fields tab in the Contact window.
b. Click the down-pointing arrow next to *Select from*, scroll down the list box, and then click *All Contact fields*.
c. Scroll down the list box and examine all of the contact fields that are available for storing information about contacts.
d. Scroll up the list box until you can see the field named *Children*. *(Note: The field names are in alphabetical order.)*
e. Click in the column labeled *Value* beside the field named *Children* to select the field and position the insertion point position inside a dotted text box.
f. Type **Brooke, Dustin, Jamie**.
g. Click Save and Close.

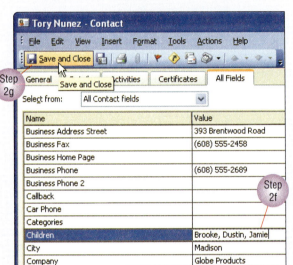

3. Add the birthday information for an existing contact by completing the following steps:
   a. Double-click the name banner for *McAllister, Kayla*.
   b. Click the Details tab in the Contact window.
   c. Drag to select the text *None* in the *Birthday* field.
   d. Type **October 15, 1979**. Outlook tracks birthdays automatically once an entry exists in the *Birthday* field and displays a reminder in the Calendar on a contact's birthday each year.
   e. Click Save and Close.
4. Click the Print button on the Standard toolbar. With *Card Style* already selected in the *Print style* section, click OK.

Adding Pictures to Contacts

Add Contact Picture

Add Picture to Contact
1. Select record in Contents Pane.
2. Click Add Contact Picture icon.
3. Navigate to drive and/or folder.
4. Double-click image file name.
5. Click Save and Close.

In Outlook 2003, you have the ability to show a picture of the individual in the contact window. Associating a face with a name is very beneficial for those contacts for whom you have an image file. Display a picture of the person in the contact window by clicking the Add Contact Picture image control box in the contact window, or click Actions, Add Picture. At the Add Contact Picture dialog box, navigate to the drive and/or folder in which the image file is stored and then double-click the file name. Outlook recognizes standard graphics file formats such as *gif*, *jpeg*, and *bmp* and resizes the image to fit within the image control, maintaining the aspect ratio so that pictures don't become distorted.

Figure 3.4 shows a contact window with an image file shown in the image control box. Once a picture has been added you can change the source image by clicking Actions, Change Picture, or remove the image by clicking Actions, Remove Picture.

FIGURE 3.4   Picture Added to Contact Window

Flagging a Contact for Follow-Up

Follow Up Flag

A reminder to follow up on an outstanding issue with a contact can be set by flagging the contact's record. To do this, select the contact record that you want to mark with a flag, click Actions, and then click Follow Up to open the Flag for Follow Up dialog box. Click the down-pointing arrow next to the *Flag to* list box, and then click the type of flag that you want to set, or type your own flag name in the *Flag to* text box. Figure 3.5 shows the flags available in the *Flag to* drop-down list.

To enter a due date for the follow-up activity, type a date in the *Due by* text box or click the down-pointing arrow to select a date from the drop-down calendar. The text box next to the date (currently reads *None*) can be used to enter a time that the activity must be completed by.

Flag Contact for Follow-Up Activity
1. Select record in Contents Pane.
2. Click Follow Up button.
3. Choose the required flag in *Flag to* list box.
4. Choose *Due by* date.
5. Click OK.

FIGURE 3.5   Flag for Follow Up Dialog Box with Flag to Drop-Down List

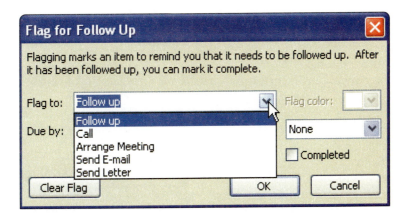

To view a list of contacts and flags in a table format, click *By Follow-up Flag* in the *Current View* section of the Navigation Pane. Contacts with flags attached to records are displayed at the top of the list.

HINT
If the *Current View* section is not currently visible in the Navigation Pane, click View, point to Arrange By, and then click Show Views In Navigation Pane.

exercise 5

FLAGGING CONTACTS FOR FOLLOW-UP

1. With Outlook open and Contacts active in Detailed Address Cards view, attach a Follow Up flag to a contact record that will remind you to schedule a meeting by completing the following steps:
   a. Click the name banner for *Taylor, Leslie*.
   b. Click Actions, and then Follow Up; or click the Follow Up button 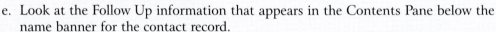 on the Standard toolbar.
   c. Click the down-pointing arrow next to *Flag to* and then click *Arrange Meeting*.
   d. Drag to select *None* in the *Due by* text box, type **one week from today**, and then click OK. Outlook allows all dates to be entered using natural language phrases. The *Due by* date will be set to one week from the current date.
   e. Look at the Follow Up information that appears in the Contents Pane below the name banner for the contact record.

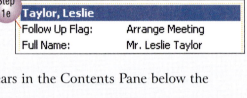

2. Double-click the name banner for *Taylor, Leslie* to view the Follow Up flag message inside the contact window.
3. Click the Close button on the Leslie Taylor - Contact window Title bar.
4. Add a Follow Up flag to the contact record for *McAllister, Kayla* by completing the following steps:
   a. Click the name banner for *McAllister, Kayla*.
   b. Click the Follow Up button on the Standard toolbar.
   c. Click the down-pointing arrow next to *Flag to* and then click *Send Letter*.
   d. Click the down-pointing arrow next to *Due by* and then click the date that is two weeks from today in the drop-down calendar.
   e. Click OK.

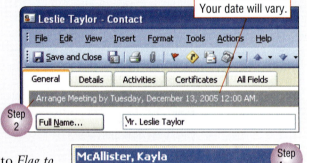

5. Change the current view to display the contact records in table format grouped by Follow Up flags by completing the following steps:
   a. Click *By Follow-up Flag* in the *Current View* section of the Navigation Pane.
   b. Double-click the miniature card icon in the first column of the row in the table for Ms. Kayla McAllister to open the contact window with the flag message displayed.

c. Click the close button on the Kayla McAllister - Contact window Title bar.
   d. Double-click the right column boundary for the *Follow Up Flag* column heading to expand the column width to the length of the longest entry.
6. Click the Print button on the Standard toolbar. With *Table Style* already selected in the *Print style* section, click OK.
7. Click *Detailed Address Cards* in the *Current View* section of the Navigation Pane.

A red flag displayed in the Flag column indicates the flag is still active. Once the contact activity has been completed, select the contact, display the Flag for Follow Up dialog box, and then click the *Completed* check box. The icon changes to a gray check mark in the flag status column in the By Follow-up Flag view.

To remove a flag from a contact record, select the contact, display the Flag for Follow Up dialog box, and then click the Clear Flag button.

A Follow Up flag that becomes overdue displays in red in the Contents Pane. For example, if you set a due date for a reminder to arrange a meeting for a contact and the due date passes without the flag being cleared or marked as completed, the data in the contact record displays in red.

Sorting Contacts

Contacts are initially displayed in the Contents Pane alphabetically sorted in ascending order by the *File As* field which defaults to the contact's last name followed by first name. In the Sort dialog box shown in Figure 3.6 you can specify up to four fields by which to sort the contact list.

QUICK STEPS

Sort Contacts
1. Click Customize Current View in Navigation Pane.
2. Click Sort button.
3. Define sort fields in Sort dialog box.
4. Click OK to close Sort dialog box.
5. Click OK to close Customize View dialog box.

FIGURE 3.6 **Sort Dialog Box**

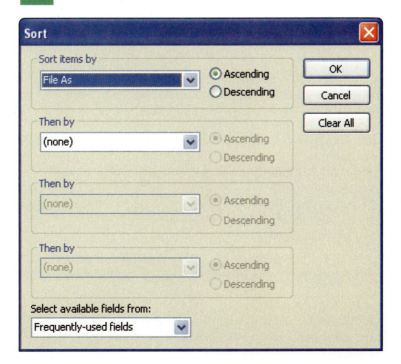

The drop-down list of fields for *Sort items by* and *Then by* defaults to *Frequently-used fields*. Click the down-pointing arrow next to the *Select available fields from* list box to change to any of the subsets of related fields or all of the contact fields.

To begin a sort, click Customize Current View in the Navigation Pane and then click the Sort button in the Customize View dialog box to define the sort criteria in the Sort dialog box.

exercise 6

SORTING CONTACTS

1. With Outlook open and Contacts active in Detailed Address Cards view, sort the contact list by company name and then by last name by completing the following steps:
   a. Click Customize Current View in the Navigation Pane.
   b. Click the Sort button in the Customize View: Detailed Address Cards dialog box.
   c. Click the down-pointing arrow next to the *Sort items by* list box, scroll up the list box, and then click *Company*. The sort order defaults to *Ascending*.
   d. Click the down-pointing arrow next to the *Then by* list box, scroll down the list box, and then click *Last Name*. The sort order defaults to *Ascending*.
   e. Click OK to close the Sort dialog box.
   f. A message box displays informing you that the field *Last Name* is not shown in the current view and asking if you want to show it. Click No. You do not need to display the *Last Name* field since the name banner for the address card displays the *File As* field which defaults to last name followed by first name.
   g. With the current sort settings displayed next to the Sort button in the Customize View: Detailed Address Cards dialog box, click OK.
   h. Examine the order of the records in the Contents Pane.

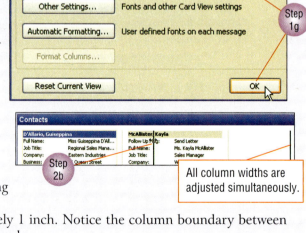

2. Expand the column widths to fully display the data in the Contents Pane by completing the following steps:
   a. Position the arrow pointer on the vertical line between the first and second columns until the pointer displays as a left- and right-pointing arrow.

   All column widths are adjusted simultaneously.

   b. Drag the pointer right approximately 1 inch. Notice the column boundary between columns 2 and 3 moves simultaneously.
3. Add the following contact by basing the record on an existing contact by completing the following steps:
   a. Select the record for Tory Nunez.
   b. Click Actions, and then click New Contact from Same Company.
   c. Type the following information in the fields noted:

100 Chapter Three

Full Name	Mr. Cal Fillmore
Job title	Sales Manager
Mobile	6085552146
E-mail	fillmore@emcp.net

   d. Click Save and Close.
   e. Notice the new record is inserted maintaining the current order of sorting first by company and then by last name within the company.
   f. Print the contact list in *Card Style*.
4. Restore the sort order to the default setting by completing the following steps:
   a. Click Customize Current View in the Navigation Pane.
   b. Click the Sort button in the Customize View: Detailed Address Cards dialog box.
   c. Click the Clear All button in the Sort dialog box.
   d. Click the down-pointing arrow next to the *Sort items by* list box, scroll down the list box, and then click *File As*. The sort order defaults to *Ascending*.
   e. Click OK to close the Sort dialog box and then click OK to close the Customize View: Detailed Address Cards dialog box.

Filtering Contacts

A filtered contact list is a subset of contact records that has been selected based on a criterion specified in the Filter dialog box. Records that do not meet the condition are temporarily removed from the Contents Pane. The message *Filter Applied* appears in the Status bar next to the total number of records to indicate that not all of the records are currently displayed.

To specify the condition upon which to display records, click Customize Current View in the Navigation Pane. Click the Filter button in the Customize View dialog box and then specify which records to display in the Filter dialog box with the Contacts tab selected shown in Figure 3.7.

QUICK STEPS

Filter Contacts
1. Click Customize Current View in Navigation Pane.
2. Click Filter button.
3. Define filter criteria in Filter dialog box.
4. Click OK to close Filter dialog box.
5. Click OK to close Customize View dialog box.

FIGURE 3.7 **Filter Dialog Box with Contacts Tab Selected**

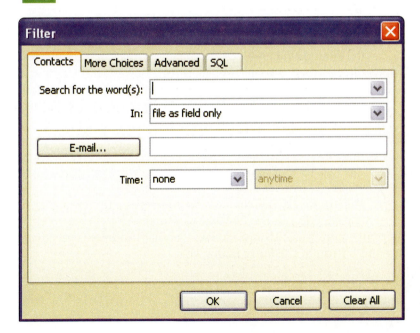

View and print the filtered list as necessary and then restore all records by completing the following steps:
1. Click *Customize Current View* in the Navigation Pane.
2. Click the Filter button in the Customize View dialog box.
3. Click the Clear All button in the Filter dialog box.
4. Click OK twice.

exercise 7

FILTERING CONTACTS

1. With Outlook open and Contacts active in Detailed Address Cards view, filter the contact list to display only those records for Globe Products by completing the following steps:
   a. Click Customize Current View in the Navigation Pane.
   b. Click the Filter button in the Customize View: Detailed Address Cards dialog box.
   c. At the Filter dialog box with the Contacts tab selected and the insertion point positioned in the *Search for the word(s)* text box, type **Globe Products**.

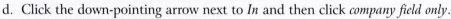

   d. Click the down-pointing arrow next to *In* and then click *company field only*.
   e. Click OK to close the Filter dialog box.
   f. With the current filter settings displayed next to the Filter button in the Customize View: Detailed Address Cards dialog box, click OK. Only two records are displayed in the Contents Pane and the message *Filter Applied* displays toward the left edge of the Status bar.
2. Print the filtered list in *Phone Directory* style by completing the following steps:
   a. Click the Print button on the Standard toolbar.
   b. Scroll down the *Print style* list box and then click *Phone Directory Style*.
   c. Click OK.
3. Restore the Contents Pane to display all contacts by completing the following steps:
   a. Click Customize Current View in the Navigation Pane.
   b. Click the Filter button in the Customize View: Detailed Address Cards dialog box.
   c. Click the Clear All button in the Filter dialog box.
   d. Click OK twice.

Grouping Contacts into Categories

Contacts can be associated with a keyword in the category list and can then be grouped or filtered by the category to produce different lists of contacts. The *By Category* option in the *Current View* section of the Navigation Pane groups contacts by the catgeory they have been assigned. The list of contacts can then be expanded and collapsed as required. The list of categories in the *Available categories* list box in the Categories dialog box is the same list as was used for appointments in the previous chapter. A contact can be associated with more than one category so that his or her name will appear on more than one list.

To create your own category name, type the category name in the *Item(s) belong to these categories* text box and then click the Add to List button.

To assign a category to an existing contact, right-click the contact name in the Contents Pane and then click Categories at the shortcut menu to open the Categories dialog box; or select the contact and then click Edit, Categories.

HINT

As an alternative to grouping related contacts using categories, you can also create separate Contact folders if you prefer to store related contacts separately.

QUICK STEPS

Assign Category to Contact
1. Right-click name banner.
2. Click Categories at shortcut menu.
3. Click category names in *Available categories* list box.
4. Click OK.

exercise 8 — CREATING CATEGORIES, ASSIGNING CONTACTS TO CATEGORIES, AND VIEWING CONTACTS IN CATEGORIES

1. With Outlook open and Contacts active in Detailed Address Cards view, create a new category and assign a contact to the new category by completing the following steps:
   a. Right-click the contact name *D'Allario, Guiseppina*.
   b. Click Categories at the shortcut menu.
   c. Click the insertion point inside the *Item(s) belong to these categories* text box and then type **Association Member**.
   d. Click the Add to List button.
   e. Look at the list in the *Available categories* list box to view the new category added in Step 1d. Notice the category is automatically checked for the current contact.
   f. Click OK. A row is added to the record in Detailed Address Cards view showing the category to which the contact has been assigned.
2. Assign categories to the remaining contacts by completing the following steps:
   a. Double-click *Fillmore, Cal*.

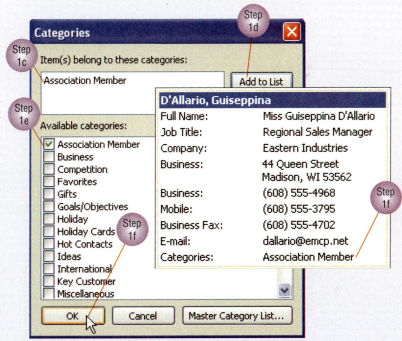

OUTLOOK — Managing Contacts

b. Click the Categories button near the bottom of the Cal Fillmore - Contact window.
c. Click *Association Member*, *Business*, and *Holiday Cards* in the *Available categories* list box and then click OK.
d. Click Save and Close.
e. Click *Miele, Henry* and then click Edit, Categories.
f. Click *Business* and *International* in the *Available categories* list box and then click OK.
g. Assign categories to contacts as follows using any of the previous methods:
   McAllister, Kayla   Association Member, Holiday Cards
   Nunez, Tory   Personal
   Taylor, Leslie   Key Customer

3. View the contacts by category in the Contents Pane by completing the following steps:
   a. Click *By Category* in the *Current View* section of the Navigation Pane. The contacts are grouped according to the categories to which they were assigned in an expanded list.
   b. Click the collapse button (minus symbol) next to *Categories: Association Member* to collapse the list. The collapse button changes to an expand button (plus symbol) for a collapsed list.
   c. Click the expand button (plus symbol) next to *Categories: Association Member* to expand the list. Notice contact names are duplicated in the table for those contacts assigned more than one category.

4. Print the contact list in *Table Style*.
5. Click *Detailed Address Cards* in the *Current View* section of the Navigation Pane.

exercise 9 — ASSIGNING CATEGORIES WHILE CREATING A CONTACT

1. With Outlook open and Contacts active in Detailed Address Cards view, assign a category while adding a new contact by completing the following steps:
   a. Scroll right if necessary and then click *Taylor, Leslie*.
   b. Click Actions and then click New Contact from Same Company.
   c. Type the following information in the fields noted:
      Full Name   Ms. Leigh Avaire
      Job title   District Sales Manager

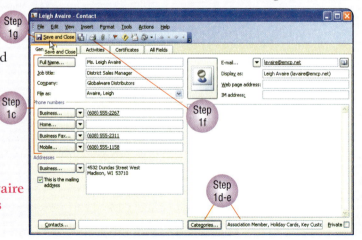

104 Chapter Three

Mobile   6085551158
  E-mail   lavaire@emcp.net

  d. Click the Categories button.
  e. Click *Association Member, Holiday Cards,* and *Key Customer* in the *Available categories* list box and then click OK.
  f. Click the Print button on the Contact window toolbar.
  g. Click Save and Close.

exercise 10 — FILTERING A CONTACT LIST BY CATEGORY

1. With Outlook open and Contacts active in Detailed Address Cards view, filter the contact list to produce a list of only those contacts in the Association Member category by completing the following steps:
   a. Click Customize Current View.
   b. Click the Filter button in the Customize View: Detailed Address Cards dialog box.
   c. Click the More Choices tab in the Filter dialog box.
   d. Click the Categories button.
   e. Click *Association Member* in the *Available categories* list box and then click OK.

   f. Click OK to close the Filter dialog box and then click OK to close the Customize View: Detailed Address Cards dialog box. Only four records are displayed in the Contents Pane as shown at the right. The message *Filter Applied* appears toward the left edge of the Status bar.

2. Print the filtered list in *Small Booklet* style by completing the following steps:
   a. Click the Print button on the Standard toolbar.
   b. Click *Small Booklet Style* in the *Print style* section of the Print dialog box.
   c. Click OK.
   d. Click Yes at the message box saying booklets should be printed double-sided and instructing you to select the double-sided printing options in the Properties dialog box for the printer. ***(Note: Small booklet style will still print on a regular 8-1/2 x 11 page without the double-sided option set on the printer.)***

3. Restore the Contents Pane to display all contacts by completing the following steps:
   a. Click Customize Current View.
   b. Click the Filter button in the Customize View: Detailed Address Cards dialog box.
   c. Click the Clear All button in the Filter dialog box.
   d. Click OK twice.

QUICK STEPS

Find a Contact
1. Click inside *Find a Contact* text box.
2. Type name or partial name.
3. Press Enter.

Finding a Contact

Once a Contacts folder contains a lot of records, browsing through the folder to find a contact record may not be feasible. Outlook provides the following three features to assist with locating a record quickly.
- The *Find a Contact* text box on the Standard toolbar
- The Find bar
- The Advanced Find dialog box

In addition to the three features listed above, the letter tabs along the right side of the Contents Pane can be used to scroll quickly to the first record that begins with the letter. For example, to move the selected record to the first contact whose last name begins with *w*, click the *w* letter tab.

Find a Contact

Find a Contact Text Box

To locate a contact record, click in the *Find a Contact* text box on the Standard toolbar (currently displays *Type a contact to find*), type the name of the individual whose record you want to see, and then press Enter. Outlook can locate records based on a partial entry such as *Joe Sm*, a first name only, a last name only, an e-mail alias, or a company name. Once you have used the *Find a Contact* text box, clicking the down-pointing arrow to the right of the box will display previously searched for entries so that you can repeat a search.

exercise 11

LOCATING CONTACTS USING LETTER TABS AND *FIND A CONTACT* TEXT BOX

1. With Outlook open and Contacts active in Detailed Address Cards view, locate and select records using the letter tabs by completing the following steps:
   a. Click the *t* letter tab along the right side of the Contents Pane. The screen scrolls right if necessary and selects the contact record for *Taylor, Leslie*.
   b. Click the letter tab that references *a*. The screen scrolls left if necessary and the contact record for *Avaire, Leigh* is selected.
   c. Click the *n* letter tab. The screen scrolls right if necessary and the contact record for *Nunez, Tory* is selected.
2. Locate and select records using the *Find a Contact* text box by completing the following steps:
   a. Click the letter tab that references *a* to return to the first record in the *Contacts* folder. In some cases, *a* will have its own letter tab while in other cases it may appear as *ab* depending on your monitor size and resolution setting.
   b. Click the insertion point inside the *Find a Contact* text box (currently reads *Type a contact to find*). The text *Type a contact to find* disappears and a blinking insertion point is positioned inside the box.
   c. Type **leslie** and then press Enter.
   d. The contact window for *Leslie Taylor* opens. Review the information in the window and then click the Close button on the Leslie Taylor - Contact window Title bar.
   e. Click the insertion point inside the *Find a Contact* text box. The recently searched for contact name, *Mr. Leslie Taylor,* is selected.
   f. Type **Worldwide** and then press Enter. Since more than one record exists for Worldwide Enterprises, Outlook opens the Choose Contact dialog box. The *Contacts* list box contains a list of all records within the folder that have Worldwide within them.

Step 2c

g. Click *Ms. Kayla McAllister* in the *Contacts* list box in the Choose Contact dialog box and then click OK.
h. Review the information in the *Kayla McAllister* Contact window and then click the Close button on the Title bar.
i. Click the down-pointing arrow next to the *Find a Contact* text box. A drop-down list of previously searched for entries appears.
j. Click *Mr. Leslie Taylor* in the drop-down list.
k. Close the Leslie Taylor - Contact window.

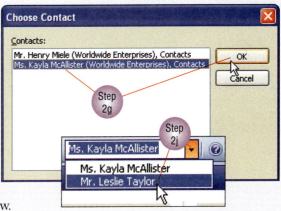

Find Bar

With the Find feature, Outlook returns a filtered list of all contacts that contain the name or other keyword specified in the *Look for* text box. The contact records that do not meet the search criteria are temporarily hidden from view. To begin a Find, click Tools, point to Find, and then click Find; or click the Find button on the Standard toolbar to open the Find bar shown in Figure 3.8.

Find

FIGURE 3.8 Find Bar

The Find bar for Contacts is used in the same manner as described for finding messages in Chapter 1. Type the name or keyword that you want Outlook to search for within the contact records in the *Look for* text box. By default, the *Search In* list box contains the name of the current folder. Click Find Now to begin the search. Outlook will list only those records that meet the search criterion in the Contents Pane. Click Clear in the Find bar to remove the filter and restore all of the contact records to the Contents Pane.

QUICK STEPS

Use Find Bar to Locate a Contact
1. Click Find button to open Find bar.
2. Type keyword in *Look for* text box.
3. Click Find Now.

exercise 12

USING THE FIND BAR

1. With Outlook open and Contacts active in Detailed Address Cards view, locate records for contacts from Globe Products using the Find bar by completing the following steps:
   a. Click the Find button  on the Standard toolbar to display the Find bar.
   b. With the insertion point positioned in the *Look for* text box, type **Globe Products**.
   c. Click Find Now. Outlook displays the records for the two contacts that meet the search criteria – *Fillmore, Cal*, and *Nunez, Tory*.

2. Click the Clear button on the Find bar. All contact records are restored to the Contents Pane.
3. Click the Find button on the Standard toolbar to close the Find bar.

Use Advanced Find to Locate a Contact
1. Click Tools, Find, Advanced Find.
2. Enter search criteria as required.
3. Click Find Now.

Advanced Find

Click Tools, point to Find, and then click Advanced Find; or click the Options button on the Find bar and then click Advanced Find to open the Advanced Find dialog box shown in Figure 3.9. The Contacts tab that is active by default contains options to locate records by typing a word that exists within the record such as a name, telephone number, or e-mail name; to search within a set of related fields such as address fields; or to restrict the search to records within a specific time frame.

FIGURE 3.9 *Advanced Find Dialog Box with Contacts Tab Selected*

Use the More Choices tab to locate contact records by the category to which they have been assigned and the Advanced tab to enter a conditional statement for a field to use as the criterion upon which to locate contact records.

LOCATING RECORDS USING ADVANCED FIND

1. With Outlook open and Contacts active in Detailed Address Cards view, locate records that have been assigned the category *Holiday Cards* using the Advanced Find dialog box by completing the following steps:
   a. Click the Find button on the Standard toolbar to display the Find bar.

    b. Click Options on the Find bar.
    c. Click Advanced Find at the drop-down menu.
    d. Click the More Choices tab in the Advanced Find dialog box.
    e. Click in the *Categories* text box and then type **holiday cards**.
    f. Click the Find Now button.
2. The dialog box expands and the records that match the search criterion are displayed in table format at the bottom of the dialog box. The Status bar at the bottom of the dialog box

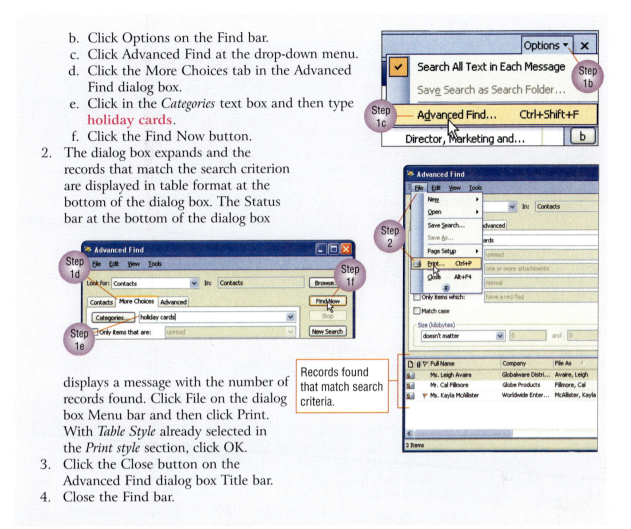

displays a message with the number of records found. Click File on the dialog box Menu bar and then click Print. With *Table Style* already selected in the *Print style* section, click OK.
3. Click the Close button on the Advanced Find dialog box Title bar.
4. Close the Find bar.

Changing the Current View

The *Current View* section of the Navigation Pane provides several options for displaying Contact information. The Address Cards and Detailed Address Cards views display the contacts in a columnar arrangement. Phone List displays the contacts in rows with the *Full Name, Company, File As*, and telephone number fields as the column headings. The By Category, By Company, By Location, and By Follow-up Flag options group related contacts together in rows of a table that you can expand or collapse.

    Additional fields can be added or existing fields removed from the current view by right-clicking a column heading and then choosing Remove This Column from the shortcut menu to delete the column, or Field Chooser to display a list of fields from which you can add to the view.

OUTLOOK   Managing Contacts

exercise 14
ADDING AND REMOVING FIELDS IN THE CURRENT VIEW

1. With Outlook open and Contacts active in Detailed Address Cards view, change the current view to Phone List and then delete columns from the view by completing the following steps:
   a. Click *Phone List* in the *Current View* section of the Navigation Pane.
   b. Scroll right to view all of the columns that are in the current view. Notice the *Home Phone* column is included in the view but contains no information.
   c. Right-click the column heading *Home Phone* and then click Remove This Column.
   d. Remove the following columns from the current view by completing a step similar to Step 1c.
      File As
      Journal
      Categories
2. Double-click the right column boundary for the *Company* field to expand the width of the column to the length of the longest entry.
3. Add a field to the current view and then expand the column width by completing the following steps:
   a. Right-click any column heading to display the shortcut menu and then click Field Chooser. A Field Chooser list box appears with the field set *Frequently-used fields* included in the list box.
   b. Scroll down the Field Chooser list box until you see the field named *Job Title*, and then drag the field button from the list box to the column header row between *Company* and *Business Phone*. As you drag the field, red arrows appear in the column header row indicating the position where the new field will be placed.
   c. Click the Close button on the Field Chooser Title bar.
   d. Double-click the right column boundary for the *Job Title* field to expand the column to the length of the longest entry.
4. Print the contact list in *Table Style* in landscape orientation by completing the following steps:
   a. Click the Print button on the Standard toolbar.
   b. Click the Page Setup button in the Print dialog box.

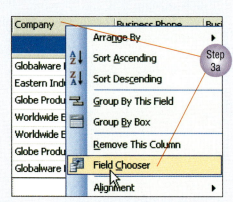

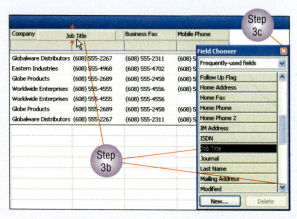

110 Chapter Three

c. Click the Paper tab in the Page Setup: Table Style dialog box.
   d. Click *Landscape* in the *Orientation* section and then click OK.
   e. Click OK in the Print dialog box.
5. Click *Address Cards* in the *Current View* section of the Navigation Pane to restore the view to the default display for the Contacts folder.

Changing Contact Options

Open the Contact Options dialog box shown in Figure 3.10 to change the fields upon which records are created, sorted, and displayed by clicking Tools, Options, and then clicking the Contact Options button in the Options dialog box with the Preferences tab selected. The default order that Outlook uses to interpret the name that is being typed in the *Full Name* text box as a new record is added is first name followed by middle name and then last name. Click the down-pointing arrow next to the *Default "Full Name" order* list box to choose *Last First*, or *First Last1 Last2*.

Change Contact Options
1. Click Tools, Options.
2. Click Contact Options.
3. Change settings as required.
4. Click OK twice.

The *Default "File As" order* list box allows you to choose the field(s) that Outlook uses to organize the Contact records. The File As setting is the default sort order for records displayed in the Contents Pane. Click the down-pointing arrow next to *Default "File As" order* to choose to organize by last name, first name, or company name. The drop-down list contains the following options:

First Last
Company
Last, First (Company)
Company (Last, First)

FIGURE 3.10 **Contact Options Dialog Box**

If you do not want Outlook to prompt you when adding a new record with a name that is the same as in a record that already exists in the folder, deselect the *Check for duplicate contacts* check box. By default, Outlook displays the Duplicate Contact Detected dialog box shown in Figure 3.11 when a name is typed in the *Full Name* text box that already exists in another record. You have the option of adding the new contact record anyway or updating the information in the current record. If you deselect the check box, Outlook defaults to adding the new record anyway.

FIGURE 3.11 Duplicate Contact Detected Dialog Box

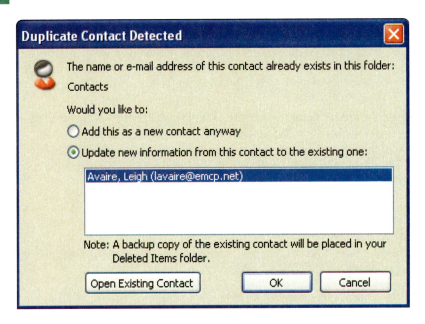

Outlook allows you to view two contact index languages at once. To specify an additional contact index that provides buttons with which you can navigate through your contacts using more than one language, click the *Show an additional Contacts Index* check box in the *Contacts Index options* section of the Contact Options dialog box. The *Additional Contacts Index* list box becomes active for you to select the language for the additional index.

Sending E-Mail Messages to Contacts

New Message to Contact

Send E-Mail to Contact
1. Select record in Contents Pane.
2. Click New Message to Contact button.
3. Type subject and message text.
4. Click Send.

You can create an e-mail message to a contact without leaving the Contacts folder and displaying the Inbox. To do this, select the contact record for the person to whom you want to send an e-mail and then do one of the following actions:
- Click File, point to New, and then click Mail Message.
- Click Actions, New Message to Contact.
- Click the New Message to Contact button on the Standard toolbar. The New Message to Contact button is also on the toolbar inside an individual contact window.

SENDING E-MAIL TO A CONTACT; REVIEWING ACTIVITIES FOR A CONTACT

1. With Outlook open and Contacts active in Address Cards view, create and send an e-mail message to a contact by completing the following steps:
   a. Click the name banner for *Taylor, Leslie*.
   b. Click the New Message to Contact button 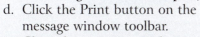 on the Standard toolbar. A message window opens with the e-mail address for Leslie Taylor already entered in the *To* text box.
   c. With the insertion point positioned in the *Subject* text box, type **New products**.
   d. Press Tab or click in the message editing window and then type the following text:

   I would like to arrange a meeting with you next week to review the new products. Please let me know what day and time work best for you.

   e. Click Send. The message window closes and you are returned to the Contents Pane for the Contacts folder.

2. View the message created for the contact from the Contacts folder by completing the following steps:
   a. Double-click *Taylor, Leslie* to open the contact window.
   b. Click the Activities tab.
   c. Double-click the message header for the message created in Step 1. The message window opens for you to review the content of what was sent to the contact. *(Note: An additional item may appear in the message window which is an undeliverable message from the mail server stating the message was not delivered. Since the e-mail address for Leslie Taylor is fictitious, the server will not be able to deliver the message created in Step 1.)*
   d. Click the Print button on the message window toolbar.
   e. Close the message window.
   f. Close the Leslie Taylor - Contact window.

Scheduling Appointments from Contacts

An appointment with a contact can be scheduled without leaving the Contacts folder and displaying the Calendar. If you already know that you are available on the required day and time, there is no need to display your Calendar to complete the scheduling. Select the contact, click File, point to New, and then click Appointment; or click Actions, New Appointment with Contact.

QUICK STEPS

Schedule Appointment with Contact
1. Select record in Contents Pane.
2. Click Actions, New Appointment with Contact.
3. Enter appointment details.
4. Click Save and Close.

OUTLOOK
Managing Contacts 113

exercise 16

SCHEDULING AN APPOINTMENT FROM CONTACTS; VIEWING ACTIVITIES FOR A CONTACT

1. With Outlook open and Contacts active in Address Cards view, schedule an appointment for a meeting with a contact by completing the following steps:
    a. If necessary, click the name banner for *Taylor, Leslie*.
    b. Click Actions and then click New Appointment with Contact. An appointment window opens with the contact's name automatically entered in the *Contacts* text box.
    c. With the insertion point positioned in the *Subject* text box, type **New products review meeting**.
    d. Press Tab or click in the *Location* text box and then type **Globalware Distributor's office**.
    e. Drag to select the current text in the *Start time* day text box and then type **one week from today**.
    f. Drag to select the current time in the *Start time* time text box and then type **noon**.
    g. Click the down-pointing arrow next to the *End time* time text box and then click *1:30 PM (1.5 hours)*.
    h. Click Save and Close.

2. View the appointment created for the contact from the Contacts folder by completing the following steps:
    a. Double-click *Taylor, Leslie* to open the contact window.
    b. Click the Activities tab.
    c. Double-click the appointment header for the appointment scheduled in Step 1. The appointment window opens for you to review the subject, location, day, and time of the appointment.
    d. Click the Print button on the Appointment window toolbar.
    e. Close the Appointment window.
    f. Close the Leslie Taylor - Contact window.

Creating a Distribution List

If you frequently send e-mail messages to the same group of people consider creating a ***distribution list*** to enable you to create the e-mail messages more quickly. A distribution list is a name associated with a group of contact records. For example, if you send a weekly status message to members of a project team you could create a distribution list named *Project Team* that contains all of the names of the people working on the project. Whenever you need to send a status message, type **Project Team** in the message window *To* text box. Outlook sends

114 Chapter Three   OUTLOOK

the message to all members stored in the distribution list. Distribution lists can also be used in meeting requests. By default, distribution lists are stored in the Contacts folder.

Click File, point to New, and then click Distribution List to open the Distribution List window shown in Figure 3.12. Type a name for the distribution list in the *Name* text box and then click the Select Members button to add names to the list.

> **QUICK STEPS**
>
> **Create a Distribution List**
> 1. Click File, New, Distribution List.
> 2. Type name for list in *Name* text box.
> 3. Click Select Members.
> 4. Double-click names of contacts to add to distribution list.
> 5. Click OK.
> 6. Click Save and Close.

FIGURE 3.12 **Distribution List Window**

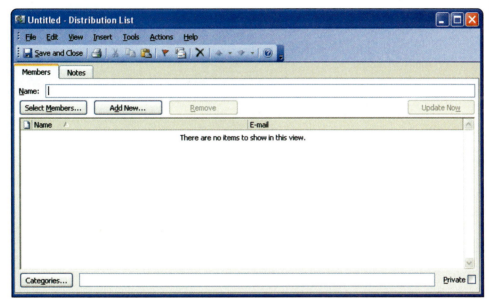

exercise 17

CREATING AND USING A DISTRIBUTION LIST

1. With Outlook open and Contacts active in Address Cards view, create a new distribution list for the sales managers by completing the following steps:
   a. Click File, point to New, and then click Distribution List.
   b. At the Untitled - Distribution List window with the Members tab selected and with the insertion point positioned in the *Name* text box, type **Sales Managers**.
   c. Click the Select Members button.
   d. At the Select Members dialog box, drag the right column boundary lines for the *Name* and *Display Name* column headings until you can view all of the text within the columns. By default, *Show Names from the* displays the names from the Contacts folder. Notice for

OUTLOOK   Managing Contacts 115

each contact, two entries exist: one for the e-mail address, and another for the business fax telephone number.

e. Double-click *Cal Fillmore (fillmore@emcp.net)* to add the e-mail address for Cal Fillmore to the *Members* text box in the *Add to distribution list* section of the Select Members dialog box.

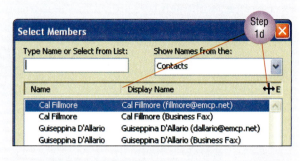

f. Double-click the following sales managers' names to add them to the list. Be sure to double-click the name with the e-mail address displayed (not the entry for Business Fax).
   Guiseppina D'Allario
   Henry Miele
   Kayla McAllister
   Leigh Avaire

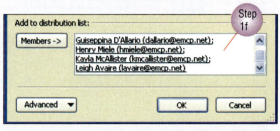

g. Click OK to close the Select Members dialog box.

h. Click Save and Close on the Sales Managers - Distribution List window toolbar. Distribution lists appear in the Contents Pane with the name of the list and the list icon in the name banner.

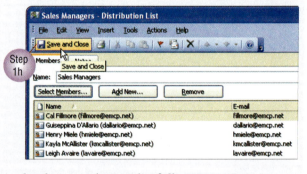

2. Send an e-mail message to the members of the Sales Managers distribution list by completing the following steps:
   a. Click the *Sales Managers* name banner in the Contents Pane.
   b. Click the New Message to Contact button on the Standard toolbar.
   c. With the insertion point positioned in the *Subject* text box, type **Supplier Web Access**.
   d. Click in the message editing window and then type the following text:

   Our new secure Web site is now operational. A member of our technical services team will be contacting you shortly with your new user name and password. Call or e-mail me if you have any questions.

   e. Click the Print button on the message window toolbar.
   f. Click Send.

Click expand button to replace list name with individual member names and e-mail addresses.

Maintaining Distribution Lists

Double-click the name banner in the Contents Pane for a distribution list to open the distribution list window with the names of the members. Click the Select Members button to add a new member to the distribution list from Contacts or click the Add New button to add a new member to the list in the Add New Member dialog box for an individual for whom you do not currently have a contact record. To delete a member from the list, click to select the member's name in the list box and then click the Remove button.

Distribution list entries are not automatically updated if a member in the list changes his or her e-mail address. Use the Update Now button in the Distribution List window to update changes to members' e-mail addresses. Click Save and Close when you have finished adding, deleting, or updating members to the distribution list.

> **HINT**
> Message recipients see all of the names in the distribution list. Display the *Bcc* field (click right arrow next to Options button, or click View, Bcc) in a message window and type the list name in the *Bcc* text box to use a list for which you do not want recipients to see other members' names and addresses.

Expanding the Distribution List in the Message Window

If you are creating a message to a distribution list and wish to view the members' individual names instead of the title of the list, click the expand button (plus symbol) that displays next to the list name in the *To* text box. Click OK at the message box indicating that once the list has been expanded it cannot be collapsed. The distribution list name is replaced with the individual names and e-mail addresses of the list members. You can add or delete names in the *To* text box for the current message without affecting the original list. For example, suppose you want to use a distribution list to send a message but want to remove one individual's e-mail address from the list since you know the person is on vacation. In this case removing the individual from the list is for a temporary period of time. In the message window, click the expand button next to the distribution list name in the *To* text box and then delete the individual's e-mail address in the expanded list. The member remains in the distribution list for future mailings.

CHAPTER summary

- The Contacts folder is used to store information you need about the individuals or companies with whom you communicate by e-mail, fax, letter, or telephone.
- The Contacts folder is a database, with the information for each individual occupying a *record* in the folder and each unit of information within the record, such as an e-mail address, referred to as a *field*.
- Add a new contact by opening a new contact window and then typing information into the General, Details, Activities, and All Fields tabs.
- A picture of a contact can be added to the contact window by clicking Add Contact Picture, navigating to the image file, and then double-clicking the file name.
- Outlook inserts text into the name and address fields based on the way in which the text is typed unless it cannot recognize the entry, in which case the

Check Full Name and Check Address dialog boxes will open automatically for you to complete the entry.
- ➤ Double-click a contact name to edit information within the fields in the contact window.
- ➤ To delete a contact record, select the contact and then press Delete or click the Delete button on the Standard toolbar.
- ➤ When there is more than one person from the same company, you can add the second or third record by basing a new record on an existing one. Select the existing record, click Actions and then click New Contact from Same Company.
- ➤ A Follow Up flag is a reminder to follow up on an outstanding issue with a contact. Display the Flag for Follow Up dialog box and then choose the type of reminder flag and a due date.
- ➤ By default, contacts are displayed alphabetically sorted in ascending order by the *File As* field which is the contact's last name followed by first name.
- ➤ Display the Sort dialog box to sort the records by up to four fields in ascending or descending order.
- ➤ A filter is a subset of contacts that has been selected based on a condition specified in the Filter dialog box. Records that do not meet the condition are temporarily removed and the message *Filter Applied* appears in the Status bar.
- ➤ A category can be assigned to a contact record so that the contact list can then be grouped or filtered by the category name to produce different lists of contacts.
- ➤ Letter tabs along the right side of the Contents Pane are used to scroll quickly to the first record that begins with the letter.
- ➤ To quickly locate and select a contact record, click in the *Find a Contact* text box, type the name of the individual, and then press Enter.
- ➤ Use the Find feature to display a filtered list of all contacts that contain the name or other keyword specified in the *Look for* text box in the Find bar.
- ➤ Use the Advanced Find feature to locate records by typing a word that exists within the record such as a name, telephone number, or e-mail name; or locate contact records by the category to which they have been assigned.
- ➤ In the *Current View* section of the Navigation Pane, Address Cards and Detailed Address Cards display contacts in a columnar arrangement; Phone List displays in a table format; By Category, By Company, By Location, and By Follow-up Flag group related contacts together and display the results in a table.
- ➤ Fields can be removed from or added to the current view by right-clicking a column heading and then choosing Remove This Column or Field Chooser.
- ➤ Open the Contact Options dialog box by clicking Tools, Options, and then clicking the Contact Options button in the Options dialog box with the Preferences tab selected, to change the fields upon which records are created, sorted, and displayed.
- ➤ You can create an e-mail message or schedule an appointment to a selected contact directly from the Contacts folder.
- ➤ Create a distribution list for a group of contacts to whom you regularly send e-mail messages. Click File, point to New, and then click Distribution List to create a new list.

FEATURES summary

FEATURE	BUTTON	MENU	KEYBOARD
Add a contact	New	File, New, Contact; or Actions, New Contact	Ctrl + N
Add contact using existing contact		Actions, New Contact from Same Company	
Add contact picture		Actions, Add Picture	
Appointment with contact		Actions, New Appointment with Contact	
Categories		Edit, Categories	
Contact Options		Tools, Options, Preferences Tab, Contact Options	
Delete a contact	X	Edit, Delete	Ctrl + D
Distribution list		File, New, Distribution List	Ctrl + Shift + L
E-mail contact		Actions, New Message to Contact	
Filter contacts		Customize Current View, Filter	
Find contacts		Tools, Find, Find	Ctrl + E
Flag for Follow Up		Actions, Follow Up	Ctrl + Shift + G
Sort contacts		Customize Current View, Sort	

CONCEPTS check

Completion: On a blank sheet of paper, indicate the correct term, command, symbol, or explanation for each description.

1. Click this button in the contact window to type the name of the contact in separate fields such as *Title*, *First*, and so on. *Check full name*
2. Click this tab in the Contact window to view a list of e-mail messages, appointments, or other items related to the contact. *Activities.*
3. Click this menu sequence to create a new contact record by basing fields upon an existing record. *Actions new contact from same company.*
4. A Follow Up flag displays in this color in the *By Follow-up Flag* view if the flag is still active. *Red.*
5. Contact records in the Contents Pane can be sorted by up to this number of fields. *4.*
6. When some contact records are temporarily removed from the Contents Pane, this message displays in the Status bar. *Filter Applied.*

OUTLOOK — Managing Contacts

7. When displaying contact records grouped by categories, click this button next to a category name to remove from view the records for the category. ~~Symbol.~~ Collapse button/minus

8. Type a contact name in this box on the Standard toolbar to quickly locate a record. Find a Contact

9. Open this bar to filter the list of contacts by a name or other keyword that is entered in the *Look for* text box. Find bar

10. Use this feature to search for contacts by typing the category to which the contact has been assigned and view the results in a separate window. Advanced Find.

11. This is the default order that Outlook uses to interpret a name that is typed into the *Full Name* text box for a new contact. First name, middle name, last name.

12. An e-mail message can be sent to a selected contact by clicking File, New, Mail Message, or this menu sequence. Actions, new message to contact

13. Open an appointment window for a selected contact by clicking either of these two menu sequences. File New Appointment, Actions, new Appointment with contact

14. Sending e-mail messages often to the same group of people in your Contacts list is made easier by creating this type of list. Distribution list

SKILLS check

Assessment 1

1. With Contacts active in Address Cards view, add the following records to the appropriate fields.

   Mr. Ji Wong
   Sales Manager, North America
   VSI International
   Bus: 717-555-5891
   Fax: 717-555-5892
   Mobile: 717-555-3126
   398 Oxford Street West
   Harrisburg, PA 17101
   jwong@emcp.net

   Ms. Hilary Lander
   Sales Representative
   Worldover Enterprises
   Bus: 717-555-6598
   Fax: 717-555-6599
   Mobile: 717-555-3485
   982 Highbury Avenue
   Harrisburg, PA 17124
   hlander@emcp.net

   Ms. Pauline Gorski
   Sales Manager
   Worldwide Marketing
   Bus: 717-555-6588
   Fax: 717-555-6589
   Mobile: 717-555-2389
   231 Forest Avenue
   Harrisburg, PA 17112
   pgorski@emcp.net

   Mrs. Edna Nadira
   District Manager
   Horizon Sales
   Bus: 717-555-3256
   Fax: 717-555-3257
   Mobile: 717-555-1279
   65 Bradley Avenue
   Harrisburg, PA 17101
   nadira@emcp.net

2. Change the current view to Detailed Address Cards.
3. Print the contact list in *Card Style*.

Assessment 2

1. With Contacts active in Detailed Address Cards view, edit the contact records as follows.

    Wong, Ji—change street address to: 12-9874 Church Street
    Nadira, Edna—change the business fax telephone number to: 717-555-4521
    Lander, Hilary—change job title to: Eastern Region Sales Manager

2. Delete the record for *D'Allario, Guiseppina*.
3. Add the following two contacts for VSI International by basing them on the record for *Wong, Ji*.

Mr. Kenneth McTague	Mrs. Meredith Abruzzi
Sales Representative	Sales Manager, Europe
Mobile: 717-555-1495	Mobile: 717-555-6987
kmctague@emcp.net	mabruzzi@emcp.net

4. Print the contact list in *Small Booklet Style*. Click Yes if prompted to proceed with printing with the double-sided settings.

Assessment 3

1. With Contacts active in Detailed Address Cards view, add Follow Up flags to contact records as follows:

    Nadira, Edna – Follow up with a call; due two weeks from today
    Abruzzi, Meredith – Arrange a meeting; due one month from today

2. Mark the Arrange meeting flag on *Leslie Taylor's* record as completed.
3. Clear the Send letter flag on *Kayla McAllister's* record.
4. Change the current view to display the records by Follow-up Flag.
5. Remove the *File As*, *Business Fax*, *Home Phone,* and *Categories* columns in the By Follow-up Flag view.
6. Print the contact list in *Table Style* in portrait orientation.
7. Change the current view to Detailed Address Cards.

Assessment 4

1. With Contacts active in Detailed Address Cards view, assign the following categories to existing contacts:

Ji Wong	Holiday Cards, Key Customer
Hilary Lander	Association Member, Business
Pauline Gorski	Association Member, Business
Edna Nadira	Holiday Cards, Key Customer
Kenneth McTague	Association Member, Business
Meredith Abruzzi	Business, International

2. Use the Advanced Find feature to locate all the records of the contacts who have been assigned the *Association Member* category.
3. Remove the following columns from the results displayed at the bottom of the Advanced Find dialog box: *File As, Home Phone, Journal,* and *In Folder*.

4. Click File on the Advanced Find dialog box Menu bar and then click Print. Change the page orientation to *Landscape* and then print the Association member contact list in *Table Style*.
5. Close the Advanced Find dialog box.
6. Change the current view to display the contact list grouped by category and then make sure all category lists are expanded.
7. Remove the *File As, Business Fax,* and *Home Phone* columns in the By Category view.
8. Expand the width of the *Company* column to accommodate the width of the longest entry.
9. Print the contact list in *Table Style*.
10. Change the current view to Detailed Address Cards.

Assessment 5

1. With Contacts active in Detailed Address Cards view, change the current view to Address Cards.
2. Sort the contact list first by *Company* in ascending order, then by *Last Name* in ascending order. Click Yes to show the *Company* field and then click No to show the *Last Name* field in the current view.
3. Print the contact list in *Card Style*.
4. Restore the sort order to sort items by *File As* in ascending order.
5. Use the Filter or Find feature to list only those contacts that are employees of VSI International.
6. Select the filtered records shown by holding down the Ctrl key while clicking each name banner. Display the Print dialog box and click *Only selected items* in the *Print range* section. Print the list in *Phone Directory Style*.
7. Clear the filter or find so that all records are restored to the Contents Pane.

Assessment 6

1. With Contacts active in Address Cards view, create an e-mail message to *Ji Wong* from Contacts as follows:

Subject	**New Price List**
Message	**A new price list has been sent today to reflect a 2% increase in all products. We will continue to honor the old prices for one week only.**

2. Print and then send the message.
3. Select the record for *Hilary Lander* and then schedule the following appointment:

Subject	**Advertising Campaign**
Location	**Room 101E**
Start time	two weeks from today at 10:00 AM
Duration	1.5 hours
Reminder	10 minutes
Label	Needs Preparation

4. Display the Calendar in Day view for two weeks from today and then print the Calendar in *Daily Style*.
5. Display Contacts in Address Cards view.

Assessment 7

1. With Contacts active in Address Cards view, add the following members to the Sales Managers distribution list:
   Meredith Abruzzi
   Pauline Gorski
   Edna Nadira
   Ji Wong
2. With the Sales Managers - Distribution List window open, click the Print button on the toolbar in the window.
3. Save and Close the window.

Assessment 8

1. Delete the *Association Member* category name from the Master Category List by completing the following steps:
   a. Click Edit and then click Categories.
   b. Click the Master Category List button in the Categories dialog box.
   c. Click *Association Member* in the list box and then click the Delete button.
   d. Click OK to close the Master Category List dialog box.
   e. Click OK to close the Categories dialog box.
2. The category name will no longer appear in the *Available categories* list box; however, existing records with the category name associated with them retain the category.

Assessment 9

1. Use the Microsoft Outlook Help feature to find information on how to share contact information with other people. In particular, find out how to send a virtual business card to someone by e-mail and how the recipient can import your contact information to his or her Contacts in Outlook, or another personal information management application.
2. Using the information you learned in Help create a new contact record for yourself in Contacts using a fictitious address and telephone number and then send your contact information by e-mail to another student in your class.

Assessment 10

(Note: In order to complete this assessment another student in your class must have sent his or her contact information to you by e-mail.)
1. Go to the Inbox folder and open the message with the contact information sent to you from Assessment 9.
2. Using the information you learned in Help in Assessment 9, import the student's record to your Contacts folder.
3. Open the contact window for the new record created in Step 2 and then click the Print button on the contact window toolbar.
4. Close the contact window.

CHAPTER 4

CREATING TASKS AND NOTES

PERFORMANCE OBJECTIVES

Upon successful completion of Chapter 4, you will be able to:
- Create, update, print, and delete tasks
- Create a recurring task
- Assign a task to someone else
- Respond to a task request
- View and track assigned tasks
- Send task information to other users
- Change the view to create task lists including customizing a view
- Change task options
- Create, edit, and delete notes
- Assign a category to a note
- Change note options
- Change the note view

(Note: There are no student data files to copy for this chapter.)

Working in Tasks is similar to maintaining a to-do list. Outlook includes the capability to track information about a job such as how much of the task is completed, the priority that has been assigned, and the due date for the task. A task request can be sent via e-mail to someone else so that you can assign him or her responsibility for completing the task. The TaskPad can be displayed while working in the Calendar so that you see the list of jobs to be completed while you are viewing your appointments for the day.

Use the Notes folder to enter small, unstructured text reminders for tasks you want to pursue or ideas for which you want to follow up. For example, you may have an idea for a new project that you do not want to forget. Typing a short description in a note will store the idea for you to follow up at a later time. A note can be placed on the desktop to place the reminder in a prominent location.

QUICK STEPS

Create a Task
1. Make active the Tasks folder.
2. Click over text *Click here to add a new Task*.
3. Type task subject.
4. Press Enter.

Creating and Updating Tasks

Adding activities in Tasks is similar to jotting down a list of jobs in a to-do list on your desk. Add tasks in the Tasks folder shown in Figure 4.1. New tasks are added by clicking the mouse over the text *Click here to add a new Task*, typing a short description of the job or activity and then pressing Enter. If you want to assign a date by which the task must be completed, click in the *Due Date* column, and then type a date or select the date from the drop-down calendar that displays by clicking the down-pointing arrow. A task that is still active after a due date has expired displays in red.

FIGURE 4.1 The Tasks Folder

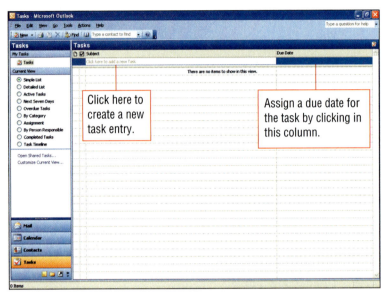

exercise 1

CREATING TASKS

1. With Outlook open, click Tasks in the Navigation Pane.
2. Add a new task to the Tasks folder by completing the following steps:
    a. Click over the text *Click here to add a new Task*.
    b. With the insertion point positioned in a blank text box in the *Subject* column, type **Assemble research on anti-virus software**.
    c. Press Tab or click in the *Due Date* column and then type **two weeks from today**.

    d. Press Enter. The task entry moves into the Task table and the insertion point appears inside another blank text box in the *Subject* column.

126 Chapter Four OUTLOOK

3. Add a task by displaying the TaskPad in the Calendar folder by completing the following steps:
   a. Click *Calendar* in the Navigation Pane.
   b. Click View on the Menu bar and then click TaskPad.
   c. If necessary, resize the TaskPad in the Calendar window by pointing to the blue border at the left edge of the TaskPad until the pointer changes to a double vertical line with a left- and right-pointing arrow and then drag left to increase the width.
   d. Click over the text *Click here to add a new Task* in the TaskPad.
   e. With the insertion point positioned in a blank text box in the TaskPad column, type **Buy extra toner for printer** and then press Enter.
   f. Click View and then click TaskPad to turn off the display of the TaskPad in the Calendar. You may prefer to leave the TaskPad turned on in the Calendar folder. Some people like to see their to-do list and appointments together within the same window.
4. Click Tasks in the Navigation Pane. Notice the task added in the TaskPad displays in the Task table with a due date of *None* assigned.
5. Click the Print button on the Standard toolbar. With *Table Style* already selected in the *Print style* section of the Print dialog box, click OK.

Tasks can also be created in the Task window shown in Figure 4.2 by clicking File, pointing to New, and then clicking Task; clicking Actions and then clicking New Task; or by clicking the New Task button on the Standard toolbar. Type a description of the task in the *Subject* text box, change other fields as required, and then click the Save and Close button on the Task window toolbar.

New Task

FIGURE 4.2 Task Window with Task Tab Selected

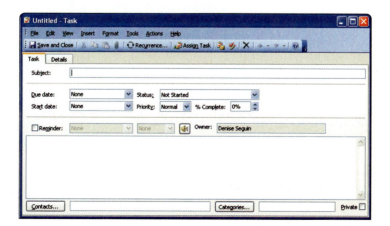

Create a Task in Task Window
1. Click New Task button.
2. Type subject text.
3. Change other options as required.
4. Click Save and Close.

The default status for a new task is *Not Started*. Enter a different status by clicking the down-pointing arrow next to the *Status* list box and then choosing from *In Progress, Completed, Waiting on someone else*, or *Deferred*. The default *Priority* of *Normal* can be changed to *Low* or *High*. Outlook inserts the name of the current user as the *Owner* of the task. The owner of a task becomes important when working with tasks that have been assigned to someone else since only the owner of a task can modify the task. Use the white text box at the bottom of the window to type additional notes or other information that you want to store with the task details.

The Details tab in the Task window contains fields in which you can record more information about the task such as the date the task was completed, the estimated number of hours to complete the task, and the actual number of hours worked on the task. Additional fields needed if the work you are doing is to be billed out include the companies to be billed, mileage, and a field for other billing information. An *Update list* field is used to save the names of individuals who have assigned the task for purposes of sending an update message when the task is modified or completed or for sending a status report.

exercise 2

CREATING A TASK USING THE TASK WINDOW

1. With Outlook open and Tasks active, add a new task using the Task window by completing the following steps:
   a. Click the New Task button [New] on the Standard toolbar.
   b. With the insertion point positioned in the *Subject* text box, type **Start budget projections for next year**.
   c. Click the down-pointing arrow next to *Status* and then click *Waiting on someone else*.
   d. Click the Save and Close button on the Task window toolbar.

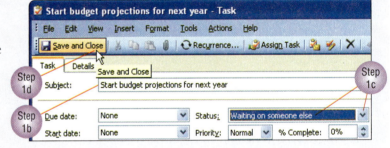

2. Print only the task entry added in Step 1 in *Memo Style* by completing the following steps:
   a. Click in the *Subject* column over the entry *Start budget projections for next year*. This selects the entry as indicated by the dotted box surrounding the row and the blue highlighting.
   b. Click the Print button on the Standard toolbar.
   c. Click *Memo Style* in the *Print style* section of the Print dialog box.
   d. Click OK.

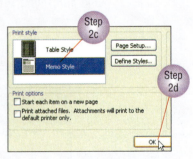

128 Chapter Four

Updating Tasks

Updating tasks can include activities such as changing the Due date, Start date, Status, Priority, or the % Complete. When a task is finished, you can either delete the task from the Task table, or change the task status to *Completed*. To do this, open the Task window and change the *Status* field to *Completed*, or click the white check box to the left of the task in the Task table. A completed task displays with a line drawn through dimmed task text. The Mark Complete button on the task window toolbar automatically changes the *% Complete* field to 100%.

Mark Complete

Delete a task by selecting it and then pressing the Delete key; clicking the Delete button on the Standard toolbar; or by clicking Edit on the Menu bar and then clicking Delete. The due date can be changed in the Task table by clicking in the *Due Date* column for the task and then typing a new date or selecting one from the drop-down calendar.

HINT
If you do not need to keep a record of the task for historical purposes, just delete a task that is finished.

Double-click a task in the Task table to open the Task window for the entry and then make changes to the task details as required. To edit the subject text only for a task, position the mouse pointer over the task entry in the Task table and then click the left mouse button. The task will be selected as indicated by a dotted box around the text and an insertion point will appear at the position where the pointer was located. Insert or delete text as required and then click in the table outside the task entry.

exercise 3

UPDATING TASKS

1. With Outlook open and Tasks active, change the status for the task entry *Assemble research on anti-virus software* by completing the following steps:
   a. Double-click over the task entry *Assemble research on anti-virus software* to open the Task window.
   b. Click the down-pointing arrow next to *Status* and then click *In Progress*.
   c. Drag to select *0%* in the *% Complete* text box and then type 40. *(Note: The up- and down-pointing arrows at the right of the % Complete text box increment the value by 25%.)*
   d. Click the Save and Close button on the Task window toolbar.
2. Change the status for the task entry *Buy extra toner for printer* to *Completed* by clicking the white check box to the left of the task in the Task table. A line is drawn through the entry as shown.

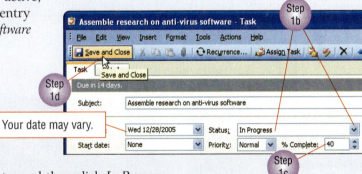

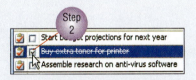

3. Change the current view and expand a column width by completing the following steps:
   a. Click *Detailed List* in the *Current View* section of the Navigation Pane. The Detailed List view adds the *Status*, *% Complete*, and *Categories* columns to the Task table.
   b. Position the mouse pointer on the right column boundary for the *Status* column until the pointer changes to a vertical line with a left- and right-pointing arrow and then double-click to expand the column to the width of the longest entry.

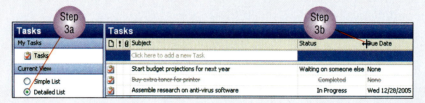

4. Click the Print button on the Standard toolbar. With *Table Style* already selected in the *Print style* section, click OK.

Creating a Recurring Task

Recurrence

A task that you perform on a regular basis can be set up in a manner similar to a recurring appointment. Recurring tasks appear one at a time in the task list. When you change the status for one occurrence of the task to *Completed*, Outlook automatically generates the next occurrence in the task list. To create a recurring task, open the Task window, type a description of the task in the *Subject* text box, click Actions on the Task window toolbar and then click Recurrence, or click the Recurrence button on the toolbar. Select the options as required in the *Recurrence pattern* and *Range of recurrence* sections of the Task Recurrence dialog box shown in Figure 4.3, and then click OK.

FIGURE 4.3 Task Recurrence Dialog Box

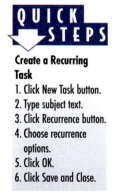

Create a Recurring Task
1. Click New Task button.
2. Type subject text.
3. Click Recurrence button.
4. Choose recurrence options.
5. Click OK.
6. Click Save and Close.

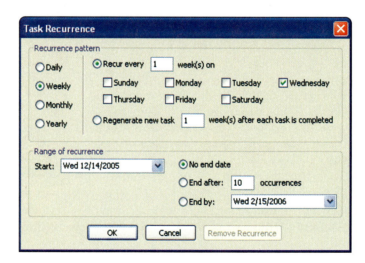

CREATING A RECURRING TASK

1. With Outlook open and Tasks active in Detailed List view, add a recurring task to the Task list by completing the following steps:
   a. Click File, point to New, and then click Task.
   b. With the insertion point positioned in the *Subject* text box, type **Compile month end sales reports**.
   c. Click the Recurrence button on the Task window toolbar.
   d. Click *Monthly* in the *Recurrence pattern* section.
   e. Click *The* in the *Recurrence pattern* section. Depending on the current date, the options next to *The* display first, second, third, fourth, or last and the current day within the week. If necessary, click the down-pointing arrow next to the occurrence list box and click *first*, and then click the down-pointing arrow next to the current day of the week and click *Thursday* so that the Recurrence pattern becomes *The [first] [Thursday] of every [1] month(s)*.

   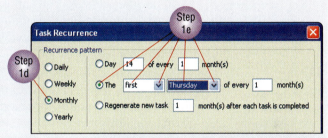

   f. Click OK to close the Task Recurrence dialog box. The gray information box in the Task window above the subject text displays the recurrence pattern details.
   g. Click Save and Close. The first recurring task is added to the Task table. Notice the icon for the recurring task in the first column of the Task table.
2. Click *Simple List* in the *Current View* section of the Navigation Pane.
3. Click the Print button on the Standard toolbar. With *Table Style* already selected in the *Print style* section, click OK.

If you created a recurring task with no end date and then want to stop the task from recurring, complete the following steps to stop the automatic generation of the next task entry:

1. Double-click the current recurring entry in the Task table to open the Task window.
2. Click the Recurrence button on the Task window toolbar.
3. Click the Remove Recurrence button at the bottom of the Task Recurrence dialog box. The Task Recurrence dialog box closes and the gray information box with the recurrence pattern details is removed from the Task window.
4. Click Save and Close in the Task window.

QUICK STEPS

Assign a Task
1. Click Actions, New Task Request.
2. Choose recipient in *To* text box.
3. Type subject text.
4. Change other options as required.
5. Click Send.

HINT

It is a good idea to use the editing window to type extra information about the task so that the task recipient understands exactly what you are expecting him or her to do.

Assigning a Task to Someone Else

You can assign a task to someone else by e-mailing the individual a task request. The recipient of the task request can choose to accept the task, decline the task, or assign the task to someone else. When the recipient accepts the task, the task is automatically added to his or her task list.

If you receive a task request and accept the task, you become the owner of the task. The owner is the only person who can make changes to the task details. By default, if the owner updates the task, Outlook sends a copy of the revision to the task originator, and when the owner changes the status of the task to *Completed*, a status report is automatically sent to the task originator.

If you decline the task, you can provide a reason why you are declining, and then the task is returned to the originator of the task request so that he or she can assign the task to someone else. To create a task request do one of the following actions:

- Click File, point to New, and then click Task Request.
- Click Actions, New Task Request.
- Click the down-pointing arrow on the New Task button and then click Task Request at the drop-down menu.
- Open a new Task window and then click the Assign Task button on the Task window toolbar.

FIGURE 4.4 Task Request

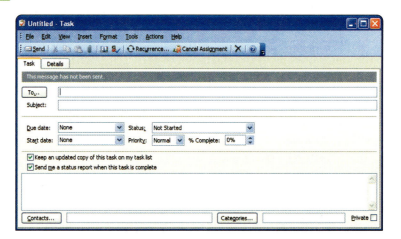

An Untitled - Task window opens with a gray information box that displays *This message has not been sent* as shown in Figure 4.4. The *To* text box is added above the *Subject* text box to type the e-mail address of the person to whom you are assigning the task. Two check boxes just above the white editing window are selected by default that instruct Outlook to keep an updated copy of the task in the originator's task table and send completed status reports to the originator. The Save and Close button is replaced with the Send button to send the task request via e-mail.

exercise 5

ASSIGNING A TASK TO SOMEONE ELSE

(Note: In this exercise you will be sending a task request by e-mail to the student that you added to your Personal Address Book [PAB] in Chapter 1. Check with your instructor if necessary for alternate instructions on to whom you should send the task request.)

1. With Outlook open and Tasks active in Simple List view, assign a task to someone else by completing the following steps:
    a. Click Actions and then click New Task Request.
    b. Click the To button. At the Select Task Recipient dialog box, click the down-pointing arrow next to *Show Names from the* and then click *Personal Address Book*.
    c. Double-click the name of the student you added to the PAB in Chapter 1 to add his or her name to the *To* list box. *(Note: You cannot send a task request to yourself—check with your instructor if necessary to be assigned to a partner for this exercise.)*
    d. Click OK to close the Select Task Recipient dialog box.
    e. Click in the *Subject* text box and then type **Research anti-virus software**.
    f. Drag to select *None* in the *Due date* text box and then type **one week from today**.
    g. Click the down-pointing arrow to the right of *Priority* and then click *High*.
    h. Click Send. The task is added to the Task table and an e-mail message is sent to the task recipient. The task icon in the first column of the Task table portrays a hand holding a clipboard to indicate the task has been assigned to someone else.
2. Double-click the entry in the Task table for the task assigned to someone else in Step 1. The task window opens with a message indicating the status of the task request. Notice that *Owner* shows the e-mail name of the person to whom you sent the task request.
3. Close the Task window.
4. View and print the e-mail message sent to the task recipient by completing the following steps:
    a. Click Mail in the Navigation Pane.
    b. Click *Sent Items* in the *All Mail Folders* section of the Navigation Pane. *(Note: Click* **Outbox** *instead of* **Sent Items** *if the message does not appear in the* **Sent Items** *folder.)*

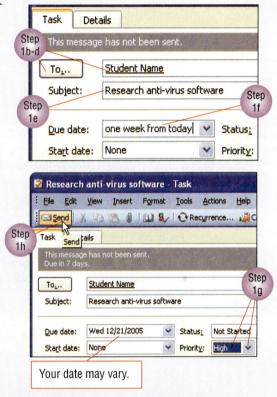

    c. Double-click the message header for the task request message sent in Step 1.
    d. Read the information in the message window.
    e. Click File on the message window Menu bar and then click Print.
    f. With *Memo Style* selected in the *Print style* section, click OK.
    g. Close the task request message window.
5. Click *Inbox* in the *All Mail Folders* section of the Navigation Pane.

Step 4c

Responding to a Task Request

The recipient of the task will receive a Task Request message in his or her Inbox similar to the one shown in Figure 4.5 when connected to a Microsoft Exchange Server. Upon opening the message, he or she can click Accept, Decline, or Assign Task if they want to delegate the task to someone else.

FIGURE 4.5   Task Request Message to Task Recipient Connected to Microsoft Exchange Server

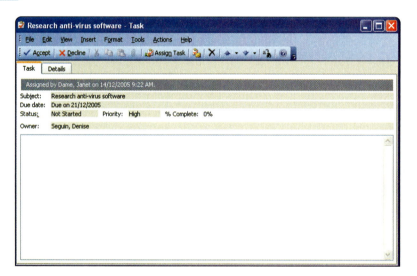

When the recipient clicks Accept or Decline, a message window appears with the information that the task will be accepted and moved into the Tasks folder for Accept; or moved to the Deleted Items folder for Decline. The recipient has the option to *Edit the response before sending* so that a few words of explanation can be appended, or *Send the response now* so that the task originator receives the default response message of *User name has accepted*. If the recipient clicks Assign Task, the message window changes to a new task request window in which the recipient can then reassign the task to someone else.

Once a task recipient accepts or declines a task, Outlook automatically deletes the task request message from the recipient's Inbox folder. A copy of the message sent to the task originator is, however, retained in Sent Items.

Outlook users who are not connected to a Microsoft Exchange Server receive a task request message similar to the one shown in Figure 4.6. Upon opening the

HINT   Outlook users not connected to an Exchange Server can track assigned tasks by sending e-mail messages. Task information has to be manually updated by the originator.

message, he or she can click the Reply button to send an e-mail message back to the originator of the task indicating whether the task is accepted or declined. In this case, the task recipient has to manually add the task to his or her Tasks folder if the task is accepted.

FIGURE 4.6 **Task Request Message to Task Recipient Connected to Internet Mail Server**

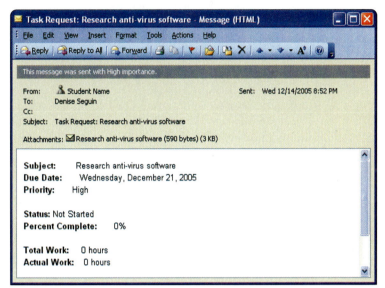

exercise 6

ACCEPTING A TASK REQUEST

(Note: To complete this exercise another student must have sent you a task request from Exercise 5. Depending on the type of server to which you are connected while using Outlook 2003, the Task Request message looks and functions differently. The following instructions include all likely scenarios; however, if your screen does not match the instructions, check with your instructor for assistance.)

1. With Outlook open and Inbox active, open the task request message and accept the task by completing the following steps:
   a. Double-click the message header with the subject *Task Request: Research anti-virus software*.
   b. Click the Accept button or click the Reply button.
   c. Click *Edit the response before sending* in the Accepting Task dialog box and then click OK. If you clicked Reply in the previous step, the Accepting Task dialog box does not appear—proceed to Step 1d.
   d. With the insertion point positioned in the message editing window, type the following text:

   Preliminary discussions with IT staff indicate that two companies offer attractive site licensing agreements. I will send a report as soon as I have completed the research.

   e. Click Send.
   f. If necessary, close the Task Request message window.
2. Click Tasks in the Navigation Pane.

3. When you accepted the task request in Step 1, Outlook automatically added the task to your Task table. Note that two tasks are shown with the subject *Research anti-virus software*. One is the task you assigned to someone else when you completed Exercise 5, and the other is the task request you accepted in Step 1 of this exercise. If you clicked Reply in Step 1b, the accepted task is not added to your task list—you will only see the task request you assigned to another student when you completed Exercise 5.

Tracking and Viewing Assigned Tasks

For users connected to a Microsoft Exchange Server, the options *Keep an updated copy of this task on my task list* and *Send me a status report when this task is complete* are active in the Task Request window, meaning Outlook automatically tracks the status of the task for the task originator. When the task owner changes any task details, Outlook generates an update and sends it to the name(s) stored in the update list of the Details tab. Generally, the update list contains only the name of the task originator; however, if a task request was sent to someone who then delegated the task to someone else, both names in the task request chain will be included. When the task originator opens and reads the task status message, Outlook updates the task copy in the Tasks folder and then deletes the status message in the Inbox.

When the task owner changes the status of an assigned task to *Completed*, Outlook sends a task completed message back to the task originator. When the originator opens the message, the task status is changed to *Completed*. Completed status messages are not deleted from the Inbox.

Click *By Person Responsible* in the *Current View* section of the Navigation Pane to display the task list grouped by task owner names. Click *Assignment* in the *Current View* section of the Navigation Pane to view a filtered list of tasks that have been assigned to others.

exercise 7

VIEWING ASSIGNED TASKS

1. With Outlook open and Tasks active in Simple List view, filter and then print a list of tasks assigned to others by completing the following steps:
   a. Click *Assignment* in the *Current View* section of the Navigation Pane. The task list is filtered to display only those tasks assigned to other users. By default the assignment list is sorted by the owner's name in ascending order and then by the due date in ascending order.

   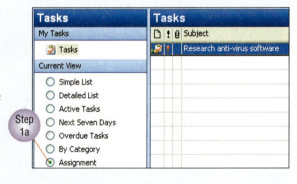

   b. Click the Print button on the Standard toolbar. With *Table Style* selected in the *Print style* section of the Print dialog box, click OK.
2. View and print the Task table in groups by the task owner by completing the following steps:

a. Click *By Person Responsible* in the *Current View* section of the Navigation Pane. The Task table displays a group heading for each task owner with his or her tasks listed below. The list is sorted by the owner's name in ascending order and then by the due date in ascending order.
   b. If necessary, adjust column widths so that data in all columns is visible.
   c. Click the Print button on the Standard toolbar. With *Table Style* selected in the *Print style* section of the Print dialog box, click OK.

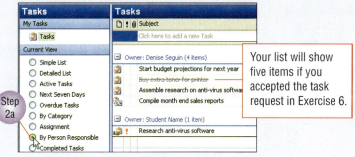

3. Click *Simple List* in the *Current View* section of the Navigation Pane.

Sending Task Information to Other Users

If you want to e-mail comments about a task to other users or report the status of the task to the task originator, open the task window, click Actions on the Task window Menu bar, and then click Send Status Report, or click the Send Status Report button on the Task window toolbar. A Task Status Report message window opens similar to the one shown in Figure 4.7. If the active task is one that was assigned to you by someone else, the name(s) of the task originator(s) in the Update list from the Details tab will automatically be inserted in the *To* text box. If the task was not an assigned task or you need to type additional status report recipients, type the required e-mail addresses in the *To* and *Cc* text boxes, type the message text for your report in the editing window, and then click Send.

Send Status Report

FIGURE 4.7 Task Status Report Message Window

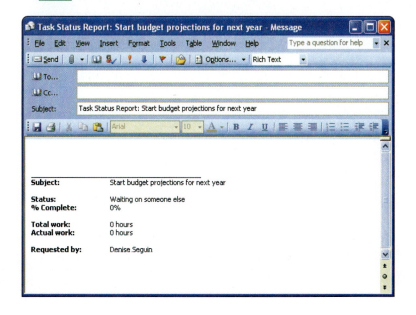

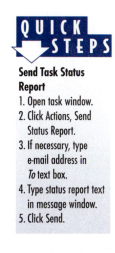

QUICK STEPS

Send Task Status Report
1. Open task window.
2. Click Actions, Send Status Report.
3. If necessary, type e-mail address in *To* text box.
4. Type status report text in message window.
5. Click Send.

Send Task Details
1. Open task window.
2. Click Actions, Forward.
3. Type e-mail address in *To* text box.
4. Type message text.
5. Click Send.

To send a copy of the task to another user, open the Task window, click Actions on the Menu bar, and then click Forward. A message window similar to the one shown in Figure 4.8 opens with the task subject automatically inserted in the *Subject* text box after *FW:*. A copy of the Task window is inserted in the message as a file attachment. Type the e-mail address of the person to whom you want to send the task information in the *To* text box, type an explanatory message in the editing window, and then click Send. The recipient will receive an e-mail message and can view the task details by double-clicking the attached task name in the message window.

FIGURE

4.8 *Forwarded Task Message Window*

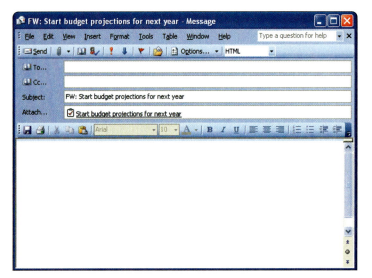

exercise 8

UPDATING AND SENDING TASK INFORMATION TO ANOTHER USER

(Note: In this exercise you will be sending task details by e-mail to the student that you added to your Personal Address Book [PAB] in Chapter 1. Check with your instructor if necessary for alternate instructions on to whom you should send the task information.)

1. With Outlook open and Tasks active in Simple List view, update the *Start budget projections for next year* task by completing the following steps:
    a. Double-click the task entry with the subject *Start budget projections for next year* to open the Task window.
    b. Click the down-pointing arrow next to *Priority* and then click *High*.
    c. Click in the editing window and then type the following text:

    Create a spreadsheet with last year's budget organized by division and then project a 1.5% increase in operating funds for next year.

138 Chapter Four

OUTLOOK

2. With the Start budget projections for next year Task window still open, send the task information to another user by completing the following steps:
   a. Click Actions on the Task window Menu bar and then click Forward. Click OK at the Microsoft Office Outlook message box stating that the original item must be saved first.
   b. Click the To button in the message window.
   c. At the Select Names dialog box, change the *Show Names from the* list box to *Personal Address Book*, double-click the name of the student you added to the PAB in Chapter 1, and then click OK.
   d. Click in the message editing window and then type the following text:
      I need your help to prepare the budget for next year. The task details with instructions are attached to this message.

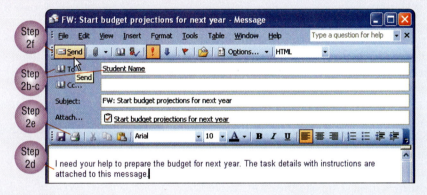

   e. Click the Print button on the message window toolbar.
   f. Click Send.
   g. Close the task window.

Changing the Task View to Create Task Lists

In Exercise 7 you changed the view to create a list of tasks that were assigned to others and a list of tasks grouped by task owner. In addition to these options and the Detailed List view, the *Current View* section of the Navigation Pane provides the ability to create the following task lists:

- *Active tasks*. A filtered list of all tasks not marked as complete and sorted in ascending order by the due date.
- *Next Seven Days*. A filtered list of all tasks with a due date that is within the next seven days and sorted in ascending order by the due date.
- *Overdue Tasks*. A filtered list of all tasks that are not marked as complete and are past the due date. The list is sorted in ascending order by due date and then in descending order by priority status.
- *By Category*. The task list is organized by groups according to the category to which they have been assigned. The list is sorted by categories in ascending order and then by due date in ascending order.
- *Completed Tasks*. A filtered list of only those tasks where the status has been changed to complete. The list is sorted in descending order by the due date.
- *Task Timeline*. The tasks are displayed in a linear calendar format with the task appearing below its respective due date.

Click <u>Customize Current View</u> in the Navigation Pane to open the Customize View dialog box in which you can change the sort or filter settings if the available views are not suited to your needs. The Sort and Filter dialog boxes are similar to those used in previous chapters. In Exercise 9 you will create a customized task list by adding and removing columns to a view.

exercise 9

CREATING A CUSTOMIZED TASK LIST; EDITING TASKS IN THE TASK TABLE

1. With Outlook open and the Tasks folder active in Simple List view, create a customized task list by completing the following steps:
    a. Click *Active Tasks* in the *Current View* section of the Navigation Pane.
    b. Right-click the *Categories* column heading and then click Remove This Column at the shortcut menu.
    c. Right-click the *Subject* column heading and then click Field Chooser at the shortcut menu.
    d. Scroll down the Field Chooser list box until you see the field named *Total Work*, and then drag the field button from the list box to the column header row between *Subject* and *Status*. As you drag the field in the column header row, red arrows appear between the column headings indicating the position where the new field will be placed.
    e. Click the Close button on the Field Chooser Title bar.
    f. If necessary, adjust column widths so that column headings and data in all columns are visible.
2. Edit the details for a task using a column in the task table by completing the following steps:
    a. Click in the *Total Work* column for the task with the subject *Start budget projections for next year*. The field becomes open for editing with an insertion point placed in the field.

    b. If necessary, use the left or right arrow keys to move the insertion point, delete *0* and then type *2* so that the field reads *2 hours*.
    c. Click in an unused area of the task table.
    d. Drag the right column boundary of the *Subject* column left approximately one inch to decrease the size of the column.
    e. Drag the right column boundary of the *Status* column right approximately one inch to increase the size of the column.
3. Click the Print button on the Standard toolbar. With *Table Style* selected in the *Print style* section of the Print dialog box, click OK.
4. Click *Simple List* in the *Current View* section of the Navigation Pane.

Changing Task Options

Open the Task Options dialog box shown in Figure 4.9 to change the color that overdue and completed tasks are displayed, or to deselect the default options for tracking assigned tasks and setting reminders. Click Tools, Options, and then click the Task Options button in the Options dialog box with the Preferences tab selected.

FIGURE 4.9 Task Options Dialog Box

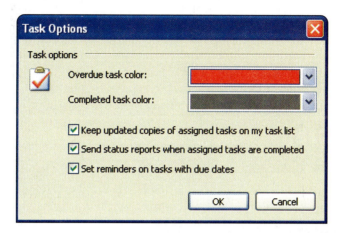

Creating and Editing Notes

A note in Outlook contains a small amount of text that is not structured in any way but is meant to act as a reminder or placeholder to store thoughts, ideas, or other types of messages that you would like to be reminded of or pursue at a later date. Important notes can be placed on the desktop in a location where they will be easily seen. To activate the Notes folder, click the Notes icon at the bottom of the Navigation Pane.

Notes

To create a new note, display the Notes folder, and then do one of the following actions:

- Click File, point to New, and then click Note.
- Click Actions and then click New Note.
- Click the New Note button on the Standard toolbar.
- Right-click in the Contents Pane and then click New Note at the shortcut menu.
- Double-click in any unused space within the Notes folder.

New Note

A yellow note window similar to the one shown in Figure 4.10 opens where you type the text that you would like to store. The note window is small since notes are meant to store short reminders or ideas. The text to the first hard return, or Enter, is used as the Note title and is displayed below the note icon in Icons view, or as a note header in Notes List view. Double-click a note icon to view the remaining text inside the Note if additional text is included. Click the Close button at the right end of the Note Title bar to close the Note window.

Create a Note
1. Make active the Notes folder.
2. Click New Note button.
3. Type note text.
4. Click Close.

OUTLOOK — Creating Tasks and Notes — 141

F I G U R E

4.10 New Note Window

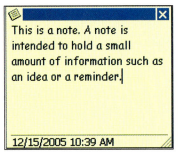

Outlook stores the day and time at which the note was created and displays this information at the bottom of the Note window. Point at the three diagonal lines at the bottom right of the Note window and then drag to make the viewing area wider and taller if you need to type more text than can fit in the current note and want the ability to view all of the text without having to scroll.

exercise 10

CREATING NOTES

1. With Outlook open, click the *Notes* icon at the bottom of the Navigation Pane.
2. Create a new note using the toolbar by completing the following steps:
    a. Click the New Note button on the Standard toolbar.
    b. With the insertion point positioned in the note window, type **Buy Birthday Present for Mom**.
    c. Click the Close button on the Note Title bar. A note icon appears in the Contents Pane with the note text displayed below the icon.

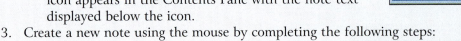

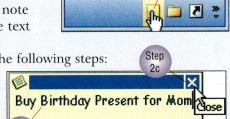

3. Create a new note using the mouse by completing the following steps:
    a. Double-click in any unused area of the Contents Pane.
    b. With the insertion point positioned in the note window, type **Project Idea**, and then press Enter twice.
    c. Type **Research market potential in India.**, and then click the Close button.
    d. Notice the text below the note icon contains only the first line of text that you typed in the note window.
4. Print the two notes created in this exercise by completing the following steps:
    a. With the *Project Idea* note currently selected, hold down the Ctrl key and then click the *Buy Birthday Present for Mom* note next to it to select both notes.
    b. Click the Print button on the Standard toolbar.
    c. With *Memo Style* selected in the *Print style* section of the Print dialog box, click OK. *(Note: Each note will print on a separate page.)*
    d. Click in any unused area in the Contents Pane to deselect the two notes.

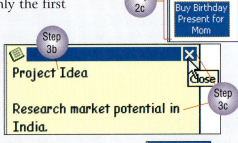

Editing and Deleting Notes

The content of a note can be edited by double-clicking the note icon to open the Note window. Insert and delete text as required and then click the Close button. A selected note can be deleted by clicking the Delete button on the Standard toolbar or pressing the Delete key.

exercise 11
CREATING, EDITING, AND DELETING NOTES

1. With Outlook open and Notes active, create a new note by completing the following steps:
    a. Click Actions and then click New Note.
    b. With the insertion point positioned in the note window, type **Renew License** and then click the Close button.
2. Edit the *Project Idea* note by completing the following steps:
    a. Double-click the *Project Idea* note icon.
    b. With the insertion point positioned at the beginning of *Project* in the note title, type **Marketing** and then press the spacebar.
    c. Click the Close button.
3. Delete the *Buy Birthday Present for Mom* note by completing the following steps:
    a. Click the *Buy Birthday Present for Mom* note icon.
    b. Click the Delete button on the Standard toolbar.
4. Print the notes in *Table Style* by completing the following steps:
    a. Click *Notes List* in the *Current View* section of the Navigation Pane.
    b. Click the Print button on the Standard toolbar.
    c. With *Table Style* selected in the *Print style* section of the Print dialog box, click OK.
5. Click *Icons* in the *Current View* section of the Navigation Pane.

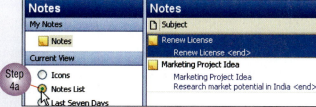

Placing a Note on the Desktop

Since notes are often used as a receptacle for storing reminders, placing a reminder note on the desktop ensures that you will see the prompt when Outlook is not open. To do this, copy a note created in the Notes folder by resizing the Outlook window until you can see a portion of the desktop, and then drag the desired note icon from the Contents Pane to the desktop. If other applications are open in the background, you may have to minimize them first before dragging and dropping the note icon. The note is copied to the desktop as a separate file with the extension *.msg*. The two notes are not linked, so that any changes made to one of the copies will not be reflected in the other. Figure 4.11 shows a copied note from the Outlook window to the desktop.

HINT
Use Notes for those quick reminders for which you are tempted to put a sticky note on your monitor!

FIGURE 4.11 Note Placed on Desktop

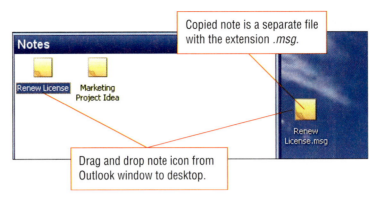

To move a note from the Notes folder to the desktop, hold down the Shift key while dragging the icon from the Contents Pane. The note will be placed on the desktop and removed from the Notes folder in Outlook.

When the reminder note on the desktop is no longer required, click the note icon on the desktop and then press the Delete key. Click Yes in the Confirm File Delete dialog box.

Assign Category while Creating Note
1. Click New Note button.
2. Type note text.
3. Click note icon at top left of window.
4. Click Categories.
5. Click categories to assign to note.
6. Click OK.
7. Close note window.

Assigning a Category to a Note

Notes can be organized by assigning them to categories and then changing to the By Category view. Assigning categories to Notes is one way of organizing the folder since notes are typically used for unstructured text. If you use notes often, the Contents Pane can quickly become filled with several notes that are not related in an obvious manner, making locating a specific note more difficult. By default, notes are not listed in the Contents Pane sorted by the note title when viewed as icons but instead in descending order by the date created.

Available categories for notes and the manner in which notes are assigned to a category is the same as for any other Outlook item. Assign a category while creating a note by clicking the note icon at the top left of the Note window and then clicking Categories at the drop-down menu that appears.

exercise 12 — ASSIGNING CATEGORIES TO NOTES

1. With Outlook open and Notes active in Icons view, create a new note using the shortcut menu and assign a category by completing the following steps:
   a. Right-click in any unused area of the Contents Pane and then click New Note at the shortcut menu.
   b. With the insertion point positioned in the Note window, type **Ask Kelly to help with the Marketing Project**.

c. Click the note icon at the top left of the Note window.
   d. Click Categories at the drop-down menu.
   e. Click *Ideas* in the *Available categories* list box and then click OK.
   f. Click the Close button.
2. Right-click the *Renew License* note icon and then click Categories at the shortcut menu. Click *Personal* in the *Available categories* list box and then click OK.
3. Click the *Marketing Project Idea* note, click Edit, and then click Categories. Click *Ideas* in the *Available categories* list box and then click OK.
4. Change the current view to By Category and then print the notes by completing the following steps:
   a. Click *By Category* in the *Current View* section of the Navigation Pane.
   b. With the notes list automatically expanded for the two categories *Categories: Ideas* and *Categories: Personal*, click the Print button on the Standard toolbar.
   c. With *Table Style* selected in the *Print style* section of the Print dialog box, click OK.
5. Click *Icons* in the *Current View* section of the Navigation Pane.

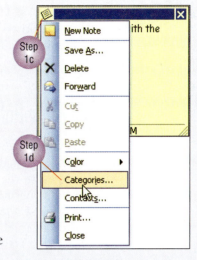

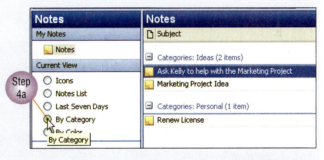

Changing Note Options

Open the Notes Options dialog box shown in Figure 4.12 to change the color of the note, the size, or the font for the note text. Click Tools, Options, and then click the Note Options button in the Options dialog box with the Preferences tab selected.

QUICK STEPS

Change Color of New Notes
1. Click Tools, Options.
2. Click Note Options.
3. Change *Color* option.
4. Click OK twice.

FIGURE 4.12 Notes Options Dialog Box

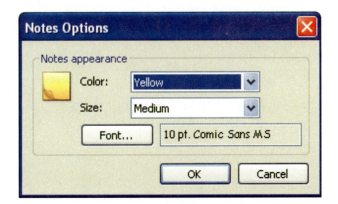

QUICK STEPS

Change Color of an Individual Note
1. Right-click note icon.
2. Point to Color.
3. Click desired color.

By default, notes are yellow in color, medium-sized, with text set in 10-point Comic Sans MS. The color of an individual note can be changed to make it stand out from the others in addition to changing the color of all new notes in the Notes Options dialog box. Using different colors is another way of organizing notes in the Notes folder.

Changing the Note View

In Icons view, the Standard toolbar contains buttons for changing the view from Large Icons to Small Icons and List. Options for changing the way in which notes are displayed in the Contents Pane available in the *Current View* section of the Navigation Pane include: *Notes List*, *Last Seven Days*, *By Category*, and *By Color*. As seen in Exercise 11, Notes List view displays the notes one below the other with the entire note text visible, the date the note was created, and the category it has been assigned. The notes are arranged in the order they were created with the most recent at the top of the list.

exercise 13

CHANGING THE COLOR OF NOTES AND THE VIEW

1. With Outlook open and Notes active in Icons view, change the color of all new notes and then create a new note by completing the following steps:
    a. Click Tools, Options, and then click Note Options in the Options dialog box with the Preferences tab selected.
    b. Click the down-pointing arrow next to *Color* and then click *Green*.
    c. Click OK to close the Notes Options dialog box.
    d. Click OK to close the Options dialog box.
    e. Click File, point to New, and then click Note.
    f. With the insertion point positioned in a green note window, type **Talk with Seth about anti-virus programs**.
    g. Click the Close button. Notice the new note created is the color green while existing notes remain yellow.
2. Right-click the *Renew License* note, point to Color at the shortcut menu, and then click Blue.
3. Change the current view to By Color and then print the notes by completing the following steps:

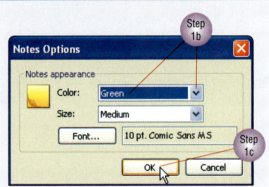

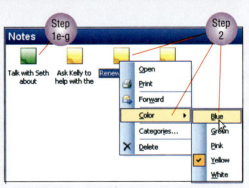

a. Click *By Color* in the *Current View* section of the Navigation Pane.
   b. With the notes list automatically expanded for the three colors *Color: Blue*, *Color: Green*, and *Color: Yellow*, click the Print button on the Standard toolbar.
   c. With *Table Style* selected in the *Print style* section of the Print dialog box, click OK.
4. Click *Icons* in the *Current View* section of the Navigation Pane.
5. Change the color of all new notes back to the default color of yellow by completing the following steps:
   a. Click Tools, Options, and then click Note Options in the Options dialog box with the Preferences tab selected.
   b. Click the down-pointing arrow next to *Color* and then click *Yellow*.
   c. Click OK twice.

CHAPTER summary

➤ Add jobs in your to-do list as tasks in the Tasks window or the TaskPad in the Calendar window.

➤ New tasks are added by clicking over the text *Click here to add a new Task*, typing a short description of the job, entering a due date if necessary, and then pressing Enter.

➤ Tasks can also be created by opening a Task window, typing a description of the task in the *Subject* text box, changing other fields as required, and then clicking the Save and Close button.

➤ Double-click a task entry to open the task window and make changes to the task details such as changing the Due date, Start date, Status, Priority, or the % Complete.

➤ When a task is finished, you can either delete the task from the Task table, or change the task status to Completed.

➤ A task that you perform on a regular basis can be set up as a recurring task. Recurring tasks appear one at a time in the task list—when you mark the existing occurrence of the task Completed, Outlook automatically generates the next occurrence in the task list.

➤ You can assign a task to someone else by e-mailing the individual a task request.

➤ The task recipient can choose to accept the task, decline the task, or assign the task to someone else.

➤ If you send a task request to someone who is not connected to a Microsoft Exchange Server, the recipient can reply to your request via an e-mail message.

➤ When you accept a task request, you become the *Owner* of the task. The owner is the only person who can make changes to the task details.

➤ For Microsoft Exchange users, by default the originator of the task request is notified whenever the owner updates the task information or marks the task complete.

➤ The *Current View* section of the Navigation Pane provides several options to create and view task lists including creating a filtered list of only those tasks that have been assigned to others or displaying all tasks grouped by the task owner's name which can then be expanded and collapsed as required.

- You can e-mail comments about a task to other users, or report the status of the task to the task originator by opening the task window, clicking Actions on the Menu bar, and then clicking Send Status Report, or click the Send Status Report button on the task window toolbar.
- A copy of a task can be sent via e-mail to another user by opening the Task window, clicking Actions on the Menu bar, and then clicking Forward.
- Change the color that overdue and completed tasks are displayed or deselect the default options for tracking assigned tasks and setting reminders in the Task Options dialog box.
- Items in the Notes folder contain small amounts of unstructured text. Notes are generally created to be reminders or placeholders to store thoughts or ideas.
- The content of a note can be edited by double-clicking the note icon to open the Note window.
- Delete a note by clicking the note icon and then pressing the Delete key or clicking the Delete button on the Standard toolbar.
- A note can be copied or moved to the desktop to place a reminder in a prominent location.
- Assigning categories to Notes is one way of organizing the folder since the Contents Pane can quickly become filled with several notes that are not related in an obvious manner.
- The color of an individual note can be changed to make it stand out from the others in addition to changing the color of all new notes in the Notes Options dialog box.
- The *Current View* section of the Navigation Pane provides options for changing the Notes folder from the default Icons view to Notes List, Last Seven Days, By Category, and By Color.

FEATURES summary

FEATURE	BUTTON	MENU	KEYBOARD
Add a task	New	File, New, Task; or Actions, New Task	Ctrl + N
Assign task to someone else		File, New, Task Request; or Actions, New Task Request	Ctrl + Shift + U
Categories		Edit, Categories	
Create a note	New	File, New, Note; or Actions, New Note	Ctrl + N
Delete task or note	X	Edit, Delete	Ctrl + D
Send task status report		Actions, Send Status Report	
Send task information		Actions, Forward	
Task or Note Options		Tools, Options	

CONCEPTS check

Completion: On a blank sheet of paper, indicate the correct term, command, symbol, or explanation for each description.

1. Tasks can be created in the Tasks folder or in this folder. *Calendar/TaskPad.*
2. Click this button in the Task window to set up a task that occurs on a regular basis. *Recurrence*
3. When you assign a new task to someone else, they are notified of the task through this communication. *E-mail message*
4. When an individual connected to a Microsoft Exchange Server receives a task request, they respond by clicking Accept, Decline, or this button. *Assign task*
5. Change to this view to create a list of only those tasks that have been assigned to someone else. *Assignment*
6. Display this list box from which you can drag new columns to the current view. *Field Chooser*
7. By default, overdue tasks are displayed in this color. *Red.*
8. A task that is finished can either be deleted from the folder or retained in the folder with this status. *Completed.*
9. A note that has been created as a reminder to do something can be copied here to place it in a more prominent location. *Desktop*
10. One way of organizing notes is to group them by these. *Categories/colors*
11. An individual note can be changed to a different color or all new notes can be changed to a different color in this dialog box. *Notes options.*
12. This view displays the notes one below the other with the entire note text visible along with the date and category. *Notes List View.*

SKILLS check

Assessment 1

1. With Outlook open, display the Calendar folder, turn on the TaskPad, and then add the following tasks in the TaskPad:

    Prepare anti-virus research presentation
    Prepare anti-virus executive summary
    Develop implementation schedule and cost projection

2. Delete the task with the subject *Start budget projections for next year.*
3. Mark the task with the subject *Assemble research on anti-virus software* completed.
4. Turn off the display of the TaskPad.
5. Display the Tasks folder and then create the following recurring task:
    a. Type Monitor budget against actual spending as the subject.
    b. The task will recur monthly on the first Friday in the month.
    c. Assign a high priority status to the task.
    d. Assign the task to the *Business* and *Goals/Objectives* categories.
6. Change the current view to Detailed List.

7. Adjust column widths as necessary so that all column headings and all data within the columns are visible.
8. Print the tasks in *Table Style*.

Assessment 2

1. With Outlook open and Tasks active in Detailed List view, create a task request as follows:

Task Recipient	Student from your Personal Address Book
Subject	Anti-virus presentation
Due date	two weeks from today
Priority	High
Notes	

    Prepare a 10-minute presentation in PowerPoint on the importance of protecting a computer from viruses and worms. Include in the presentation recommendations for safe computer usage.

2. With the task request window open, print the task in *Memo Style*.
3. Send the task request.

Assessment 3

(Note: In order to complete this assessment, you must have received the task request in Assessment 2 from another student.)

1. With Outlook open and Tasks active in Detailed List view, display the Inbox.
2. Open the *Task Request: Anti-virus presentation* message and then respond to the request as follows:
    a. Decline the task request and then type the following response to the task originator:

    Please accept my regrets, but I cannot complete this task for you as I have just learned I have been transferred to another division effective immediately. Kelly is filling in for me on existing work until a replacement is found; however, I have been instructed not to give any new assignments to Kelly.

    b. Print the response message.
    c. Send the response message to the originator.
3. Display the Tasks folder.

Assessment 4

1. With Outlook open and Tasks active in Detailed List view, double-click the entry in the Task table with the subject *Compile month end sales reports*.
2. Click the Assign Task button on the Task window toolbar to delegate this task to someone else.
3. Click the To button and then add the name of the student you added to your Personal Address Book as the task recipient.
4. Send the task request.

Assessment 5

1. With Outlook open and Tasks active in Detailed List view, double-click the entry in the Task table with the subject *Prepare anti-virus executive summary*.
2. Update the task as follows:
    a. Change the *% Complete* to *75%*.
    b. Type the following text in the editing window.

        Waiting for more information from Symantec on site licensing options.

    c. Click the Details tab.
    d. Change the value in the *Actual Work* field to *2.5 hours*.
3. With the task window open, print the task in *Memo Style*.
4. Save and Close the task window.

Assessment 6

1. With Outlook open and Tasks active in Detailed List view, change the current view to Assignment.
2. Print the task list in *Table Style*.
3. Change the current view to By Person Responsible.
4. Print the task list in *Table Style*.
5. Change the current view to Simple List.

Assessment 7

1. With Outlook open and Tasks active in Simple List view, change to the Notes folder.
2. Create the following two notes:

    Order a case of photocopy paper
    Find out when next performance evaluation is due

3. Change the current view to Notes List.
4. Print the notes in *Table Style*.

Assessment 8

1. With Outlook open and Notes active in Notes List view, change the current view to Icons.
2. Change the color of the following individual notes:

Find out when next performance evaluation is due	*Blue*
Order a case of photocopy paper	*Green*

3. Change the current view to By Color.
4. Print the notes in *Table Style*.
5. Change the current view to Icons.

CHAPTER 5

CUSTOMIZING, INTEGRATING, AND ARCHIVING OUTLOOK COMPONENTS

PERFORMANCE OBJECTIVES

Upon successful completion of Chapter 5, you will be able to:
- ➤ Use and customize the Outlook Today page
- ➤ Change the folder that Outlook displays on startup
- ➤ Hide the Navigation Pane
- ➤ Customize the Navigation Pane
- ➤ Specify e-mail options
- ➤ Change the e-mail editor and viewer
- ➤ Customize desktop alerts
- ➤ Understand search folders
- ➤ Create a private appointment
- ➤ Use the Letter Wizard to create a letter to a contact
- ➤ Create an e-mail merge using contacts
- ➤ Create and use a new Outlook data file
- ➤ Archive Outlook data
- ➤ Use the Mailbox Cleanup utilities
- ➤ Compact and back up your Outlook information store

(Note: There are no student data files for this chapter.)

A multitude of options are available for customizing Outlook to operate in the way that best suits your preferences and work habits. Data is easily integrated between Outlook folders and between Outlook and other applications within the Microsoft Office suite such as Microsoft Word. Backing up, restoring, and clearing Outlook folders of outdated information are important routines that keep your data file a manageable size. In this chapter you will learn the more popular options that you might want to use to customize and integrate Outlook and how to manage your information store which contains all of your Outlook data.

Using and Customizing Outlook Today

Outlook Today

Display Outlook Today Page
1. Click View, Toolbars, Advanced.
2. Click Outlook Today icon.

The Outlook Today page provides a glimpse of your current day and the next few days by displaying a list of appointments, tasks, and the number of e-mail messages that you have received or not sent. You can instruct Outlook to display Outlook Today as the starting page whenever you open the program. The layout of the Outlook Today page and the content that is displayed can be customized to suit your needs.

Display the Advanced toolbar and then click the Outlook Today icon to display the Outlook Today page shown in Figure 5.1, or click the top level in the *All Mail Folders* section of the Navigation Pane. For Microsoft Exchange clients, the top level displays *Mailbox – your name* where your mailbox name on the server (usually your first and last name) is substituted for *your name*. For Internet Mail Clients, the top level displays *Personal Folders*. By default, five days of appointments, meetings, and events from the Calendar are displayed in the first column. Active tasks are displayed in the second column in descending order by due date with overdue tasks in red. The third column provides the number of messages that are currently not read in the Inbox, as well as any messages that may be saved in Drafts or the Outbox.

FIGURE 5.1 Outlook Today Page

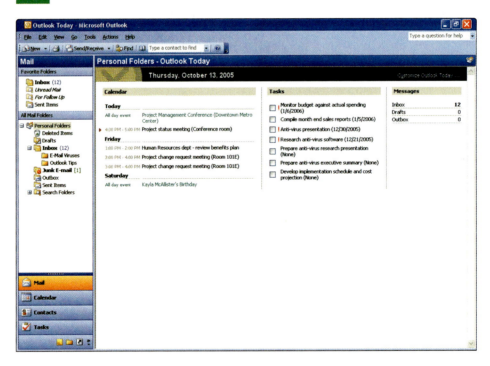

Each entry on the page is a link to the individual window or folder so that you can click an appointment, task, or folder name and view the details directly from Outlook Today.

exercise 1

USING AND CUSTOMIZING OUTLOOK TODAY

1. With Outlook open, click Mail in the Navigation Pane.
2. Click the top level of folders in the *All Mail Folders* section of the Navigation Pane. The top level name is either *Personal Folders* or *Mailbox – your name* where the name of your mailbox on the mail server is substituted for *your name*. This displays the Outlook Today page in the Contents Pane.
3. View folder contents and update tasks from the Outlook Today page by completing the following steps:
    a. Click Inbox in the *Messages* section. Notice *Inbox* appears underlined and the pointer changes to a hand with the index finger pointing upwards as in a hyperlink when pointing at the word *Inbox*.
    b. With the Inbox folder active, return to the Outlook Today page using the Advanced toolbar by completing the following steps:
        1) Right-click over the Standard toolbar and then click Advanced at the shortcut menu.
        2) Click the *Outlook Today* icon on the Advanced toolbar.
    c. Click the check box next to the task *Prepare anti-virus executive summary*.
4. Customize the appearance of Outlook Today and set it as the page that is displayed whenever Outlook is started by completing the following steps:
    a. Click Customize Outlook Today located at the right side of the current date banner.
    b. Click the *When starting, go directly to Outlook Today* check box in the *Startup* section of the Customize Outlook Today window to insert a check mark.
    c. Click the down-pointing arrow next to *Show this number of days in my calendar* in the *Calendar* section, and then click *2*.
    d. Click the down-pointing arrow next to *Show Outlook Today in this style* in the *Styles* section and then click *Winter*.
    e. Click Save Changes at the right side of the Customize Outlook Today banner. The Outlook Today page with the new settings appears in the Contents Pane.
5. Click File and then Exit to close Microsoft Outlook. In the next step you will reopen Outlook to verify that Outlook Today is the default page shown.
6. Start Outlook. If necessary, enter your user name and password to connect to the

server. The customized Outlook Today page appears in the Outlook window. Click the Print button on the Standard toolbar and then click OK at the Print dialog box.
7. Restore Outlook Today to the default settings by completing the following steps:
   a. Click *Customize Outlook Today* at the bottom of the *Messages* section.
   b. Click the *When starting, go directly to Outlook Today* check box in the *Startup* section of the Customize Outlook Today window to deselect it.
   c. Click the down-pointing arrow next to *Show this number of days in my calendar* in the *Calendar* section and then click *5*.
   d. Click the down-pointing arrow next to *Show Outlook Today in this style* in the *Styles* section and then click *Standard*.
   e. Click Save Changes at the right side of the Customize Outlook Today banner.
8. Right-click either toolbar and then click Advanced at the shortcut menu to turn off the display of the Advanced toolbar.

Specifying the Startup Folder

Normally Inbox is the active folder that is displayed when Outlook is started, or, as seen in the previous topic, Outlook Today can be set as the starting page. Open the Advanced Options dialog box shown in Figure 5.2 to change the startup folder to any of the other Outlook folders. For example, you may prefer to have the Calendar folder automatically displayed whenever Outlook is started so that you can immediately see the day's appointments, meetings, and events.

FIGURE

5.2 **Advanced Options Dialog Box**

Specify Startup Folder
1. Click Tools, Options, Other.
2. Click Advanced Options button.
3. Click Browse button.
4. Click desired folder name.
5. Click OK three times.

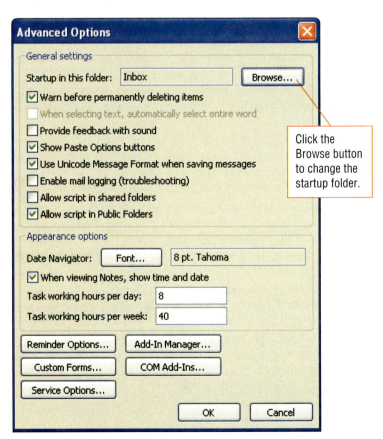

To open the Advanced Options dialog box, click Tools, Options, click the Other tab in the Options dialog box, and then click the Advanced Options button in the *General* section.

exercise 2

CHANGING TO CALENDAR AS THE STARTUP FOLDER

1. With Outlook open and the Outlook Today page displayed, change the startup folder to the Calendar by completing the following steps:
   a. Click Tools and then click Options.
   b. Click the Other tab at the Options dialog box.
   c. Click the Advanced Options button in the *General* section of the Options dialog box with the Other tab selected.
   d. Click the Browse button next to *Startup in this folder* in the *General settings* section.
   e. At the Select Folder dialog box, click *Calendar* in the *Start in this folder* list box and then click OK.
   f. Click OK to close the Advanced Options dialog box.
   g. Click OK to close the Options dialog box.

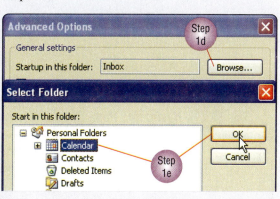

2. Click File and then Exit to close Microsoft Outlook. In the next step you will restart Outlook to verify that the Calendar is displayed when Outlook is reopened.
3. Start Outlook. If necessary, enter your user name and password to connect to the server. The Calendar is displayed when Outlook is opened.
4. Change the startup folder back to the Inbox by completing the following steps:
   a. Click Tools, click Options, and then click the Other tab at the Options dialog box.
   b. Click the Advanced Options button.
   c. Click the Browse button next to *Startup in this folder* and then click *Inbox* in the *Start in this folder* list box at the Select Folder dialog box.
   d. Click OK to close the Select Folder dialog box.
   e. Click OK to close the Advanced Options dialog box.
   f. Click OK to close the Options dialog box.

Customizing the Navigation Pane

By default, the Navigation Pane displays buttons for the four most popular folders in Outlook: Mail, Calendar, Contacts, and Tasks. You can show more or fewer buttons and/or change the order in which the buttons are displayed to suit your personal work habits. Click the Configure buttons button at the bottom right of the Navigation Pane to display the Navigation Pane menu shown in Figure 5.3. Click Navigation Pane Options at the menu to open the Navigation Pane Options dialog box in which you change the order that the buttons are displayed as shown in Figure 5.4.

QUICK STEPS

Show/Hide Navigation Pane
1. Click View.
2. Click Navigation Pane.

FIGURE 5.3 Navigation Pane Menu

FIGURE 5.4 Navigation Pane Options Dialog Box

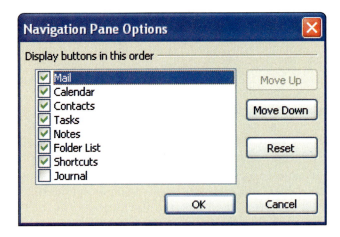

HINT You can also increase or decrease the width of the Navigation Pane by dragging the right blue border right or left.

To free up more space in the Contents Pane, you may choose to hide the Navigation Pane while viewing a folder with a large amount of information. Hide the Navigation Pane by clicking View and then Navigation Pane to remove the check mark next to the menu option. Redisplay the Navigation Pane after hiding it by clicking View and then Navigation Pane. As an alternative, use the shortcut keys Alt + F1 to toggle the Navigation Pane on and off.

exercise 3

HIDING, REDISPLAYING, AND CUSTOMIZING THE NAVIGATION PANE

1. With Outlook open and Calendar active, hide the Navigation Pane, change folders and views, and then redisplay the Navigation Pane by completing the following steps:
    a. Click View on the Menu bar and then click Navigation Pane to remove the check mark next to the Navigation Pane option.
    b. Click Go on the Menu bar and then click Contacts to display the Contacts folder in the Contents Pane.

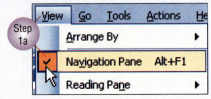

158 Chapter Five

c. Click View, point to Arrange By, point to Current View, and then click Detailed Address Cards. *(Note: Skip this step if your Contacts folder is already displayed in Detailed Address Cards view.)* Notice that without the Navigation Pane, more of the information in Contacts is visible.

d. Press Alt + F1 to redisplay the Navigation Pane.
2. Customize the appearance of the Navigation Pane using the Navigation Pane menu and using the mouse by completing the following steps:
   a. Click the Configure buttons button at the bottom right of the Navigation Pane.
   b. Click Show Fewer Buttons at the Navigation Pane menu. The Tasks button is removed from Navigation Pane.
   c. Repeat Steps 2a-2b to remove the Contacts button from the Navigation Pane. Each time you click Show Fewer Buttons, the bottommost button is removed from the Navigation Pane.
   d. Point at the dark blue border at the top of the Mail button in the Navigation Pane until the pointer displays as a double-headed up- and down-pointing arrow and then drag up until the Contacts and Tasks buttons are redisplayed.
3. Change the order of the buttons in the Navigation Pane by completing the following steps:
   a. Click the Configure buttons button and then click Navigation Pane Options at the Navigation Pane menu.
   b. At the Navigation Pane Options dialog box, click *Tasks* in the *Display buttons in this order* list box and then click the Move Up button twice.
   c. Click OK to close the Navigation Pane Options dialog box. Tasks is now the second button in the Navigation Pane, positioned below the Mail button.
4. Restore the Navigation Pane to the default order by completing the following steps:
   a. Click the Configure buttons button and then click Navigation Pane Options at the Navigation Pane menu.
   b. At the Navigation Pane Options dialog box, click *Tasks* in the *Display buttons in this order* list box and then click the Move Down button twice.
   c. Click OK to close the Navigation Pane Options dialog box.

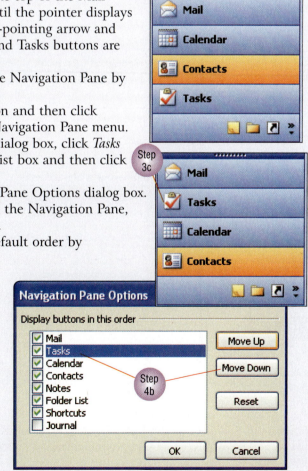

Setting E-Mail Options

Set E-mail Options
1. Click Tools, Options.
2. Click E-mail Options button.

In Chapter 1 you learned how to specify message options for individual messages, create signatures, and create rules with which to process messages as they are received in the Inbox. In this chapter, you will explore some of the other message handling and advanced e-mail options available in Outlook. The *Message handling* section of the E-mail Options dialog box shown in Figure 5.5 allows you to control the actions that occur when messages are sent, received, and deleted. The *On replies and forwards* section provides options for how the original message text is threaded within messages that you reply to or forward to someone else. Click Tools, Options, and then click the E-mail Options button in the *E-mail* section of the Options dialog box with the Preferences tab selected to open the dialog box shown in Figure 5.5.

FIGURE 5.5 **E-mail Options Dialog Box**

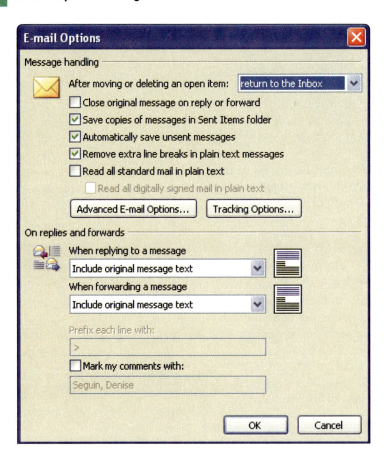

Set Advanced E-mail Options
1. Click Tools, Options.
2. Click E-mail Options button.
3. Click Advanced E-mail Options button.

The Advanced E-mail Options button in the E-mail Options dialog box displays a dialog box with additional features for controlling the actions that occur when messages are saved, messages are received, and when messages are sent as shown in Figure 5.6. The Advanced E-mail Options dialog box is divided into three sections: *Save messages*, *When new items arrive in my Inbox*, and *When sending a message*.

FIGURE 5.6 Advanced E-mail Options Dialog Box

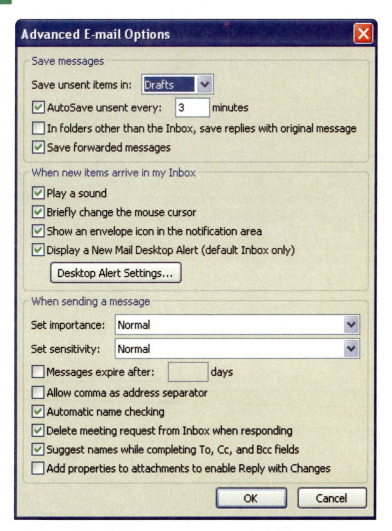

The Tracking Options button in the E-mail Options dialog box allows you to control how read receipts are processed. For example, in the dialog box shown in Figure 5.7 you can specify that you want a delivery or read receipt for all messages sent by you.

F I G U R E

5.7 Tracking Options Dialog Box

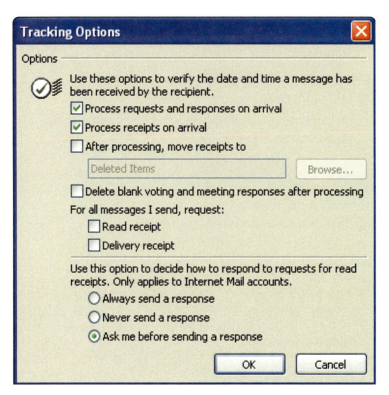

In the next three exercises, you will examine the available e-mail options and experiment with changing the default settings.

exercise 4

CHANGING E-MAIL OPTIONS

1. With Contacts the active folder, instruct Outlook to close the original message window when you reply or forward a message by completing the following steps:
   a. Click Mail in the Navigation Pane.
   b. Click Tools, click Options, and then click the E-mail Options button in the *E-mail* section of the Options dialog box with the Preferences tab selected.
   c. Read each option shown in the *Message handling* section of the E-mail Options dialog box.
   d. Click the *Close original message on reply or forward* check box. *(Note: Skip this step if this check box is already selected.)*
2. With the E-mail Options dialog box still open, increase the time interval that Outlook saves unsent messages in Drafts by completing the following steps:
   a. Click the Advanced E-mail Options button.

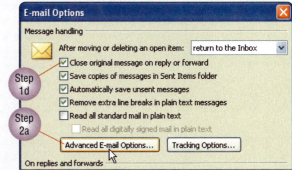

Step 1d

Step 2a

162 Chapter Five

b. Drag across the current value in the *AutoSave unsent every* [] *minutes* text box, and then type 5. *(Note: If this box is currently empty, click the check box next to AutoSave to turn the feature on.)*

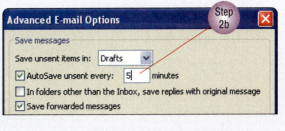

c. Click OK to close the Advanced E-mail Options dialog box.
3. Click OK to close the E-mail Options dialog box.
4. Click OK to close the Options dialog box.

exercise 5

CHANGING MORE ADVANCED E-MAIL OPTIONS

1. With Outlook open and Inbox active, instruct Outlook not to save copies of forwarded messages, not to show an envelope in the notification area when a new message arrives, and not to delete meeting requests after you have responded by completing the following steps:
   a. Click Tools and then click Options.
   b. Click the E-mail Options button in the *E-mail* section of the Options dialog box with the Preferences tab selected.
   c. At the E-mail Options dialog box, click the Advanced E-mail Options button.
   d. Click to deselect the *Save forwarded messages* check box in the *Save messages* section. *(Note: Skip this step if* **Save forwarded messages** *is already deselected.)*
   e. Click to deselect the *Show an envelope icon in the notification area* check box in the *When new items arrive in my Inbox* section. *(Note: Skip this step if* **Show an envelope icon in the notification area** *is already deselected.)*
   f. Click to deselect the *Delete meeting request from Inbox when responding* check box in the *When sending a message* section. *(Note: Skip this step if* **Delete meeting request from Inbox when responding** *is already deselected.)*
   g. Click OK to close the Advanced E-mail Options dialog box.
   h. Click OK to close the E-mail Options dialog box.
   i. Click OK to close the Options dialog box.

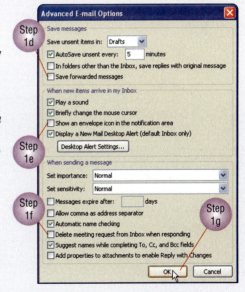

2. Create and send a message to yourself and then forward the message to another student to test the new options by completing the following steps:
   a. With Inbox the active folder, click the New Mail Message button on the Standard toolbar.

OUTLOOK Customizing, Integrating, and Archiving Outlook Components

b. With the insertion point positioned in the *To* text box, type your own e-mail address.
c. Click in the *Subject* text box and then type **Advanced E-mail Options**.
d. Click in the message editing window and then type the following text:

   This message is to test the changes made to the advanced e-mail options.

e. Click Send.
f. In a few seconds, the message should appear in your Inbox. Watch the notification area at the bottom right of the screen. Notice the new mail icon does not appear after the message arrives.
   (Note: If the message does not appear within a few seconds, click the Send/Receive button on the Standard toolbar.)

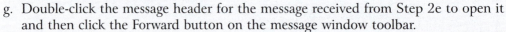
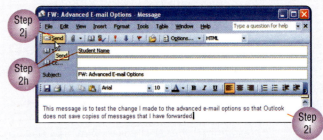

g. Double-click the message header for the message received from Step 2e to open it and then click the Forward button on the message window toolbar.
h. Click the To button, change to the Personal Address Book at the Select Names dialog box, double-click the name of the student you added to the PAB in Chapter 1, and then click OK.
i. Click in the message editing window and then type the following text:

   This message is to test the change I made to the advanced e-mail options so that Outlook does not save copies of messages that I have forwarded.

j. Click Send. Notice the original message window is automatically closed as soon as you send the forwarded message. This is a result of the change you made to the e-mail options in Exercise 4, Step 1d.
k. Click Sent Items in the *All Mail Folders* section of the Navigation Pane. In the Contents Pane, notice that Outlook has not retained a copy of the forwarded message—only the original message that you sent to yourself is shown.
l. Click Inbox in the *All Mail Folders* section of the Navigation Pane.

RESTORING E-MAIL OPTIONS TO THE DEFAULT SETTINGS

1. Restore the e-mail options back to the original default settings by completing the following steps:
   a. Click Tools, Options, and then click the E-mail Options button at the Options dialog box.
   b. Click the *Close original message on reply or forward* check box to deselect it.
   c. Click the Advanced E-mail Options button.
   d. Change the value in the *AutoSave unsent every* [ ] *minutes* to 3.
   e. Click the *Save forwarded messages* check box to select it.

f. Click the *Show an envelope icon in the notification area* check box to select it.
g. Click the *Delete meeting request from Inbox when responding* check box to select it.
h. Click OK to close the Advanced E-mail Options dialog box.
2. Click OK to close the E-mail Options dialog box.
3. Click OK to close the Options dialog box.

Changing the Mail Editor and Viewer

On an initial installation of Outlook, Microsoft Word is the default application in which to create and edit messages. Word is set as the default editor in order to take advantage of Word's capabilities such as automatic spelling and grammar checking, tables, and backgrounds to name a few. Display the Options dialog box with the Mail Format tab selected to choose whether to use Word as the e-mail editor or Outlook. In the *Message format* section, click the *Use Microsoft Office Word 2003 to edit e-mail messages* to deselect the option if you want to use Outlook as the mail editor. A separate option is available in which you specify which application to use to read rich text e-mail messages.

When you deselect Word as the mail editor, the message window shown in Figure 5.8 appears when you start a new message. The menu items and toolbars have fewer options now that you do not have access to Word's editing features.

Change Mail Editor
1. Click Tools, Options.
2. Click Mail Format tab.
3. Check or clear Use Microsoft Office Word 2003 to edit e-mail messages.

Change Mail Format for Single Message
1. Click Actions.
2. Point to New Message Using.
3. Click desired mail format.

FIGURE 5.8 **Message Window with Outlook as the Mail Editor**

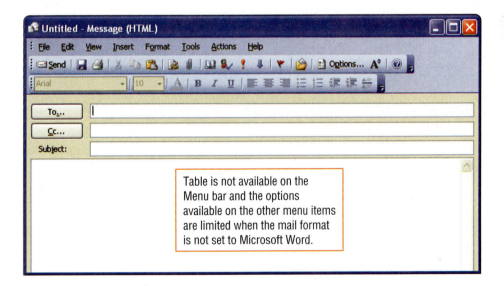

With Word turned off as the default mail editor, you can still create an individual message using Word by clicking Actions on the Menu bar, pointing to New Mail Message Using, and then clicking Microsoft Office Word 2003 (HTML) as shown in Figure 5.9.

FIGURE

5.9 Choosing Mail Format for an Individual Message Using Actions Menu

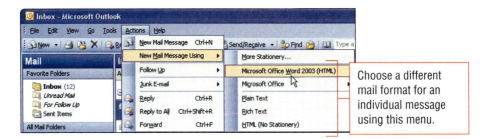

HINT

By default, a message created in Outlook Rich Text is automatically converted to HTML format when sent to an Internet mail recipient.

Other mail format options available include Plain Text, Rich Text, and HTML. Plain Text does not include any formatting options. Rich Text displays formatting features such as font changes, text alignment, and bullets; and HTML displays features in addition to rich text such as backgrounds and horizontal lines commonly seen in Web pages. Generally, use Rich Text messages only when you are sending messages to others on your network with Outlook connected to a Microsoft Exchange server. In this case, you can be assured that the recipient will see all of the formatting applied within the message. When sending a message to others over the Internet to a recipient outside your network, use HTML to retain formatting.

To change the mail format within a message window, click Format on the message window Menu bar and choose the desired mail format at the drop-down menu.

exercise 7

CHECKING THE DEFAULT MAIL EDITOR AND VIEWER AND CHANGING MAIL FORMAT FOR AN INDIVIDUAL MESSAGE

1. With Outlook open and Inbox active, check the current setting for e-mail editing and viewing on the computer you are using and if necessary, turn on Word as the e-mail editor by completing the following steps:

    a. Click Tools and then click Options.
    b. Click the Mail Format tab at the Options dialog box.
    c. Look in the *Message format* section at the check boxes for *Use Microsoft Office Word 2003 to edit e-mail messages* and *Use Microsoft Office Word 2003 to read Rich Text e-mail messages*. If one or both check boxes have a check mark then Word is the default editor and/or viewer. If the boxes are empty then Outlook is the default editor and/or viewer.
    d. If necessary, click *Use Microsoft Office Word 2003 to edit e-mail messages* to turn on Word as the mail editor. Skip this step if the check box is already selected.
    e. Click OK to close the Options dialog box.
2. Create a new message using a different mail format by completing the following steps:
    a. Click Actions on the Menu bar, point to New Mail Message Using, and then click Plain Text.

b. Type your own e-mail address in the *To* text box.
c. Type **Mail Format** in the *Subject* text box.
d. Type the following text in the message window:

   Text in plain text messages defaults to 10-point Courier New as the font. All formatting options, even bold and italics, are not available! Most people type an asterisk before and after a word to *emphasize* it in a plain text message.

e. Notice all of the buttons on the formatting toolbar are dimmed, meaning none of the options are available for use in the message text.
f. Click Send.

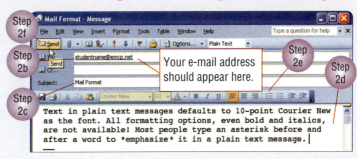

Customizing Desktop Alerts

As you learned in Chapter 1, a desktop alert displays when you are online and a new mail message is received in the Inbox. The alert displays the sender's name, the subject, and the first two lines of text within the message. By default, the alert remains visible for 7 seconds after which the alert fades away. The transparency value for the alert is 20 percent, which can be adjusted to display the alert inside a more solid or clear box. To increase or decrease the time interval or change the transparency value, display the Desktop Alert Settings dialog box shown in Figure 5.10 by clicking the Desktop Alert Settings button in the *When new items arrive in my Inbox* section of the Advanced E-mail Options dialog box.

QUICK STEPS

Customize Desktop Alert
1. Click Tools, Options.
2. Click E-mail Options button.
3. Click Advanced E-mail Options button.
4. Click Desktop Alert Settings button.
5. Change duration or transparency setting.
6. Click OK four times.

FIGURE 5.10 *Desktop Alert Settings Dialog Box*

CUSTOMIZING THE DESKTOP ALERT

1. With Outlook open and Inbox active, customize the desktop alert to display for a longer period of time inside a solid box by completing the following steps:
   a. Click Tools, Options, and then click the E-mail Options button at the Options dialog box.
   b. Click the Advanced E-mail Options button at the E-mail Options dialog box.
   c. Click the Desktop Alert Settings button in the *When new items arrive in my Inbox* section of the Advanced E-mail Options dialog box.
   d. At the Desktop Alert Settings dialog box, drag the slider in the *Duration* section right until the time interval below the slider displays *15 seconds*.
   e. Drag the slider in the *Transparency* section left to *Solid* so that the value below the slider displays *0% transparent*.
   f. Click the Preview button.
   g. Click OK to close the Desktop Alert Settings dialog box.
   h. Click OK three times.

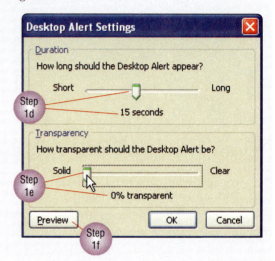

Understanding Search Folders

A new feature in Outlook 2003 called **Search Folders** provides a new tool for finding messages. The search folders do not store messages. Instead they store filter or search settings so that when you click the search folder name, Outlook displays in the Contents Pane those messages that meet the saved criteria. For example, the search folder named For Follow Up displays messages in the Contents Pane that have a flag attached.

To use a search folder, expand the folder named Search Folders in the *All Mail Folders* section of the Navigation Pane and then click the name of the search folder for the contents that you want to view as shown in Figure 5.11. The search folder name initially appears in italics with a dimmed folder icon; however, once the Contents Pane displays the messages that meet the criteria, the name changes to bold and the icon is no longer dimmed.

FIGURE

5.11 *Using Search Folders*

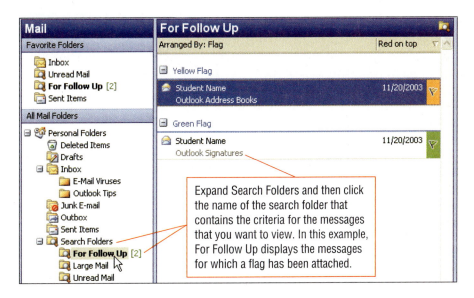

Expand Search Folders and then click the name of the search folder that contains the criteria for the messages that you want to view. In this example, For Follow Up displays the messages for which a flag has been attached.

You can create your own search folder by right-clicking Search Folders and then clicking New Search Folder at the shortcut menu. At the New Search Folder dialog box, choose one of the predefined search folders or click Create a Custom Search Folder and define your own criteria with which to display items.

Creating a Private Appointment

When another user has access to your Calendar either as a delegate or through permissions on the folder properties, he or she can view all of the appointments in your Calendar folder. If you are creating an appointment and do not want other users to see the appointment details, click the *Private* check box in the Appointment window. The appointment details appear when you view your folder but the details are hidden from view for other users.

To mark an existing appointment private, right-click over the appointment box in the calendar, and then click Private at the shortcut menu.

For Exchange Server clients, grant others permission to open your Calendar folder using the Permissions tab in the Calendar Properties dialog box. Various permission options provide you with control over the other user's viewing and editing abilities.

QUICK STEPS

Create a Private Appointment
1. Open Appointment window.
2. Add appointment details as required.
3. Click *Private* check box.
4. Click Save and Close.

exercise 9

CREATING A PRIVATE APPOINTMENT

1. With Outlook open and Inbox active, click Calendar in the Navigation Pane.
2. Press Ctrl + G to open the Go To Date dialog box, type **10/14/2005** in the *Date* text box, and then press Enter or click OK.
3. Create a new appointment and mark it as private by completing the following steps:
   a. Double-click next to *12 pm* in the Appointment area to open an Appointment window.
   b. With the insertion point positioned in the *Subject* text box, type **Doctor's appointment**.

c. Change the *End time* to *1:00 PM*.
d. Click the *Private* check box in the lower right corner of the Appointment window.
e. Click Save and Close. The appointment appears in the Appointment area with an icon of a key indicating to you the appointment is private.
4. Click the Print button on the Standard toolbar. With *Daily Style* selected in the *Print style* section of the Print dialog box, click OK.
5. Make Inbox the active folder.

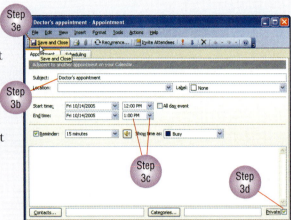

QUICK STEPS

Create Letter to Contact
1. Click Contacts.
2. Click name banner for contact.
3. Click Actions, New Letter to Contact.
4. Complete Letter Wizard in Microsoft Word.
5. Print letter.
6. Exit Word.

Creating a Letter to a Contact

A letter can be generated to a contact within the Contacts folder using the Letter Wizard that is available in Microsoft Word. Select the contact record for which you want to send a letter, click Actions on the Menu bar, and then click New Letter to Contact. Microsoft Word opens with the Letter Wizard Step 1 of 4 dialog box open. The Letter Wizard walks you through the process of creating the letter by choosing the letter format, inserting recipient information, including letter elements such as an attention line, and typing the sender information.

When the Letter Wizard is complete, the selected contact's name and address are automatically inserted in the inside address section of the letter. Type the body of the letter in the document, save, print, and then exit Word to return to the Contacts folder in Outlook.

exercise 10

CREATING A LETTER TO A CONTACT

1. With Outlook open and Calendar active, click Contacts in the Navigation Pane and then click *Address Cards* in the *Current View* section of the Navigation Pane.
2. Start a letter to a contact by completing the following steps:
    a. Click the name banner for *Miele, Henry*.
    b. Click Actions on the Menu bar and then click New Letter to Contact. Microsoft Word opens with the Letter Wizard started. *(Note: If Microsoft Word does not automatically open, look on the Taskbar for the Word document button. Clicking the Word button on the Taskbar will switch to Microsoft Word where you can complete the exercise.)*
3. Finish the letter in Microsoft Word by completing the following steps:
    a. At the Microsoft Word Letter Wizard - Step 1 of 4 dialog box with the Letter Format tab selected, complete the following steps:

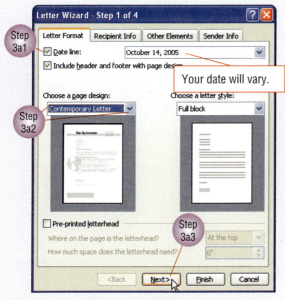
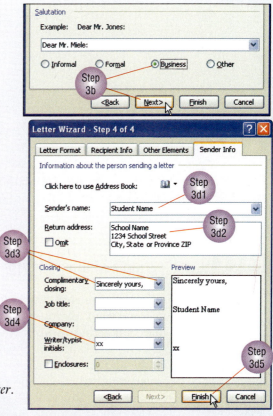

1) Click the *Date line* check box. The current date appears in the adjacent text box.
2) Click the down-pointing arrow next to the *Choose a page design* list box and then click *Contemporary Letter*.
3) Click Next.

b. At the Letter Wizard - Step 2 of 4 dialog box with the Recipient Info tab selected, click *Business* in the *Salutation* section and then click Next.

c. Click Next at the Letter Wizard - Step 3 of 4 dialog box with the Other Elements tab selected.

d. Enter the sender information in the Letter Wizard - Step 4 of 4 dialog box with the Sender Info tab selected by completing the following steps:
   1) Type your first and last name in the *Sender's name* text box.
   2) Type the name and address of your school in the *Return address* text box.
   3) Click the down-pointing arrow next to *Complimentary closing* and then click *Sincerely yours,*.
   4) Type your initials in the *Writer/typist initials* text box.
   5) Click Finish.

e. If necessary, switch to Print Layout view and then type the following text as the body of the letter. *(Note: The letter is formatted to double-space between paragraphs automatically. You will only need to press Enter once between paragraphs.)*

   We are now finished with the implementation of our new order processing system.

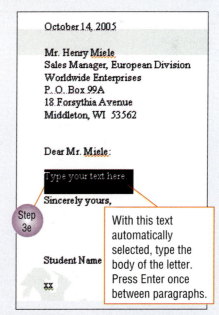

OUTLOOK

Customizing, Integrating, and Archiving Outlook Components

> Products are in stock and ready to ship to Europe. We encourage you to advise your representatives in the European division to proceed with entering orders into our system.
>
> With our streamlined process, we anticipate faster shipments and fewer returns for errors and omissions. Thank you for your patience during this setup time.

   f. Click File, Page Setup, and then click the Layout tab at the Page Setup dialog box. Click the down-pointing arrow next to *Vertical alignment* in the *Page* section, click *Center*, and then click OK. This will vertically center the letter on the page.
4. Click the Print button on the Standard toolbar.
5. Exit Microsoft Word to return to Contacts in Outlook. Click No when prompted to save changes.

QUICK STEPS

Create Mail Merge to Contacts
1. Click Contacts.
2. Change to view that displays required fields for merge.
3. Add or remove fields as needed to the view.
4. If necessary, select records to be merged.
5. Click Tools, Mail Merge.
6. Change required merge options.
7. Click OK.
8. Create main document in Microsoft Word.
9. Click required Merge button on Mail Merge toolbar.
10. Exit Word.

Creating a Standard Letter to Multiple Contacts

You can filter or sort data in Contacts, and then use the data as the data source in a mail merge in Microsoft Word. A *mail merge* is the term used when a list of names and addresses from one file, called the ***data source***, is used to create form letters, mailing labels, or envelopes. A second file, called the ***main document***, contains the standard text for each letter, label, envelope, catalog, or e-mail. Formatting instructions and field codes that instruct Word as to the placement of the name and address fields is also included in the main document.

The contact information for the selected contacts is sent to a temporary mail merge file while the main document is created in Word. Save the data source file in Word if you want to use the same contact data for future merges.

Performing a mail merge using Outlook and Word requires completion of the following three steps:
1. Export the contact data as a data source from Outlook.
2. Create the main document in Word by typing standard text and inserting the merge fields as required.
3. Merge the data source with the main document to a new document, directly to the printer, or to e-mail.

Exporting Data from Contacts to Create a Data Source

Complete the following steps to create a data source from the Contacts folder:
1. Change to the view that contains the fields you want to merge and then sort or filter the data in the Contacts folder in the order you want the letters or messages generated. Remove any fields from the current view that are not required in the merged document. If you do not want a letter, label, e-mail, or envelope generated to each record, select the contact records to include in the merge. For example, use Ctrl + click to select nonadjacent records, or click the first record and then Shift + click the last record to select adjacent contacts.
2. Click Tools and then click Mail Merge to open the Mail Merge Contacts dialog box shown in Figure 5.12. *All contacts in current view* is selected by default in the *Contacts* section. If you had selected multiple contact records before opening the Mail Merge Contacts dialog box, the *Only selected contacts* option would be active instead.

3. Click *Contact fields in current view* in the *Fields to merge* section. The default option *All contact fields* sends all contact data to the data source file. In most cases, it is unnecessary to include all of the fields in contact records for generating a letter.
4. Click *New document* in the *Document file* section, or click *Existing document* and then browse to the folder and file name of the existing data source.
5. If you want to save the exported contact information for future mail merges, click the *Permanent file* check box in the *Contact data file* section and then browse to specify the folder and file name in which to store the data source.
6. In the *Merge options* section, select the type of main document that you will be creating in Word in the *Document type* drop-down list. You can choose *Form Letters, Mailing Labels, Envelopes,* or *Catalog.*
7. Select where the merged records are to be sent in the *Merge to* list box. The data can be merged to *New Document, Printer,* or *E-mail.* When you select E-mail, a text box is added to the dialog box in which you type the subject text for the e-mail messages.
8. Click OK.
9. Microsoft Word opens where you complete the merge process.

FIGURE 5.12 **Mail Merge Contacts Dialog Box**

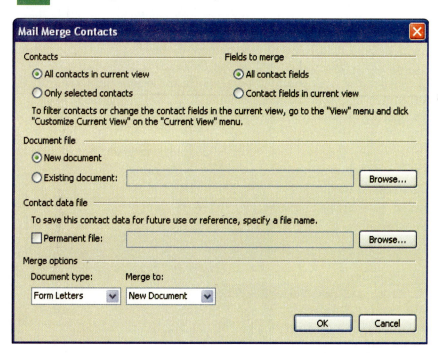

Completing the Merge in Word

When the data from Contacts has finished exporting, you will be at a Microsoft Word editing window with the Mail Merge toolbar automatically opened. Insert the required fields and text to complete the letters, and then click the Merge to New Document, Merge to Printer, or Merge to E-mail button on the Mail Merge toolbar. Microsoft Word generates an individual letter or e-mail message to each record in the data source.

Insert Merge Fields

To create the main document, type the text in the form letter to the point where you need to insert the recipient's name and/or address. Click the Insert Merge Fields button on the Mail Merge toolbar, click the required field at the Insert Merge Field dialog box, click the Insert button, and then click the Close button. Press Enter or insert spaces or other punctuation as required between the fields. Continue inserting merge fields and typing text until the form letter is complete. You can save the main document if you want to use it for future merges.

exercise 11 — CREATING AND SENDING A FORM LETTER BY E-MAIL TO CONTACTS

1. With Outlook open and Contacts active in Address Cards view, start a mail merge to create a standard letter to contacts by completing the following steps:
   a. Click *By Company* in the *Current View* section of the Navigation Pane.
   b. Remove the following columns from the current view:
      Company
      File As
      Department
      Home Phone
      Categories
   c. Add the *E-mail* field to the current view by completing the following steps:
      1) Right-click any column heading and then click Field Chooser at the shortcut menu.
      2) Click the down-pointing arrow next to *Frequently-used fields* and then click *E-mail fields*.
      3) Drag the *E-mail* field button from the *Field Chooser* list box to the column headings row between the *Job Title* and *Business Phone* columns.
      4) Double-click the right column boundary for the *E-mail* field to adjust the column width to the length of the longest entry.
      5) Close the *Field Chooser* list box.
   d. Click the contact record for *Ms. Kayla McAllister*. Hold down the Shift key and then click the contact record for *Ms. Pauline Gorski*. Three contact records are selected as shown below.

   e. Click Tools and then click Mail Merge.
   f. At the Mail Merge Contacts dialog box, click *Contact fields in current view* in the *Fields to merge* section.
   g. Click the down-pointing arrow next to the *Merge to* list box in the *Merge options* section and then click *E-mail*.
   h. Click in the *Message subject line* text box and then type **New secure Web site**.
   i. Click OK.

2. Outlook exports the selected records as a data source in Microsoft Word. Microsoft Word opens with a clear document screen and the Mail Merge toolbar below the Standard and Formatting toolbars. Create the main document by completing the following steps:
    a. Type **We are in the process of setting up our new secure Web site for processing orders. Your company,**
    b. Press the spacebar and then click the Insert Merge Fields button on the Mail Merge toolbar.
    c. At the Insert Merge Field dialog box, click *Company* in the *Fields* list box and then click the Insert button.
    d. Click the Close button to close the Insert Merge Field dialog box.
    e. Type **indicated an interest in using this Web-based ordering system.** and then press Enter twice.
    f. Type **To ensure our records are accurate, please indicate the following information is correct:** and then press Enter twice.
    g. Click the Insert Merge Fields button. Click *Full_Name* in the *Fields* list box, click the Insert button, and then click the Close button.
    h. Press Enter.
    i. Repeat Steps 2g-2h to add the *Job_Title* and *Business_Fax* fields below *Full_Name*.

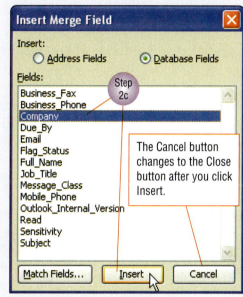

3. Merge the main document with the data source to e-mail by completing the following steps:
    a. Click the Merge to E-mail button on the Mail Merge toolbar.
    b. At the Merge to E-mail dialog box, click OK. The main document is merged with the three contact records and a message is sent automatically to each contact's e-mail address.

4. Exit Microsoft Word. Click No when prompted to save changes.
5. With Outlook active in Contacts, click *Address Cards* in the *Current View* section of the Navigation Pane.
6. Click Mail in the Navigation Pane and then click Sent Items in the *All Mail Folders* section.
7. Note the three messages sent to the contacts selected in Step 1. Since the e-mail addresses for the contacts are fictitious you will receive undeliverable messages from the mail server for these messages.

8. Double-click the message header for the message sent to *hmiele@emcp.net*. Notice the data placed in the message where you inserted merge fields in the main document for *Company, Full_Name, Job_Title,* and *Business_Fax*.

   Step 8

   To: 'hmiele@emcp.net'
   Cc:
   Subject: New secure Web site

   We are in the process of setting up our new secure Web site for processing orders. Your company, Worldwide Enterprises indicated an interest in using this Web-based ordering system.
   To ensure our records are accurate, please indicate the following information is correct:

   Mr. Henry Miele
   Sales Manager, European Division
   (608) 555-4556

9. Click the Print button on the message window toolbar and then close the message window.
10. Click Inbox in the *All Mail Folders* section of the Navigation Pane.

Creating a Personal Folders File

QUICK STEPS

Create a PST File
1. Click File, New, Outlook Data File.
2. With *Office Outlook Personal Folders File (.pst)* selected, click OK.
3. Browse to drive and/or folder and type file name.
4. Click OK.
5. Type name to display in *All Mail Folders* section at Create Microsoft Personal Folders dialog box.
6. Click OK.

HINT

For Exchange Server clients, moving messages from the server mailbox to a personal folders file helps to keep the mailbox under the size limit set by the system administrator.

All of the data in the Outlook folders is stored in a single file that is referred to as a **personal information store** and has the file name extension *.pst*. Outlook users who are connected using a Microsoft Exchange Server have all of their data stored on the central Exchange server in a file referred to as **private store**.

Creating multiple personal folders is one of many methods available for organizing your Outlook data. For example, you may be working on a project in which you send and receive several e-mail messages. Creating a personal folders file for the project and moving the messages to the folder will keep all of the information in one place. Managing the project data file separately from your main folder also makes it easier to archive the project.

If you are using Outlook connected to an Exchange server, you may want to create a personal folders file to move or copy messages from the server's centralized file to a pst file stored on your computer's hard drive. This ensures that you have access to the messages whether you are connected to the server or not.

Complete the following steps to create a personal folders file.
1. Click File, point to New, and then click Outlook Data File.
2. At the New Outlook Data File dialog box shown in Figure 5.13, with *Office Outlook Personal Folders File (.pst)* selected in the *Types of storage* list box, click OK. If you need to create a pst file for use in a version of Outlook prior to Outlook 2003, select *Outlook 97-2002 Personal Folders File (.pst)*. For Outlook 2003, Microsoft changed the file format for the personal folders file, and data in Outlook 2003 pst files is not compatible with data in the earlier versions.
3. At the Create or Open Outlook Data File dialog box, browse to the location in which to store the pst file, type a name in the *File name* text box, and then click OK.
4. At the Create Microsoft Personal Folders dialog box, type in the *Name* text box a unique name to describe the personal folders file. For example, type the name of the project for which you are creating the separate pst file.
5. If you want to password protect the pst file as a security precaution, type the password in the *Password* and *Verify Password* text boxes.
6. Click OK. Outlook creates the new pst file and automatically makes it the active folder.

FIGURE

5.13 New Outlook Data File Dialog Box

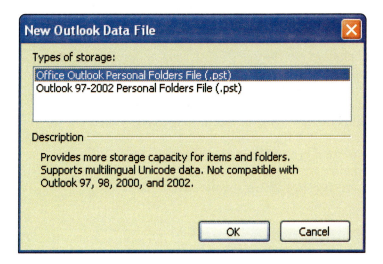

Once the personal folders file is created, you can move or copy Outlook items to it by creating new folders within the pst file and then dragging and dropping items to the new folders.

exercise 12

CREATING AND USING A PERSONAL FOLDERS FILE

(Note: Make sure your Outlook data disk is in the drive before starting this exercise.)

1. With Outlook open and Inbox active, create a new personal folders data file by completing the following steps:
    a. Click File, point to New, and then click Outlook Data File.
    b. With *Office Outlook Personal Folders File (.pst)* selected in the *Types of storage* list box at the New Outlook Data File dialog box, click OK.
    c. At the Create or Open Outlook Data File dialog box, click the down-pointing arrow next to *Save in* and then click *3½ Floppy (A:)*.
    d. Select the default name in the *File name* text box and then type StudentName where your name is substituted for *StudentName*.
    e. Click OK.

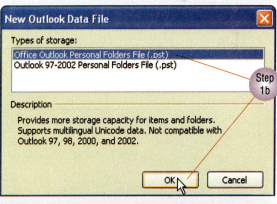

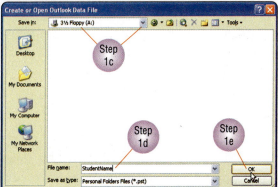

OUTLOOK
Customizing, Integrating, and Archiving Outlook Components 177

f. At the Create Microsoft Personal Folders dialog box, type **Learning Outlook** in the *Name* text box, and then click OK.
2. With Learning Outlook the active folder, create a new folder for storing e-mail messages and then move a message to the new folder by completing the following steps:
   a. Right-click Learning Outlook in the *All Mail Folders* section of the Navigation Pane.
   b. Click New Folder at the shortcut menu.
   c. With the insertion point positioned in the *Name* text box at the Create New Folder dialog box, type **Training**, and then click OK.
   d. Click Inbox in the *All Mail Folders* section of the Navigation Pane.
   e. Position the mouse pointer over the message header with the subject *Advanced E-mail Options*, and then drag the message header to the folder named Training in the *All Mail Folders* section of the Navigation Pane.
   f. Click the Training folder name in the *All Mail Folders* section of the Navigation Pane to view the message header for the moved message.
3. Make Inbox the active folder.

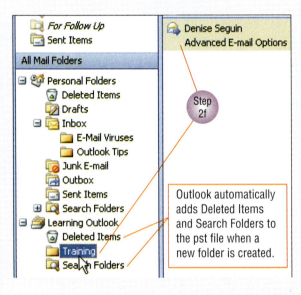

Archiving Folders

Change Global AutoArchive Settings
1. Click Tools, Options.
2. Click Other tab.
3. Click AutoArchive button.
4. Change settings as required.
5. Click OK twice.

If you receive on average ten messages per day, that means your Inbox folder will have approximately 300 messages at the end of the month! Over time, your mail folders can grow quite large due to the number of messages stored in them. If you use e-mail for business communication, you should archive the messages instead of deleting them so that you maintain essential records. An *archive* is a file containing old messages that have been purged from the mail folder. The archived messages can be retrieved if necessary by opening the archive folder.

You can manually transfer old items to the archive file, or you can rely on the global **AutoArchive** feature to have Outlook do the transferring automatically. Items are considered for archiving when they reach a specified age. The default setting is for AutoArchive to run every 14 days and clean out items that are older than 6 months. If you prefer, you can set different options for each Outlook folder. AutoArchive can either delete the items or move old items to the storage file. The default setting is to move the old items to a file named *archive.pst*.

To change the default options for AutoArchive, display the Options dialog box, click the Other tab, and then click the AutoArchive button. In the AutoArchive dialog box shown in Figure 5.14, choose the options that you want, and then click OK.

> **HINT**
> Before running an archive, clean out from the mail folders any messages that do not need to be retained to avoid using unnecessary disk space.

FIGURE 5.14 AutoArchive Dialog Box

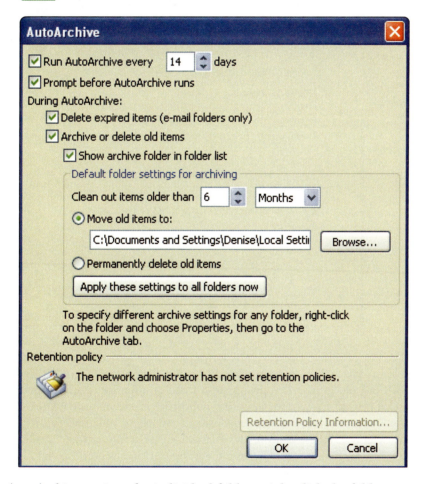

To set AutoArchive options for individual folders, right-click the folder name in the *All Mail Folders* section of the Navigation Pane, click Properties, and then click the AutoArchive tab at the Properties dialog box. Choose one of the following three options: *Do not archive items in this folder, Archive items in this folder using the default settings*, or *Archive this folder using these settings*. When you click *Archive this folder using these settings*, the options shown in Figure 5.15 become active. Choose the time period you want items archived in the *Clean out items older than* text boxes, choose the location to move the items to, or choose to delete the old items. Changes made to individual folder AutoArchive properties override the global settings in the Options dialog box.

FIGURE 5.15 Inbox Properties Dialog Box with AutoArchive Tab Selected

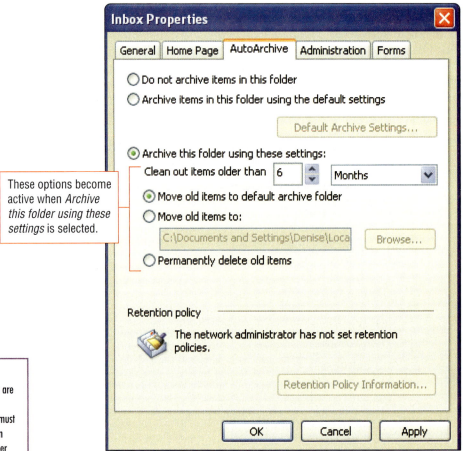

These options become active when *Archive this folder using these settings* is selected.

HINT
E-mail messages are valid business documents and must be retained in an organized manner subject to record retention rules for any other business document.

QUICK STEPS

Perform Manual Archive
1. Click File, Archive.
2. Click *Archive this folder and all subfolders*.
3. Click desired folder to archive.
4. Choose date in *Archive items older than* text box.
5. Type archive file name.
6. Click OK.

The AutoArchive process runs automatically whenever you start Outlook and by default, you will be prompted to click Yes if you want AutoArchive to proceed to clean out old items. The properties of each folder are checked by date, and old items are moved to your archive file. Following is the default AutoArchive option for the Outlook folders: Calendar, Tasks, Sent Items, and Deleted Items have the option selected *Archive items in this folder using the default settings,* and Inbox, Junk E-mail, Notes, Drafts, and Outbox have the option selected *Do not archive items in this folder*. Contacts does not have an AutoArchive tab in the Properties dialog box since contacts are not time-sensitive items.

Manually Archiving Items

To archive at your discretion, you can choose to turn off AutoArchive by clearing the *Run AutoArchive every [] days* check box in the AutoArchive dialog box, or leave the option on and click No whenever you are prompted to AutoArchive. When you are ready to start a manual archive, click File, and then click Archive to open the Archive dialog box shown in Figure 5.16. Click *Archive all folders according to their AutoArchive settings* to start the archive process for all folders based on each folder's AutoArchive properties. To choose an individual folder to archive, click *Archive this folder and all subfolders*, and then click the folder name in the list box.

Change the date in the *Archive items older than* text box, type an archive file name in the *Archive file* text box, or use Browse to navigate to a drive and/or folder and type a name. Click OK to begin the manual archive.

FIGURE
5.16 **Archive Dialog Box**

The status bar displays the message *Archiving 'folder name'* as the archive process is running and you will see the messages in the folder being removed if the folder is active in the Contents Pane.

exercise 13 — CHECKING AUTOARCHIVE SETTINGS AND MANUALLY ARCHIVING SENT ITEMS

(Note: Check with your instructor before completing the manual archive in Step 3 of this exercise for a location that you have write access to on the network or hard drive as archive files might become too large to store on a floppy disk. As an alternative, delete unnecessary messages in the Sent Items folder before completing this exercise to reduce it to the smallest possible size.)

1. With Outlook open and the Inbox folder active, check the global AutoArchive settings on the computer you are using by completing the following steps:
    a. Click Tools and then click Options.

b. Click the Other tab at the Options dialog box.
c. Click the AutoArchive button in the *AutoArchive* section of the Options dialog box with the Other tab selected.
d. Review the settings in the AutoArchive dialog box and then click OK.
e. Click OK to close the Options dialog box.

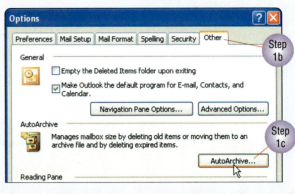

2. View and then change AutoArchive settings for the Inbox folder by completing the following steps:
   a. Right-click Inbox in the *All Mail Folders* section of the Navigation Pane.
   b. Click Properties at the shortcut menu.
   c. Click the AutoArchive tab at the Inbox Properties dialog box and then review the current settings for archiving the Inbox folder.
   d. Click *Archive this folder using these settings*. *(Note: Skip this step if the option is already active.)*
   e. Click the up- or down-pointing arrow next to the value in *Clean out items older than* until the number is *2*, and then click OK.

3. Manually archive the Sent Items folder by completing the following steps:
   a. Click File and then click Archive.
   b. If necessary, click *Archive this folder and all subfolders*.
   c. Click *Sent Items* in the list box containing the folder names. *(Note: You may have to scroll down the list box.)*
   d. Click the down-pointing arrow next to *Archive items older than* and then click a date in the drop-down calendar that is two days prior to the current date.
   e. Delete the file name in the *Archive file* text box and then type **A:\SentItemsArchive**. *(Type a different drive and/or include a folder name if your instructor has advised that you have write access to a location other than the floppy disk.)*
   f. Click OK. Outlook displays a message at the right end of the Status bar indicating the archive is taking place. Depending on the number of messages in Sent Items, archiving may take a few moments to complete.

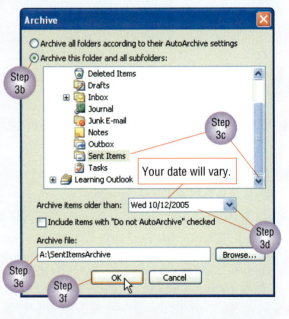

4. Display Sent Items in the Contents Pane. Only the messages sent in the last two days are shown.
5. Make Inbox the active folder.

Once an archive has been run, it is a good idea to copy the archive.pst file to a removable disk, such as a CD/R or CD/RW for record retention purposes. E-mail archiving and records management are increasingly becoming critical functions as businesses do more and more transactions and communication by e-mail.

Mailbox Cleanup Tool

Click Tools and then click Mailbox Cleanup to open the Mailbox Cleanup dialog box shown in Figure 5.17. From this dialog box you can view the current size of your mailbox and the individual folders, find old items, start an AutoArchive process, or view and empty the Deleted Items folder. The advantage of using the Mailbox Cleanup feature is that all of the folder maintenance tools can be accessed from one dialog box.

FIGURE 5.17 *Mailbox Cleanup Dialog Box*

Restoring Archived Items

To retrieve items in an archive file, use the Open command on the File menu to open the archive file name. Click File, point to Open, and then click Outlook Data File. Browse to the location of the archive file and then double-click the file name. An archive folder is added to the folder list. Display the contents of the required archive folder, open and view messages as required. You can also copy or move items from the archive folder to current folders if necessary. Right-click the archive folder name and then click Close "Archive Folders" at the shortcut menu when finished.

Another method that can be used to restore items that have been archived is to import the archive file. To do this, click File and then click Import and Export to start the Import and Export Wizard. At the first dialog box, choose *Import from another program or file* in the *Choose an action to perform* list box. Click *Personal Folder File (.pst)* in the *Select file type to import from* list box at the second dialog box. Follow the prompts in the remaining dialog boxes to complete the Import. When you import, you can select to move all of the archived items back into the folders from which they were archived, or you can choose to import the archived items into a new folder.

Compacting PST Files

PST files become very large in size after working in Outlook for a while. When you delete items in Outlook, the file size does not decrease. Outlook includes a compact feature that you should run periodically to keep the size of the pst file as small as possible. Complete the following steps to compact a pst file:

1. Click File and then click Data File Management.
2. Click the name of the file that you want to compact in the Outlook Data Files list box.
3. Click the Settings button.
4. Click the Compact Now button at the Personal Folders dialog box. A message displays telling you the file is being compacted.
5. Click OK to close the Personal Folders dialog box.
6. Click Close to close the Outlook Data Files dialog box.

Depending on the amount of data in the selected file, compacting can take a few moments to complete.

Compact PST File
1. Click File, Data File Management.
2. Click name of data file to compact.
3. Click Settings button.
4. Click Compact Now button.
5. Click OK.
6. Click Close.

Backing Up the PST File

HINT
You can download the Microsoft Outlook Personal Folders Backup tool from Microsoft Office Online. Once installed, this utility makes short work of pst file backups!

Use the normal Windows copy and paste commands to copy the pst file to a removable device for back up purposes. To find the location in which the pst file is stored, click File and then click Data File Management. At the Outlook Data Files dialog box shown in Figure 5.18, expand the right column boundary for the *Filename* column until you can see the entire path.

Users connected to a Microsoft Exchange Server need not be concerned with backing up the information stored on the server since the system administrator for the server would be running daily backups. However, a personal folders file created on the user's local hard drive would need to be copied periodically for backup purposes.

FIGURE 5.18 Outlook Data Files Dialog Box

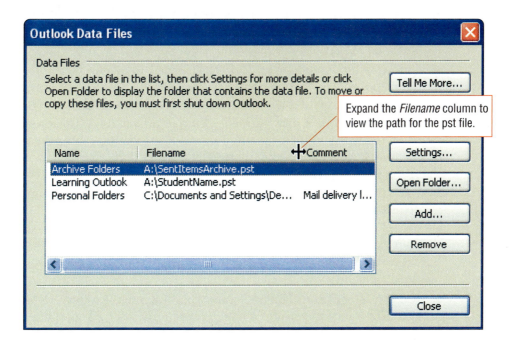

CHAPTER summary

➤ Outlook Today provides a glimpse of your current day by displaying a list of appointments, tasks, and the number of e-mail messages that you have received or not sent.

➤ Outlook Today can be set as the starting page whenever you load Outlook and the appearance and content can be customized.

➤ Any Outlook folder can be set as the starting page in the Advanced dialog box which is found on the Other tab of the Options dialog box.

➤ Customize the Navigation Pane by showing more or fewer buttons or changing the order in which the buttons are shown. Click the Configure buttons button to display the Navigation Pane menu.

➤ Click View and then click Navigation Pane to show or hide the Navigation Pane in the Outlook window.

➤ Open the E-mail Options and/or the Advanced E-mail Options dialog box to modify the default settings for handling mail messages.

➤ The Advanced E-mail Options dialog box is divided into three sections: *Save messages*, *When new items arrive*, and *When sending a message*.

➤ By default, Microsoft Word is the application that is used to create, edit, and view messages in order to take advantage of Word features such as automatic spelling and grammar checking, tables, and themes.

- Display the Options dialog box with the Mail format tab selected to choose whether to use Word as the e-mail editor or Outlook.
- Click Actions, point to New Mail Using, and then click a mail format option to create a message in a format other than the default.
- Mail formats available for creating and sending e-mail are Plain Text, Rich Text, and HTML.
- Customize the time interval and transparency setting for Desktop Alerts at the Desktop Alert Settings dialog box by clicking Tools, Options, E-mail Options, Advanced E-mail Options, and then Desktop Alert Settings.
- Search Folders are a new feature added to Outlook 2003. Click a search folder name to display in the Contents Pane the messages that meet the criteria for the folder. A search folder is essentially a folder that stores search and/or filter settings.
- Click the *Private* check box in the Appointment window to hide appointment details from other users of your calendar.
- Create a letter to a contact by selecting the name banner for the contact in the Contacts folder and then clicking Actions, New Letter to Contact. Microsoft Word opens with the Letter Wizard started in which you complete the document.
- You can filter or sort data in Contacts and then select records to be exported as a data source to perform a mail merge in Microsoft Word. Once the data is exported, create the main document with the merge fields inserted wherever variable information is positioned in a Word document. The data source is then merged with the main document and individual letters are created for printing or e-mailing.
- Data in Outlook folders is stored in a single file referred to as a *personal information store*.
- Create multiple personal folder files to organize groups of related data in different folders.
- Once a new pst file is created, create a new folder within the personal folders file and then drag and drop Outlook items to the new folders.
- An archive is a file containing old messages that have been purged from the active mail folders.
- Outlook folders can be set to automatically archive old items based on the age of the item, or you can manually transfer old items to the archive file.
- The AutoArchive dialog box accessed from the Options dialog box is used to set the global archive options.
- Open the Properties dialog box for an individual folder to set different AutoArchive options that override the global options.
- Click File and then click Archive to perform a manual archive for a folder.
- The Mailbox Cleanup dialog box accessed from the Tools menu provides all of the folder maintenance features in one location.
- Archived items can be restored by opening or importing the archive.pst file into Outlook.
- Since pst files can become very large in size, Outlook includes a compact feature that you should run periodically to keep the size of the pst file as small as possible.

➤ Back up a pst file using standard Windows copy and paste commands.
➤ Display the Outlook Data Files dialog box to determine the location in which the pst file is stored.

FEATURES summary

FEATURE	MENU	KEYBOARD
Advanced e-mail options	Tools, Options, E-mail Options, Advanced E-mail Options	
Archive	File, Archive	
AutoArchive	Tools, Options, Other, AutoArchive	
Compact pst file	File, Data File Management, Settings	
Create letter to contact	Actions, New Letter to Contact	
Create mail merge to contacts	Tools, Mail Merge	
Create personal folders file	File, New, Outlook Data File	
Desktop Alert Settings	Tools, Options, E-mail Options, Advanced E-mail Options, Desktop Alert Settings	
E-mail options	Tools, Options, E-mail Options	
Mailbox Cleanup	Tools, Mailbox Cleanup	
Outlook Data Files	File, Data File Management	
Set startup folder	Tools, Options, Other, Advanced Options	
Set default e-mail editor and/or viewer	Tools, Options, Mail Format	
Show/Hide Navigation Pane	View, Navigation Pane	Alt + F1

CONCEPTS check

Completion: On a blank sheet of paper, indicate the correct term, command, symbol, or explanation for each description.

1. Click this button to change the appearance of the Outlook Today page. *(Customize)*
2. Display this dialog box to change the default folder that Outlook displays whenever Outlook is opened. *Advanced Options.*
3. These are the shortcut keys that toggle the Navigation Pane on or off. *Alt + F1.*
4. Message handling options are available in this dialog box. *E-mail options.*
5. The actions that Outlook performs when a new mail message is received can be set at this dialog box. *Advanced E-mail options.*

6. Click this tab in the Options dialog box to set the e-mail editor and/or viewer. *Mail format*
7. The time interval for which a desktop alert displays can be increased or decreased at this dialog box. *Desktop Alert Settings*
8. Search folders do not store messages but instead update the list in the Contents Pane to meet this (these) setting(s). *Filter/Search settings*
9. Click this check box in the Appointment window to prevent other users from viewing details about your appointment. *Private*
10. This wizard starts in Microsoft Word after clicking Actions, Create New Letter to Contact. *Letter Wizard*
11. Use this feature to export selected contact records to Microsoft Word where you can combine them with standard text to create personalized letters or e-mails. *Mail Merge*
12. This Outlook feature globally scans the Outlook folders and transfers items to a separate file used to store old data. *Auto Archive*
13. Open this dialog box for an individual folder to change the time period for which items should be purged from the current folder. *Properties*
14. These are the two methods with which data that has been purged from the Outlook folders can be restored.

    ① File, Import & Export, follow steps of the Import wizard. Either or

15. Click this menu sequence to open the Outlook Data Files dialog box from which you can determine the path for the files or choose a file to compact. *File - Outlook data file*

File - open, Outlook data file, browse to location of archive file, double click archive file name, copy or move items to current folders.

SKILLS check

Assessment 1

1. With Outlook open, display the Outlook Today page and then customize the appearance of Outlook Today as follows:
   a. Make Outlook Today the startup page.
   b. Show 1 day in the calendar.
   c. Show Today's tasks only in the task list.
   d. Change to the *Summer* style.
2. Save the changes and then print the Outlook Today page.
3. Exit Outlook.
4. Restart Outlook to make sure Outlook Today is the starting page.
5. Restore Outlook Today to the default settings as follows:
   a. Remove Outlook Today as the startup page.
   b. Show 5 days in the Calendar.
   c. Show all tasks in the task list.
   d. Change to the *Standard* style.
6. Save the changes made to the Outlook Today page.
7. Display the Inbox.

Assessment 2

1. With Outlook open, change the startup folder to Tasks.
2. Exit Outlook.
3. Restart Outlook to make sure Tasks is the starting folder.
4. Change the startup folder to Inbox.

Assessment 3

1. With Outlook open, change the actions that are performed when a new mail message arrives in your Inbox to disable the sound that is played as the message arrives.
2. Create and then send a message to yourself as follows:
   a. Type **Mail Options** as the subject text.
   b. Type **This is a test of disabling the sound when a new message arrives.** in the message editing window.
3. As the message is placed in the Inbox notice that no sound is played. If necessary, click the Send/Receive button on the Standard toolbar to receive the message immediately.
4. Change the actions that are performed when a new mail message arrives so that the sound is restored for new messages.

Assessment 4

1. With Outlook open, change the Desktop Alert Settings to the default options as follows:
   a. Change the duration to *7 seconds*.
   b. Change the transparency to *20% transparent*.
2. Preview the default settings.

Assessment 5

1. With Outlook open, expand the Search Folders list in the *All Mail Folders* section of the Navigation Pane.
2. Click the For Follow Up search folder name and then review the messages in the Contents Pane.
3. Click the Large Mail search folder name and then review the messages in the Contents Pane if any are listed.
4. Click the Unread Mail search folder name and then review the messages in the Contents Pane if any are listed.
5. Collapse the Search Folders list and then display the Inbox in the Contents Pane.

Assessment 6

1. With Outlook open and Inbox active, change to the Contacts folder.
2. Create a letter to *Pauline Gorski* using the Letter Wizard as follows:
   a. Include the current date and choose the *Professional Letter* page design.
   b. Choose the *Formal* salutation.
   c. Click Next at the Letter Wizard - Step 3 of 4 dialog box to add no other elements to the letter.
   d. Type your first and last name as the Sender's name.
   e. Type your school name and address as the Return address.
   f. Choose an appropriate closing for the letter.
   g. Type your initials as the Writer/typist initials.
   h. Type the following text as the body of the letter.

      Our new product line is now available for shipping and we have launched an extensive advertising campaign to coincide with the holiday season.

> The advertising campaign is both print and Web-based and includes a toll-free number to our call center where we have customer service representatives available 24/7.
>
> If you have any questions about the new products, please feel free to call or e-mail me at any time.

     i. Center the letter vertically on the page.
     j. Print the letter.
3. Exit Microsoft Word. Click No when prompted to save changes.
4. Make Inbox the active folder.

Assessment 7

1. With Outlook open and Inbox active, expand the Learning Outlook folder in the *All Mail Folders* section of the Navigation Pane if it is not already expanded.
2. Create a new folder within the Learning Outlook personal folders file and name it *E-mail Viruses*.
3. Display in the Contents Pane the contents of the E-mail Viruses folder within the Inbox folder and then copy all of the messages to the E-mail Viruses folder within Learning Outlook.
4. Display in the Contents Pane the contents of the Outlook Tips folder within the Inbox folder and then copy all of the messages to the Training folder within Learning Outlook.
5. Make Inbox the active folder.

Assessment 8

1. With Outlook open and Inbox active, right-click the Inbox folder name and then click Properties at the shortcut menu.
2. Click the AutoArchive tab in the Inbox Properties dialog box and then restore the AutoArchive properties to the default settings as follows:
   a. Change *Clean out items older than* to *6 months*.
   b. Click *Do not archive items in this folder*.
3. Click OK to close the Inbox Properties dialog box.

Assessment 9

1. With Outlook open and Inbox active, delete the E-Mail Viruses and Outlook Tips folders within Inbox.
2. Open the Mailbox Cleanup dialog box.
3. Click the Empty button to permanently delete the items in the Deleted Items folder, and then click Yes at the Microsoft Office Outlook message box asking if you are sure.
4. Open the Outlook Data Files dialog box.
5. Select *Personal Folders* in the *Name* list box and then click the Settings button.
6. At the Personal Folders dialog box, click the Compact Now button.
7. When the compact operation is complete, close all of the open dialog boxes.

Assessment 10

1. With Outlook open and *Inbox* active, delete the personal address book created in Chapter 1 by completing the following steps:
   a. Click Tools and then E-mail Accounts.
   b. Click *View or change existing directories or address books* in the *Directory* section and then click Next.
   c. Click *Personal Address Book* in the Directories and Address Books list box and then click the Remove button.
   d. Click Yes at the Account Manager dialog box asking if you are sure you want to remove the Personal Address Book.
   e. Click Finish to close the E-mail Accounts dialog box.
2. Exit Outlook.

INDEX

A

Accept Meeting Response dialog box, 72
Actions menu: mail format chosen for message with, 166
Active tasks list, 139
Activities tab: in New Contact window, 89
Adaptive menus, 7
Add Contact Picture dialog box, 96
Add Contact Picture image control box, 96
Add New button, 117
Add New Member dialog box, 117
Addresses: in To text box, 9
Address Book
 entries added to, 20–22
 maintaining, 18–22
Address Cards view, 109
Add to List button, 103
Advanced dialog box, 185
Advanced E-mail Options button, 160
Advanced E-mail Options dialog box, 161
 sections within, 185
Advanced Find dialog box, 106
 with Contacts tab selected, 108
Advanced Find feature, 29, 118
 records located with, 108–109
Advanced Options dialog box, 156
 opening, 157
Advanced tab, 29
All Fields tab: in Contact window, 94, 95–96
All Mail Folders option, 29
Anniversaries, 57, 87
Appointment Recurrence dialog box, 55
Appointments, 3, 81
 automatic formatting of, 67–68
 categories assigned to, 64–66
 editing, deleting, and moving, 58–59, 81
 grouping, 81
 hiding details about, 186
 private, 169–170
 recurring, 55–56
 scheduling, 51, 52–55
 scheduling from contacts, 113–114
 viewing by category, 64–66
Appointment window: scheduling appointment with, 53
Appointment window toolbar: Recurrence button on, 55
Archive dialog box, 181
Archive files: retrieving items in, 184
archive.pst file, 186
copying, 183
Archives, 178, 186
Archiving
 features summary, 187
 folders, 178–184
 manual, 180–183, 186
Ask a Question text box, 42, 45
Attachment formats: changing, 24
Attachments: saving to disk, 17–18
AutoArchive dialog box, 179, 186
AutoArchive feature, 178
AutoArchive settings: creating, 181
Automatic Formatting dialog box, 66, 67
Auto-Select option, 24

B

Bcc button, 19
Bcc field, 117
BINHEX, 24
Birthdays, 57, 87
Blocked file attachment messages, 16
Blue flags, 30
bmp format, 96
Browse button, 23
By Category task list, 139

C

Cable modem, 8
Calendar
 capabilities with, 51
 changing options in, 77–79
 customizing, 78–79, 81
 deleting meetings from, 74
 displaying more than one, side-by-side, 79–80, 81
 features summary, 82
 formatting, 66
 as startup folder, 157
Calendar Coloring button, 60, 66
Calendar Current View menu, 60
Calendar folder, 5, 157
 appointments viewed in, 169
 creating, 81
 TaskPad in, 127
Calendar Options dialog box, 77
Calendar options section of, 78
Calendar Properties dialog box: Permissions tab in, 169
Calendar view: changing, 60–63
Categories
 assigning, while creating contacts, 104–105
 assigning to appointments, 64–66
 assigning to notes, 144–145, 148
 contact, 118
 filtering contact lists by, 105
Categories dialog box, 64, 103
Categories text box, 24, 53
Category names: creating, for contacts, 103
Cc button, 19
Cc text box, 137
Certificates tab: in New Contact window, 89
Check Address dialog box, 92
Check for duplicate contacts check box, 112
Check Full Name dialog box, 92
Choose Folders option, 29
Clear Flag button, 99
Collapse button, 33
Color
 for calendar, 60
 for message flags, 44
 for message headers, 34–36
 for messages, 44
 note, 145, 146–147, 148
 for overdue and completed tasks, 148
Completed flags, 32–33
Completed Tasks list, 139
Condition button, 67
Conferences: scheduling, 51, 57
Configure buttons button, 157
Confirm Delete Meeting Message Box: to attendee, 74
Contact index languages: viewing, 112
Contact lists: filtering by categories, 105
Contact options: changing, 111–112
Contact Options button, 111
Contact Options dialog box, 111
Contact records: deleting, 118
Contacts, 3. *See also* Multiple contacts
 adding, 88–93, 117
 creating/sending form letter by e-mail to, 174–176
 editing, 92–93, 118
 e-mail messages sent to, 112–113

features summary, 119
filtering, 101–102, 186
finding, 106–109, 118
flagging for follow-up, 97–99, 118
grouping into categories, 103–104
letters created for, 170–172, 186
linking messages to, 24
locating with Advanced Find, 108
locating with letter tabs and Find a Contact text box, 106–107
managing, 87–123
new, from existing contacts, 94
personal information about, 89
pictures added to, 96, 117
reviewing activities for, 113, 114
scheduling appointments from, 113–114
sorting, 99–101, 118
viewing in categories, 103–104
Contacts button, 24
Contacts folder, 5, 23, 157
adding records to, 88–92
address book linked to, 18
letter generated to contact within, 170
uses for, 87, 117
Contacts text box, 53
Contacts window, 88
Contents Pane, 28, 30
contents viewed in, 44
flagging messages in, 31–32
freeing up space in, 158
mail items grouped in, 44
messages arranged in, 33–34
overdue Follow-Up flags in, 99
Create New Folder dialog box, 37, 45
Create Rule button, 39
Create Rule dialog box, 39
Create Signature dialog box, 28

Current View menu, 44, 81
By Category option on, 64
fields added/removed in, 110–111
Current View section
changing, 109
in Navigation Pane, 63
Customized task lists: creating, 140
Customize View dialog box, 100

D

Data: exporting from Contacts to create data source, 172–173
Data source: creating, 172–173
Date Navigator, 52
changing way calendar displays in, 78
Dates
for contact follow-up activities, 97
task, 126
Default format: for attachments, 24
Delete button, 15, 58, 92, 129, 143
Deleted Items folder, 36, 44, 45
emptying, 15–16, 39
Delete key, 129
Delete Meeting Message Box: to meeting organizer, 74
Delivery and read receipts, 23
Desktop alerts
customizing, 167–168, 186
for new message received, 11
Desktop Alert Settings dialog box, 167, 186
Desktop Information Management program, 3
Detailed Address Cards view, 109
Details tab
in Contact window, 94, 95–96
in Task window, 128

Dial-up connection, 8
Digital modem, 8
Digital signature, 23
DIM program. See Desktop Information Management program
Distribution lists
creating, 114–116, 118
expanding in message window, 117
maintaining, 117
Distribution List window, 115
DSL, 7
Due by text box, 30
Duplicate Contact Detected dialog box, 112

E

Edit Calendar Labels dialog box, 60
Editing notes, 143
Edit Signature dialog box, 28
E-mail (Electronic mail)
archiving, 183
features summary, 45–46
E-mail Accounts Wizard, 18
E-mail messages
creating, 118
creating and sending, 7–10
sending to contacts, 112–113
E-mail options
changing, 162–163
changing advanced, 163–164
restoring to default settings, 164–165
setting, 160–162
E-mail Options dialog box: Message handling section of, 160
E-mail profile, 8
server types and, 8
setting up, 4
Encoding methods: changing, 24
Encryption, 23, 89
End times: for appointments, 53
End time text box, 53
Etiquette, 7

Events, 81
adding, 57–58
scheduling, 51, 52, 57
Existing contacts: new contacts added from, 94
Expires after text box, 24

F

Fields, 88, 117
about contacts, 94
adding/removing, 110–111, 118
in Task window, 128
File attachments: saving to disk, 17–18
Files: attaching to messages, 16–17, 44
Filter dialog box
with Contacts tab selected, 101
opening, 67
Filtered contact lists, 101, 118
Filtering messages, 33–34
Find a Contact text box, 106, 118
Find bar, 28, 44, 106, 107
Find feature, 107, 118
Find Now, 29
First-rank options, 6
Flag Complete, 30
Flag for Follow Up dialog box, 30, 99
with Flag to Drop-Down list, 97
Flagging
contacts for follow-up, 97–99, 118
messages, 44
Flags
clearing, 32–33, 44
removing from contact records, 99
Folders, 44
archiving, 178–184
creating, 36–37, 38, 40–41, 45
creating rule to move messages to, 39
managing, 36–42
messages moved in, 37–39
Outlook, 5
personal, 176, 186
search, 168–169, 186

setting as starting page, 185
startup, 156–157
viewing contents of, 6
Folders list box, 29
Follow up flag: attaching to message, 31–32
For Follow Up folder, 30
Formatting: in Calendar, 66
Formatting toolbar, 7, 9
Forward button, 13
Forwarded Task message window, 138

G

gif format, 96
Global Address List, 18, 19, 23
Global AutoArchive settings: changing, 178
Go To Date: using, 62–63
Graphics file formats, 96
Green flags, 30

H

Help: using, 42–43, 45
HTML, 165, 166, 186
Hypertext Transfer Protocol (HTTP), 8, 44

I

iCal (Internet Calendar) item, 71
Icons view, 146
Images: adding to contacts, 96
IMAP. *See* Internet Message Access Protocol
Importance: High button, 23
Importance: Low button, 23
Importing archive files, 184
Inbox, 44
   Contents Pane of, 11
   mail messages in, 15
   rules and controlling size of, 41
Inbox component, 3, 5
Inbox folder, 5, 36, 45
Inbox option, 29

Inbox Properties dialog box: with AutoArchive tab selected, 180
Indexes: contact, 112
Information management programs, 3
Insert File button, 16
Insert Merge Field dialog box, 174
Insert Merge Fields button, 173, 174
Instant messaging addresses, 88
Internet: calendar information shared over, 94
Internet Mail clients: Outlook Today for, 154
Internet Mail Server, 44
   task request message to task recipient connected to, 135
   using Outlook connected to, 8
Internet Message Access Protocol, 8, 44
In text box, 29

J

jpeg format, 96
Junk E-mail Filter, 41–42
Junk E-mail folder, 41, 45
Junk Email Options dialog box, 41, 45
   with Options tab selected, 42

L

Label list box: color coding appointments in, 53
LAN. *See* Local area network
Letters
   to contacts, 186
   creating, to contacts, 170–172
   to multiple contacts, 172–173
Letter Wizard, 170, 186
Local area network, 8
Location text box: appointment locations in, 53
Look for text box, 107

M

Mailbox Cleanup dialog box, 183, 186
Mailbox Cleanup feature, 183
Mail client, 7
Mail component, 5
Mail editor
   changing, 165–166
   default, checking, 166
Mail folder, 157
Mail format, 186
   changing for individual message, 166–167
   choosing for message using Actions menu, 166
   options, 165–166
Mail I Received option, 29
Mail I Sent option, 29
Mail merge: with Outlook and Word, 172
Mail Merge Contacts dialog box, 173
Mail Merge toolbar: Insert Merge Fields button on, 173, 174
Mail server, 7
Main document, 172
Manually archiving, 180–183
Manually archiving folders, 186
Mark Complete button, 129
Master Category List, 64
Meeting attendees
   changing or rescheduling, 81
   updating, 76
Meeting requests
   accepting, 72–73
   creating, 68
   responding to, 71–72
Meeting responses: manually tracking, 76–77
Meetings, 3
   canceling, 81
   deleting from Calendar, 74
   scheduling, 51, 68–71, 81
   scheduling and updating, 74–75
   updating and

canceling, 73–76
Meeting window, 69
   Tracking tab in, 81
Menu bar, 5
Menus: using, 6–7
Message Flag button, 30
Message headers: color applied to, 34–36
Message options: assigning, 23–26
Message Options dialog box, 23, 44
Message rules, 36
   creating, 40–41, 45
   creating to move messages to folder automatically, 39
Messages
   clearing flags from, 32–33
creating and sending, 9–10
   deleting, 15, 44
   expiring, 24
   files attached to, 16–17, 44
   filtering, 33–34, 44
   finding, 28–30
   finding with Search Folders, 168–169
   flagging, 30–32, 44
   forwarding, 11, 12
   moving form one folder to another, 45
   moving in folders, 37–39
   opening, 44
   opening, printing, replying to, and forwarding, 11, 13–14, 44
   reading and printing, 11
   receiving, 44
   replying to, 11, 12
   storing, 45
Microsoft Exchange clients: Outlook Today for, 154
Microsoft Exchange Server, 18, 19, 26, 44, 184
   task request message to task recipient connected to, 134
   tracking/viewing tasks and, 136
   using Outlook connected to, 7–8
Microsoft Internet Explorer, 43

Microsoft NetMeeting, 94
Microsoft Office Internet Free/Busy Service, 72
Microsoft Office Online option, 43
Microsoft Office Online Web page, 43
Microsoft Office Outlook dialog box, 29
  with Advanced Find option, 30
Microsoft Office Outlook Help window, 42
Microsoft Office Outlook 2003 window: exploring, 4–5
Microsoft Outlook
  customizing, integrating and archiving components of, 153–190
  customizing features summary, 187
  for e-mail, 3–50
  message window with Outlook as mail editor, 165
  navigating components within, 5
  starting for first time, 4
Microsoft Word, 165
  creating, editing, and viewing messages in, 185
  data used as data source in mail merge in, 172
  merge completed in, 173–174
MIME, 24
Modems, 7, 8
More Choices tab, 29
.msg extension, 143, 144
Multiple contacts: creating standard letter to, 172–173

N

Names: adding to Address Book, 18
Natural language phrases, 58
Navigation Pane, 6
  All Mail Folders section of, 36, 41, 154, 168
  Configure buttons button in, 158
  Current View section of, 109, 147, 148
  Customize Current View in, 100, 101, 140
  customizing, 157–159, 185
  Favorite Folders section in, 30
  hiding, redisplaying, and customizing, 158–159
  My Calendars section of, 79
  Notes icon at bottom of, 141
  Tasks in, 126
  views displayed in, 63
Navigation Pane Options dialog box, 158
New Appointment button, 52
New Contact button, 88
New Contact from Same Company, 118
New Contact window:
  with General tab selected, 89
New Mail Message button, 8, 44
New messages: composing, 8–10
New Message to Contact button, 112
New Note window, 142
New Outlook Data File dialog box, 177
New Search Folder dialog box, 169
New Task button, 127
Next Seven Days task list, 139
Note options: changing, 145–146
Notes, 3
  categories assigned to, 144–145, 148
  color of, 145, 146–147, 148
  copying, 148
  creating, 140–142, 143
  deleting, 148
  editing, 143, 148
  features summary, 148
  placing on the desktop, 143–144
Notes folder, 5, 118, 148
  activating, 141
  moving note from, to desktop, 144
Notes Options dialog box, 145
Note view: changing, 146

O

Online meetings, 94
Options button, 23
Options dialog box
  displaying, 186
  Note Options button in, 145
  with Preferences tab selected, 111
Orange flags, 30
Outbox folder, 36, 45
Outlook. *See* Microsoft Outlook
Outlook Data Files dialog box, 184, 185, 187
Outlook Today, 185
  page, 154
  setting up as starting page, 156, 185
  using and customizing, 154–156
Outlook 2003 Startup Wizard, 4
Overdue Tasks list, 139

P

PAB extension, 18
Paper clip icon, 16
Password, 7
Personal Address Book, 23, 44
  adding entries to, while creating message, 21–22
  creating, 18–19, 20–21
Personal folders file: creating and using, 176–178
Personal Information Manager program, 3
Personal information store, 176, 186
Phone List: contacts displayed in, 109
Pictures: adding to contacts, 96, 117
PIM program. *See* Personal Information Manager program
Plain Text, 166, 186
Plus symbol (+): next to folder name, 36, 37
Post Office Protocol 3 (POP 3), 8, 44
Print button, 12
Private appointments: creating, 169–170
Private check box, 53
Private store, 176
Properties dialog box:
  AutoArchive tab at, 179
Propose New Time button, 72
Propose New Time dialog box, 72
Propose Time button, 72
Protection levels: changing, 42, 45
.pst file extension, 176, 186
PST files
  backing up, 184, 187
  compacting, 184, 187
Purple flags, 30

R

Reading Pane, 11
  adjusting size of, 12
  displaying, 61–63
  Message Options Information Box in, 25
Read receipt, 44
Read receipt messages, 25, 26
Read report messages, 25, 26
Records, 88
  contacts, 117
  locating, with Advanced Find, 108–109
  retention of, 183

Records management:
importance of, 183
Recurrence button, 55
Recurring appointments:
scheduling, 56
Recurring tasks: creating,
130–131
Red flags, 30
Reminder check box, 53
Remove button, 117
Remove from Calendar
button, 73
Reply button, 13
Reply to All button, 13
Rich Text, 166, 186
Rules
automatic formatting in
Calendar and, 66
creating, 45
creating, to move
messages to folder
automatically, 39
message, 36

S

Scheduling meetings,
68–71, 81
Search Folders, 168–169,
186
Search In list box, 29
Search Results task pane,
42
Second-rank options, 6
Security, 23
Security Settings button,
23
Select Folders dialog box,
29
Select Members button,
115, 117
Select Names button, 23
Select Names dialog box,
19, 20, 44
Seminars, 57
Send Status Report
button, 137
Send Update button, 73,
81
Send Update to Attendees
Message Box, 76
Sent Items folder, 15, 36,
45
Settings: changing, 23

Show time as list box, 53
Signature: creating, 26–28,
44
Sort dialog box, 99
Spam, 41–42, 45
Standard toolbar, 5, 7
Address Book icon, 20
Calendar Coloring
button on, 60, 66
Create Rule button on,
39
Delete button on, 15,
58, 92, 129, 143
Find a Contact text box
on, 106
Find button on, 28, 107
Foward button on, 13
New Appointment
button on, 52
New Mail Message
button on, 8, 44
New Message to
Contact button on,
112
New Task button on,
127
Print button on, 12
Reply or Reply to All
button on, 13
Start button, 4
Start times: for
appointments, 53
Startup folder: specifying,
156–157
Status bar, 5
Storage: of deleted
messages, 15
Subfolders, 36, 37, 45
Subject box, 9
Subject text box:
appointment
description in, 53

T

Taskbar: Start button on, 4
Task details: changing, 147
Task lists
changing task view for
creation of, 139–140
customized, 140
Task options: changing,
141

Task Options dialog box,
141
TaskPad, 118
Task Recurrence dialog
box, 130
Task requests, 118, 132
accepting, 135–136, 147
responding to, 134–135
Tasks
adding, 147
assigning to someone
else, 132–134, 147
creating, 147
creating and updating,
126–130
default status for new
tasks, 128
deleting, 129, 147
editing in task table, 140
e-mailing comments
about, 148
features summary, 148
recurring, 130–131
reporting status of, 148
sending copies of, via
e-mail, 148
sending information
about to others,
137–139
tracking and viewing
assigned, 136–137
updating, 129–130
Tasks folder, 5, 126, 157
Task Status Report
message window, 137
Task table: tasks edited in,
140
Task Timeline list, 139
Task view: changing to
create task lists,
139–140
Task window
opening, 147
tasks created in, 128
with Task tab selected,
127
Threads, 13
Times: appointment, 53
Time Zone: changing, 78
Title bar, 5
Titles: contact, 92
To-do lists, 3
Toolbar Options button, 7

Toolbars: using, 6–7
To text box, 9, 137
Tracking Options button,
161
Tracking Options dialog
box, 162
Trade shows: scheduling,
57
Training sessions, 57

U

Untitled Message window,
8, 9
Update Now button, 117
User name, 7
Using Colors: Way to
Organize Inbox Pane
with, 35
UUEncode, 24

V

Vacations: scheduling, 57
Viewer: default checks,
166
Views: displaying in
Navigation Pane, 63
Viruses, 16
Voting and tracking, 23
Voting buttons, 23

W

Ways to Organize Inbox
pane, 34, 44
Automatic Formatting
in, 36
Word. *See* Microsoft Word
Worms, 16

Y

Yellow flags, 30